Prescription Drugs

By the Editors of CONSUMER GUIDE®
with Thomas A. Gossel, R.Ph., Ph.D.
and Donald W. Stansloski, R.Ph., Ph.D.

Beekman House

New York

Contents

2

Manufactured in the United States of America
  2 3 4 5 6 7 8 9 10

Library of Congress Catalog Card Number: 79-91204

This edition published by:
Beekman House
A Division of Crown Publishers, Inc.
One Park Avenue
New York, NY 10016

Cover Design: Frank E. Peiler
Cover Photo: Mel Winer

Introduction

WE LIVE in a drug-oriented society, with a pill or potion for almost any ailment. Nevertheless, people are becoming increasingly reluctant to take medication on faith alone or just because "my doctor says so."

This reluctance may stem from a lack of trust of the medical profession, the disappearance of the family doctor and the emergence of depersonalized health care, and the ever-rising costs of treatment. Undoubtedly another important factor is the influence of the consumer movement. People want to participate in their own health care; they want to be able to make decisions that affect their treatment.

To make these decisions wisely, you need information. You must know about the drugs you take—how they work, when potential dangers may arise, and what side effects to expect from drug use.

This book intends to provide such information. Written by pharmacists and the Editors of CONSUMER GUIDE®, it explains what the experts know in easy-to-understand language. The book not only contains detailed profiles of the most commonly prescribed drugs but also presents valuable information about the way drugs are manufactured and used. You'll learn how to read a prescription and how to save money when you purchase medications. You will discover which possible side effects are common to some medications and which are danger signals that require immediate attention from your physician.

Of course, this book is not a substitute for consulting your doctor. Your doctor and your pharmacist are your primary reference sources. But, we hope this book will supplement your knowledge of prescription and over-the-counter medications so you can work with these health care professionals to develop a harmonious relationship.

> *Note: Every effort has been made to assure that the information in this book is accurate and current at time of printing. However, new developments occur almost daily in drug research, and the authors and publisher suggest that the reader consult his physician or pharmacist for the latest available data on specific products.*

The Evolution Of A Miracle

A modern miracle occurs every time you take a pill or capsule or swallow a teaspoon of medicine: modern because most of the potent drugs used today were developed in the past 20 or 30 years; a miracle because the drug you take may cure illness, relieve pain, or preserve life.

IN THE BEGINNING

Drug use is as old as civilization itself—perhaps even older. Three thousand years before the birth of Christ, the Babylonians wrote about the drugs they used, and they described more than 350 items.

Egyptian papyri dating back to about 1900 B.C. describe prescriptions compounded from almost every plant and animal in the environment—spider webs steeped in syrups, the testicles of the black ass, the eggs of the babzu bird, and oil from the hippopotamus. Mothers' milk was a common medical item; but not the milk from any mother, only from one who had borne a son.

Hippocrates, author of the "Hippocratic Oath" and called "the Father of Medicine," lived around 400 B.C. He, as many others of that time, believed in the theory of "The Four Humors," that is, that the humors (blood, phlegm, black bile, and yellow bile) were responsible for health or caused sickness. When the humors were "in harmony," a person was healthy. When the humors "were out of harmony," he was ill. The physician Galen later taught how the humors determined one's temperament. People in whom blood was dominant were optimistic and buoyant; those with too much phlegm were sluggish; black bile accounted for a quick temper; and yellow bile explained melancholy.

The theory of "The Four Humors" was popular until the 19th

NOTE: All trade names of drugs used in the text of this book are capitalized.

century when scientists discovered bacteria and began to understand the real causes of many diseases. But until that time, physicians used more than 400 drugs to return the balance of the humors to normal. And some of these drugs, such as morphine and certain vitamins, are still used today.

The earliest physicians administered many substances to treat particular ailments: earthworms rolled in honey (for gastritis), owl brain (for headache), sheep brain (for insomnia), deer heart (for heart disease), fox lung (for tuberculosis), goat liver (for jaundice), powdered human skull and the blood of a dying gladiator (for epilepsy), rabbit testicles (for bladder disease and impotence), and cow dung (for eye infections).

In the 16th and 17th centuries, plants and animal parts gave way to chemicals as the mainstay of drug therapy.

Use of chemicals was not without its problems. Many of the chemicals—lead, mercury, arsenic, copper—have since been shown to be toxic. One can only surmise that patients who improved after receiving these chemicals had been given smaller doses and that many of those who died did so because of their "treatment" rather than their disease.

By the 18th century, thousands of items had been tried as drugs. Of these, only a few dozen were effective. Colchicine, derived from the root or seeds of a plant, was used in the treatment of arthritis and gout. Even today, it is the drug of choice for acute attacks of gout. Then and now, ergot is unequaled for controlling bleeding after childbirth. Digitalis, once used specifically for dropsy, has kept more people with heart disease alive than any other drug. Morphine—first used as a sedative—is now one of the most valuable and powerful painkillers.

THE ADVENT OF MODERN MEDICINE

When did "modern medicine" begin? Modern medicine may date back to Harvey's discovery of blood circulation (1628), Pasteur's work with bacteria (1862), or Lister's development of antiseptic techniques (1865).

Modern drug therapy, however, began in 1935, with the introduction of the first sulfa drug, prontosil. Before this time, there were no drugs to conquer infections. The slightest cut or bruise might initiate infection and lead to sudden death. A chest cold that today can be resolved with several days of modern drug therapy frequently led to pneumonia, then death, before the discovery of prontosil. At first, many regarded prontosil as just "another drug in the pharmacy." But as dozens, then hundreds, of lives were saved by using prontosil for infections, researchers took a closer look.

The drug prontosil was first developed by German and French scientists. The American drug industry viewed it as the beginning of a new era in drug therapy because of its positive effect in saving lives and began to invest millions of dollars in medical research. This research uncovered several dozen new, more potent sulfa drugs. Penicillin was developed in the early 1940s, and new penicillin compounds are being developed today.

Severe disorders of the heart and blood pressure were brought under control in the 1950s with the development of hydralazine and rauwolfia. Further research on rauwolfia isolated reserpine, which, along with another new drug, Thorazine phenothiazine, almost emptied the nation's mental wards. Later that same decade, drugs that could be taken by mouth became available to treat diabetes. And later, research would progress toward the control of other diseases, such as smallpox, arthritis, and polio.

THE RIGHTS OF THE CONSUMER

In spite of all the miracles of the past and those promised for the future, and despite the discovery of drugs that have saved lives and have prevented misery, the authors are somewhat critical of the drug industry.

We take the same kinds of drugs that you do, and, as consumers, we share a common interest—to know the facts about what we buy.

Many of the drugs you take are prescribed by your doctor; so you frequently rely on his experience and judgment. Your doctor usually chooses drugs carefully, and he often follows a general rule known as the five R's—"The right drug for the right patient in the right dose by the right route at the right time."

Now you may add a sixth R, another kind of "right"—the right to be informed about the drugs that may reduce your suffering and perhaps prolong your life. You have the right to know about a drug's harmful effects as well as its beneficial ones. You should be aware of a drug's limitations and what to expect after you have taken it. Since so many drugs are available and used in the United States, you must know when not to take a drug and when two or more drugs should not be taken at the same time.

Perhaps you know an elderly person who is becoming senile or a stroke victim who is weak, forgetful, dizzy, and has slurred speech. Both are likely to receive prescriptions for papaverine capsules. Papaverine is used as a smooth muscle relaxant. It increases the flow of blood to the brain and, at least in theory, should help relieve the symptoms of senility and the aftereffects of a stroke. However, the theory has not been proved, at least with the recommended doses of papaverine when used orally.

Papaverine may or may not help a senile patient or a stroke victim, but members of the medical community believe the drug is worth trying because the theory is sound and should work. The patient, meanwhile, pays for a drug that may not help him. If he buys a leading brand of papaverine, the patient pays from $14 to $18 for a month's supply of capsules. If he buys capsules under the generic name of papaverine, the patient pays from $5 to $7 for a month's supply. Is he getting his money's worth? Yes, as long as the drug itself relieves his symptoms. But is it the drug that's helping, or is the patient getting better on his own? We know that the power of positive thinking is very real.

This example illustrates why you should be informed about the drugs you take. You should decide whether or not you wish to spend money on a drug that may not help you. You may choose to abide by your doctor's orders, but you should have all the facts at your command.

MODERN DRUG INDUSTRY

The drug industry in the United States is financially successful and can take credit for major achievements in drug development. Because it sponsors laboratory and clinical research, the drug industry has discovered many of the finest and strongest drugs available to anyone in the world today. The American drug industry, however, has been accused of claiming discovery of drugs that were developed in other countries—for example, Thorazine phenothiazine, developed in France; Orinase oral antidiabetic, developed in Germany; reserpine, developed in India; and insulin, developed in Canada.

For years, the American drug industry has been scrutinized and criticized by the federal government and the public. Profit of 9 percent a year, the critics say, is too much. Not so, answer the drug companies. They argue that drug manufacture is a high-risk industry. But since few drug companies fail, the risk does not seem to be too great. Drug companies also argue that a major portion of their income is devoted to research and development of new products. Drug companies certainly conduct research, but their research—say the critics—is directed toward developing marketable products and determining market trends instead of discovering significant new drugs. In fact, the claim is made that many companies spend more for advertising than for research.

Critics of the American drug industry also question the way drug companies price their products. They say that the same drug from the same drug company in the same quantity should cost the same. But, in fact, purchasers are charged different prices—the federal government pays little when it buys a drug to use in federal institutions. The next most favored customer is a hospital pharmacy, and the least favored customer is the neighborhood pharmacy. Because hospitals pay less for a drug, consumers pay more for it. The price you pay for a drug at your local drugstore is higher to make up for the low prices charged to the government and hospitals. Your pharmacist doesn't like this any more than you do, but there's nothing he can do about it.

HOW DRUGS ARE MADE

In ancient times, drugs were prepared by one person or family. The tribal medicine man or village wise woman gathered the necessary ingredients and mixed the potions. Today, drugs are prepared in large factories scattered throughout the world.

Pharmacists compound a small number of prescriptions in their pharmacies, but this "one-at-a-time" system has yielded to factory mass production for the same reason industrialization took the place of piecework—it is more efficient.

To prepare a drug, a company might obtain some type of vegetation—the root of a plant that grows in India, the stem of a plant that is common to Africa, or a leaf from a tree that flourishes in the Pacific Northwest. Or it might obtain the organs and tissues of animals. The pancreas from a cow or pig is used to make insulin; the urine from pregnant mares is collected to make female hormones.

Drugs also may be made by chemical synthesis. Chemical synthesis is the building up of complex compounds from simpler compounds, much like placing brick upon brick to build a house. For instance, the manufacturer might start with a natural substance—such as coal tar, cotton, or extracts from plants or animals—or with a man-made chemical and add other chemicals to it until the desired result is achieved. Most drugs nowadays are made this way.

PRESCRIPTION VS. NONPRESCRIPTION DRUGS

Some drugs can be purchased without a prescription. These are referred to as over-the-counter (OTC), or patent, drugs and are sold in a wide variety of settings such as drug and grocery stores and hotel lobbies. There are no legal requirements or limitations on who may buy or sell them.

Other drugs require a prescription before they can be purchased. Doctors and dentists may dispense them from their offices; but, in general, their sales are limited to pharmacies under the direction of a registered pharmacist.

Drug items that are sold OTC are safer to use than are those that require a prescription. They are safer because they are usually less active than are prescription medications. Drugs that require a prescription are both more potent and more dangerous to use than OTC drugs.

The manufacturers of a new drug decide whether it should be an OTC item or sold only with a prescription. The Food and Drug Administration (FDA) then either agrees or disagrees, based upon evidence of what the drug is intended to do and how safe it is.

Occasionally, a drug will be safe to use, but the FDA will still require a prescription to purchase it. Decisions of this nature are based on the idea that some diseases shouldn't be self-treated, or treated without a doctor's assistance. For example, an earache can usually be relieved with eardrops containing the local anesthetic benzocaine. Although benzocaine is a component of many OTC items for itching, hemorrhoids, etc., the FDA has ruled that eardrops that contain it require a prescription. The reason for this ruling is that an earache can be caused by a number of different illnesses, some of them serious. Use of eardrops containing benzocaine could mask symptoms of a serious ailment and thereby delay proper diagnosis and treatment. Therefore, the FDA has ruled that you must see your doctor before you can obtain such drops.

Working With
Your Doctor
And Pharmacist

A DRUG taken without obtaining the advice of a doctor or a pharmacist can be a time bomb, ready to explode the minute your body's defenses are down.

You wouldn't take a car into expressway traffic without first learning to drive. You wouldn't rewire an electrical outlet without first carefully reading and understanding how to do it. So why would you take a drug without first knowing all about it?

Your doctor and your pharmacist are your best sources of information. Each has been trained in a different field, and their areas of expertise complement one another. The two of them working together can provide better health care than either working alone.

To take advantage of their combined knowledge, you must know how to select a doctor and a pharmacist and how to communicate with them. You must know what questions to ask and how to be sure you get the answers.

TRAINING AND QUALIFICATIONS

Doctors and pharmacists are highly trained professionals. Both are college-educated. After four years of premedical college training, medical students begin four years of study in medical schools, followed by periods of internship and residency. After two years of prepharmacy college education, students of pharmacy complete three years of college training, followed by internships and residencies. And in the near future, schools of pharmacy may require an additional year of training.

A doctor's training concentrates on the recognition and treatment of illness. A pharmacist's training centers on drugs and how they are used.

Specialists

There are almost as many kinds of doctors as there are parts of the body: doctors who specialize in diseases of the heart (cardiologists), urinary tract (urologists), ear, nose, and throat (otorhinolaryngologists), for example. Based on their education, doctors may hold one of two degrees. The most common is the MD, or "Doctor of Medicine," degree. More than 300,000 MDs are currently licensed to practice medicine in the United States.

The other is the DO, or "Doctor of Osteopathy," degree. Holders of a DO degree are osteopaths or osteopathic physicians. Osteopaths were looked upon with less than complete confidence in the past. But today's osteopathic physicians receive training comparable to that received by MDs. In fact, much of a DO's training is conducted by MDs or professionals who may have either an MD or a DO degree. Currently, over 16,000 DOs practice in the United States.

Pharmacists may also specialize. The individual you see in the drugstore is the community pharmacist. The community pharmacist fills prescriptions and may tend to the rest of the store as well. The hospital pharmacist fills drug orders in a hospital, frequently without ever seeing a patient. The manufacturing pharmacist works for a company that makes large quantities of drugs. Finally, the clinical pharmacist is responsible for monitoring a patient's drug therapy for accuracy. He often does not dispense drugs and usually works in a hospital or clinic alongside physicians.

Like all doctors, all pharmacists have the same basic education. The training differs in the supplemental course study or practical experience required to perform specialized work.

Writing Prescriptions

A pharmacist can fill your prescription; he cannot write one. By law, MDs and DOs can write prescriptions, regardless of their specialty. Some health care professionals do not have one of these degrees, and they cannot write prescriptions—for example, optometrists and psychologists. Ophthalmologists, psychiatrists, and anesthesiologists (professionals who administer drugs to induce unconsciousness to avoid pain during surgery) can write prescriptions.

Dentists can legally write prescriptions for drugs related to the dental needs of their patients. Podiatrists can write prescriptions for drugs to treat foot problems, and veterinarians can write prescriptions for animals. No one else can legally sign a prescription.

HOW TO SELECT THE RIGHT HEALTH CARE PROFESSIONAL

You must be able to rely on the professionals you entrust with your health care. You must have confidence in their knowledge and skill and feel comfortable enough to ask questions when you are worried or puzzled.

Choosing Your Doctor

In the past, the family doctor, or general practitioner (GP), was practically a member of the family. He delivered a baby, treated his childhood illnesses, and danced at his wedding 20 years later. Today, medicine is so specialized that patients may have to see a different doctor for different ailments.

But medicine may be returning to the bygone era of the GP. One of the most popular new specialties is family practice. The family practitioner is a general practitioner who has had specialized training as well.

The family practitioner or community physician can be your first line of defense. He may suggest that you see a specialist for some specific treatment, but he is your family doctor, the one who knows about all the medical care you are receiving. He can concentrate on you as a whole person rather than just on the part of your body that temporarily has gone awry.

But how do you choose a family doctor? Choosing a family physician may be a long and complex process, or a short and simple one. You can follow some general guidelines, but remember that guidelines are not hard-and-fast rules etched in granite.

By the way, you should begin this process now—before you need a doctor. Give yourself time to shop around. You wouldn't buy a used car without first inspecting it. So why place your health in the hands of a doctor before knowing something about him?

Get Some Names—You may ask doctors in your community or your previous doctor, if you are moving, for names of family practitioners. The city or county medical society may suggest several physicians, but remember, not all doctors belong to these societies. You may ask the administrator of your local hospital for a list of the doctors on its staff, or you may call nearby medical schools and request the names of doctors who are accepting new patients in your area. You may contact your local Department of Health or your local pharmacist.

Examine Qualifications—Most of us accept the first doctor who agrees to see us without asking about his qualifications. However, since we are talking about your health, and possibly your life, do your homework.

Begin by asking others. Check with friends or family members who have seen the physician or with his other patients. Then, judge the physician's qualifications by visiting his office yourself. Request a complete physical examination or the diagnosis of a malady that has plagued you for years (such as a sore arm, a cyst on the neck, a wart on the toe, or even falling hair) and carefully note what happens.

Does he take a complete medical history? Does he ask you about your previous illnesses, hospitalizations, and dietary habits? Does he inquire about your home life? Does he ask about any previous pregnancies—their number, ease of delivery or complications? Does he want to know about allergies or unusual responses to foods or drugs? Does he completely answer all the questions you ask in terms you can easily understand?

Consider how the physician conducts his practice. Is his office clean or cluttered? Do you have to wait a long time before he sees you? Do you know if he attends regular continuing education seminars and meetings? Can you find out if his practice is covered by a colleague when he is away? Does he seem willing to consult with another doctor if necessary? Does he discuss his fees openly? Do you believe he will make every effort to protect you against excessive charges from hospitals or consulting physicians? And, perhaps most important, does he appear to be interested in you as a person and not just as another $20 fee?

A good doctor is intelligent and knowledgeable but willing to admit his deficiencies. Above all, the doctor who is good for you is one whose personality and manners are compatible with yours.

Once you've chosen a doctor, you're still only halfway home. Now, you must find a pharmacist.

Choosing Your Pharmacist

Just as you have taken time to select a competent doctor, you must take time to choose a capable pharmacist.

Before you pick a pharmacist, consider how he keeps records. Does he record all the prescription drugs he dispenses to his patrons? Does he maintain a file or card that lists all of the drugs they are receiving? If he does not have files or cards for his customers, he cannot assess the accuracy of their drug therapy. Nor can he detect any possible life-threatening drug interactions. And without such records, you may not be able to find out from him why you react strangely or have nausea, itching, palpitations, or blurred vision.

Look at the pharmacy itself. Does the pharmacist provide a separate room or a corner where he can talk with you privately? No doubt you wouldn't want to discuss your personal health problems in an "open shop" or where others may overhear.

Finally, judge the pharmacist's attitude. Is he willing to talk to you about your drugs? Are his directions clear? Does he make sure you understand them? Does he ask you to repeat his instructions? And does he appear to be unhurried and interested in you?

If you can answer "yes" to all the questions, you've found a capable pharmacist.

THE IMPORTANCE OF COMMUNICATION

One way to choose health care professionals is on the basis of their willingness to answer your questions. Equally important is your willingness to answer theirs—or your eagerness to volunteer information. You should know what to tell your doctor and your pharmacist as well as what to ask.

Talking to Your Doctor

What should you tell your physician about the drugs you are taking? Mention all the over-the-counter nonprescription drugs you take—even an occasional aspirin tablet. Aspirin may cause significant problems, such as stomachache, itching, or difficulty in breathing. It may interact with a drug your doctor wishes to prescribe and could cause serious bleeding. Discuss with your doctor any laxatives, "stay awake" tablets, or vitamins you use. A laxative such as mineral oil may be responsible for a tired, run-down feeling; and, if you take a laxative at the wrong time, it may interfere with the action of an antibiotic you may also be taking.

Also, remind your physician about birth control pills. Let him know if you have seen another doctor or dentist recently or plan to soon. Keep him thoroughly informed.

Do not ask him how much a prescription will cost. He probably does not know. The question is important to you, but it is one you should save for your pharmacist.

Talking to Your Pharmacist

Give the same information to your pharmacist that you gave to your doctor. Doctors and pharmacists should complement one another. If one misses an important possible drug interaction or toxicity or has made an error in drug dosage, the other should catch it. And if your pharmacist is to check for possible drug interactions, he must know about drugs you get from another drugstore or those the doctor dispenses directly to you.

What information should you get in return? You should be informed if the drugs can cause drowsiness or nausea. You should be told what to expect from the medication and about how long you will have to take it. Of course, people's treatments vary tremendously, but you should know whether you will have to take medication for five to ten days (for example, to treat a mild respiratory infection) or for a few months (for example, to treat a kidney infection).

Your pharmacist should advise you of possible side effects and describe their symptoms in terms you can understand. And he should tell you which side effects require prompt attention from your physician. For example, one of the major side effects of the drug Butazolidin is a blood disorder. One of its first symptoms is a sore throat. Your pharmacist should tell you to consult your physician if you develop a sore throat.

Your pharmacist should also explain how to take your medicine. "One tablet four times a day" is not enough. He should tell you whether to take the drug before or after a meal or along with it. When you take a drug can make a big difference, and the effectiveness of each drug depends on following the directions for its use. Your pharmacist should describe what "as needed," "as directed," and "take with fluid" mean. You may take water with some drugs but not milk. With other drugs, you should take milk. Your pharmacist should tell you how many refills you may have and whether you may need them. You should know all this information before putting a tablet, capsule, or spoonful of liquid medication in your mouth.

Do not ask your pharmacist questions he cannot or will not answer. "What is this drug used for?" is a question to ask your doctor. Most drugs have several uses. Your pharmacist may tell you about only one of them; if it is not the one for which your doctor prescribed the drug, you may become worried needlessly. Second, your pharmacist may not be able to answer such questions as, "Will this drug work for me," or "Will it cure me?" He can only give you a general answer. And remember, your doctor prescribed it because he believed it would work for you. On the other hand, a few drugs may have side effects, and you should know about possible side effects in advance.

How Your Pharmacist Can Save You Money

One way your pharmacist can save you money is by recommending a generic drug. More about that later.
Another way your pharmacist can help you save money is by recommending self-therapy or the use of over-the-counter drugs. Many people visit a doctor for ailments that can be treated effectively by taking nonprescription drugs. Actually, some prescriptions are written for such drugs. But if your pharmacist recommends that you not take over-the-counter drugs, take his advice.

Reading Your Prescription

YOU DO NOT have to be a doctor, nurse, or pharmacist to read a prescription, but you must learn how. After all, the prescription describes the drug you will be taking—the drug to treat your condition. You should understand what your doctor has written on the prescription blank to be sure he hasn't made a mistake and to be sure the label on the drug container you receive from your pharmacist coincides with the prescription.

Also, when you understand what has been written on a prescription, you will be able to pay closer attention to detail and to follow your doctor's directions.

Prescriptions are not mysterious, and they contain no secret message. Many of the symbols and phrases doctors use on prescriptions are abbreviated Latin or Greek words, and they are holdovers from the days when doctors actually wrote in Latin. For example, "gtts" comes from the Latin word *guttae,* which means drops, and "bid" is a shortened version of *bis in die,* Latin for twice a day.

Now, let's see how easy it is to read a prescription.

First, study the chart in this chapter that lists the most commonly used symbols and abbreviations on prescriptions. Then, look at the sample prescriptions.

One prescription is for Darvon Compound-65 (Darvon Cpd. 65) analgesic. The prescription tells the pharmacist to give you 24 capsules (#24), and it tells you to take one capsule (cap i) every four hours (q̄4h) as needed (prn) for pain. The prescription indicates that you may receive five refills (5x) and that the label on the drug container should state the name of the drug (yes).

Look at the prescription for a 3 percent solution of Isopto-Carpine ophthalmic solution. It states you will receive 15 ml (disp: 15 ml) of these eyedrops. Isopto-Carpine solution is packaged in 15-ml containers; the pharmacist will give you one bottle. The bottle's label will direct you to place two drops (ggts ii) in your left eye (OL) every (q̄) morning (AM) and evening (PM) as directed (ut dict). No refills are indicated; so you or your pharmacist must contact your doctor before you can have the prescription refilled. And the prescription states that the name of the drug should be on the bottle's label (✔).

John D. Jones MD
Anytown, U.S.A.

DEA#123456789   PHONE #123-4567

NAME _Your name_   AGE _25_
ADDRESS _Anytown, U.S.A_   DATE _10-15-79_

℞ Darvon cpd - 65
        #24
        Sig: cap ī q̄ 4h prn pain

REFILLS _5x_   _John D. Jones, MD_
LABEL _yes_   MD

John D. Jones MD
Anytown, U.S.A.

DEA#123456789   PHONE #123-4567

NAME _Your name_   AGE _25_
ADDRESS _Anytown, USA_   DATE _10-15-79_

℞ Isopto - Carpine 3%
        disp: 15 ml
        Sig: gtt ii OL q̄ AM & PM ut dict

REFILLS _____   _John D Jones, MD_
LABEL _✓_   MD

```
                  John D. Jones MD
                  Anytown, U.S.A.
DEA#123456789                    PHONE #123-4567

NAME    Your name              AGE 25
ADDRESS Anytown, U S A         DATE 10-15-79

Rx    Lanoxin  0.125
      dtd  C
      sig: iii stat, ii tomonow AM ⊤ then
          i q̄ AM c̄ OJ

REFILLS  prn        John D Jones, M.D.
LABEL    ✓                          MD
```

Look at the last prescription. It shows you will receive 100 (dtd
C) tablets of Lanoxin heart drug, 0.125 mg. You will
take three tablets at once (iii stat), then two (ii) tomorrow morning
(AM), and one (i) every (q̄) morning (AM) with (c̄) orange juice
(OJ). You may receive refills as needed (prn), and the name of
the drug will be on the package (✓).

Do remember to check the label on the drug container. If the
label is not the same as the prescription, question your
pharmacist. Make doubly sure that you are receiving the right
medication and the correct instructions for taking it.

DOSAGE

One of the least understood aspects of drug therapy is dosage.
Most Americans believe that dosage is the amount of the drug to
be taken. But dosage also involves when to take the drug.

Obviously, the amount of a drug to take is important. People
can become seriously ill by taking an overdose, and taking just a
little too much can often cause problems. Many cases of aspirin
poisoning in children are caused by parents or guardians when

they give just "a little too much" aspirin just "a little too soon." On the other hand, diabetics may go into shock if they wait too long between injections of insulin or if they miss an injection.

If medicine were a perfect science, each patient would have the dosage of his drug precisely adjusted to his needs. The label on a drug container might read, "One tablet every four hours and 37 minutes," because the patient would need another dose of the drug at such intervals. Or a small computer might measure when

COMMON ABBREVIATIONS AND SYMBOLS USED IN WRITING PRESCRIPTIONS

Abbreviation	Meaning	Derivation and Notes
A_2	both ears	*auris* (Latin)
aa	of each	*ana* (Greek)
ac	before meals	*ante cibum* (Latin)
AD	right ear	*auris dextra* (Latin)
AL	left ear	*auris laeva* (Latin)
AM	morning	*ante meridiem* (Latin)
AS	left ear	*auris sinistra* (Latin)
bid	twice a day	*bis in die* (Latin)
c̄	with	*cum* (Latin)
cap	capsule	—
cc or cm^3	cubic centimeter	30 cc equals one ounce
disp	dispense	—
dtd#	give this number	*dentur tales doses* (Latin)
ea	each	—
ext	for external use	—
gtts	drops	*guttae* (Latin)
gutta	drop	*gutta* (Latin)
h	hour	*hora* (Latin)
H_2O or HOH	water	two molecules of hydrogen, one of oxygen
HS	bedtime	*hora somni* (Latin)
M ft	make	*misce fiat* (Latin)
mitt#	give this number	*mitte* (Latin)
ml	milliter	30 ml equals one ounce
O	pint	*octarius* (Latin)
O_2	both eyes	*oculus* (Latin)
OD	right eye	*oculus dexter* (Latin)

a patient needed another dose of a drug and dispense it automatically.

But medicine is not a perfect science, and doctors often simplify dosage instructions. Yet, to be effective, a drug must be taken on schedule.

A prescription that states "one tablet four times daily" seems plain enough. But what does four times a day mean?

For some antibiotics that are prescribed for serious infections, it

---

COMMON ABBREVIATIONS AND SYMBOLS USED IN WRITING PRESCRIPTIONS

Abbreviation	Meaning	Derivation and Notes
OJ	orange juice	—
OL	left eye	*oculus laevus* (Latin)
OS	left eye	*oculus sinister* (Latin)
OU	each eye	*oculus uterque* (Latin)
pc	after meals	*post cibum* (Latin)
PM	evening	*post meridiem* (Latin)
po	by mouth	*per os* (Latin)
prn	as needed	*pro re nata* (Latin)
q̄	every	*quaqua* (Latin)
qd	once a day	*quaqua die* (Latin)
qid	four times a day	*quater in die* (Latin)
qod	every other day	—
s̄	without	*sine* (Latin)
Sig	label as follows	*signetur* (Latin)
sl	under the tongue	*sub lingua* (Latin)
SOB	shortness of breath	—
sol	solution	—
ss	half-unit	*semis* (Latin)
stat	at once, first dose	*statim* (Latin)
susp	suspension	—
tab	tablet	—
tid	three times a day	*ter in die* (Latin)
top	apply topically	—
ung or ungt	ointment	*unguentum* (Latin)
UT	under the tongue	—
ut dict	as directed	*ut dictum* (Latin)
x	times	—

may mean one every six hours around the clock. For some medications used for nervous conditions, it may mean one in the morning, one at noon, one in the early evening, and one at bedtime. And for medication to treat intestinal worms, it may mean one every hour for the first four hours after you get up in the morning.

For example, the prescription for Darvon Compound-65 analgesic tells you to take one capsule every four hours as needed. How many capsules can you take each day—four, six, eight or more? The phrase "as needed" is not clear, and unless you completely understand your prescription, you may leave the pharmacy with unanswered questions.

The phrases "as needed," "as directed," "with meals," and "on an empty stomach" seem specific. Your doctor and pharmacist understand these phrases and sometimes assume that you do too. But these phrases are not always as clear as they seem. To get the most benefit from your medication and to minimize harmful side effects, you must take drugs as directed. So do not be afraid to ask your pharmacist for an explanation. After all, you wouldn't begin a journey without a road map. So why start on a drug therapy program without knowing the plan and how to follow it?

REFILLS

A word about refilling prescriptions. While some prescriptions can be refilled anytime, others cannot be refilled without consulting your doctor. Whenever you receive a prescription, ask your doctor about refills.

Buying And Storing Drugs

I N A PRESCRIPTION, your doctor specifies exactly how many tablets or capsules or how much liquid medication you will receive. But if you must take a drug for a long period of time, or if you are very sensitive to drugs, you may want to get a different quantity.

The amount of medication to buy depends on several factors. The most obvious is how much money you have or, for those who have a comprehensive insurance program, how much the insurance company will pay for each purchase. These factors may help you decide how much medication to buy. But you must also consider the kind of medication you will be taking. For example, you should buy enough antibiotics to last ten days unless your doctor has specifically directed otherwise. Antibiotics often cure an infection within ten days. If you have more than a ten-day supply, you may waste money on medication you do not need. Also, a liquid antibiotic preparation may have lost its potency after ten days.

But medication to treat heart disease, high blood pressure, diabetes, or a thyroid condition may be purchased in large quantity. Patients with such chronic conditions take medication for prolonged periods of time, and chances are they will pay less per tablet or capsule by purchasing large amounts of drugs. Generally, the price per dose decreases with the amount of the drug purchased. In other words, a drug that generally costs six cents per tablet may cost $4 or $5 for 100 tablets, or four or five cents per tablet, if you buy a supply of 100 at a time. Many doctors prescribe a month's supply of drugs that will be taken for a long period of time. If you wish to buy more, check with your pharmacist.

When buying drugs, also consider how far away from the pharmacy you live and how many trips you will have to make to get a prescription refilled. Above all, buy enough medication to be economical but not so much that you may have to throw some away.

By the way, if you have been plagued with annoying side effects or have had allergic reactions to some drugs, ask your pharmacist to dispense only enough medication on initial prescriptions for a few days or a week to determine whether the drug agrees with you. Pharmacists cannot take back prescription drugs once they have left the pharmacy. You may have to pay more by asking the pharmacist to give you a small amount of the drug, but at least you will not be paying for a supply of medication you cannot take. And be sure you can get the remainder of the prescribed amount of the drug. With some drugs, such as narcotics, after you have received part of the intended amount, you cannot receive more without obtaining another prescription.

SHOPPING AROUND

Should you shop around to get the best price on your prescription drugs? We don't think so. When you get your drugs at different pharmacies, it's extremely difficult to detect drug interactions or find other potential errors. Don't play around with your health. Stick to one pharmacy.

You should select a competent pharmacist who is truly interested in you as a person rather than just as another customer. Tell him you plan to purchase all of your prescription items from him. He'll appreciate hearing that you plan to give him all of your prescription business. And, don't be afraid to mention early on that you're on a limited income, or that you have exceptionally high medical bills. You could even just come out and ask for a discount. Many pharmacists are willing to give discounts to persons over 60, to other health professionals such as nurses, or to school teachers, or to any person who is financially disabled. We're willing to bet that he'll give you a special price if you identify yourself.

And by the way, don't ever think that the bigger the pharmacy, the cheaper its prices and vice versa. It's the people within that make the difference.

EXPIRATION DATES

All prescription drugs have expiration dates. Drug manufacturers establish expiration dates, or the time beyond which the drugs may no longer be totally effective. An expiration date usually is set for five years after the drug was made, and it is usually based on the time at which 5 percent of the drug will have been destroyed or converted.

The expiration date on certain antibiotics, such as the

tetracyclines, is especially important because it indicates when the antibiotic may become toxic. Case studies in the medical literature have reported deaths of patients who took outdated tetracycline. After the expiration date, tetracycline converts into another chemical that is damaging to the kidneys. Patients who take outdated tetracycline develop symptoms of severe kidney disease and may die. Other antibiotics, such as penicillin, do not become toxic after their expiration date, but they do lose potency.

While a drug may be effective beyond its expiration date, you cannot be sure and should not take chances. So, never use a prescription drug after the date stated on the manufacturer's label. Be sure your pharmacist indicates the expiration date on your prescription label.

STORING YOUR DRUGS

If drugs are stored in containers that do not protect them from heat or moisture, they may lose potency. Some drugs lose potency if the lids of the containers in which they are stored do not fit tightly. Consequently, you should follow some basic rules for keeping prescription drugs.

You can safely store most prescription drugs at room temperature and out of direct sunlight. Some drugs are dispensed in colored bottles or containers that reflect light. Nevertheless, remember to keep all prescription drugs out of direct sunlight.

One of the worst places to keep a drug is in the glove compartment of your car during the summer. The temperature inside the glove compartment may reach 160°F or more, and the drug may be destroyed completely in a short time.

Some drugs require storage in the refrigerator. But the statement "keep in the refrigerator" does not mean that you can keep the drug in the freezer. If frozen and thawed, some liquid medications will separate into layers that cannot be remixed. And sugar-coated tablets may crack when frozen and thawed.

Other drugs cannot be stored in the refrigerator. For example, in liquid form, the antibiotic Cleocin will thicken as it becomes cold and will not pour from the bottle. Some people keep nitroglycerin tablets in the refrigerator because they believe the drug will be more stable. Nitroglycerin, however, should not be stored in the refrigerator.

Many people keep prescription drugs and other medications in the bathroom medicine cabinet. But this is one of the worst places to keep drugs. Small children can easily climb onto the sink and reach drugs stored above it. The temperature and humidity in the bathroom vary greatly over the course of the day, and the changes in humidity and temperature may adversely affect the stability of prescription drugs.

Of course, prescription drugs and over-the-counter medications must be kept away from children. Remember that "children see, children do"—that is, if a child sees you taking medicine, he wants to take it too. And he can take a deadly dose.

If you have small children, keep drugs locked up. You can get an inexpensive lock for a cabinet or closet at your local hardware store. But remember to use it.

Perhaps you have fought to open one of the "child-resistant" drug containers and have muttered angrily about the "confounded things." Child-resistant caps and containers, however, have reduced the number of accidental poisonings. If you do not lock up drugs, have them packaged in child-resistant containers.

If you have trouble opening child-resistant containers, ask your pharmacist to place your medication in a regular container. But please remember to store these containers out of the reach of any children.

Many regular drug containers are more difficult to open than they once were because the container tops and lids fit more tightly to prevent moisture in the air from causing the drugs to deteriorate. Containers with tightly fitting lids can help assure the safety and effectiveness of the drugs they house.

DISPOSE OF OLD DRUGS

Do not keep prescription drugs that you no longer need. Flush any leftover medication down the toilet or pour it down the sink, and wash and destroy the empty container. Regularly clean out your medicine cabinet and discard all drugs you are no longer using. These drugs can be dangerous to your children, and you might be tempted to take them in the future if you develop similar symptoms. Though similar, the symptoms may not be due to the same disease, and you may complicate your condition by taking medication prescribed to treat a different ailment. So be cautious—always dispose of leftover prescription drugs.

Poisoning—And What To Do When It Happens

HOW MANY Americans are poisoned by drugs each year? The reported figures range from one to several million. Many poisonings are not reported, however, and the reported figures most likely are lower than the actual number. In fact, a study showed that only one out of every 50 cases of poisoning was reported. The number of Americans poisoned each year is unknown.

What is known is that over half of all poisonings are caused by drugs. Drugs are the most common cause of accidental poisoning.

CHILDREN ARE MOST SUSCEPTIBLE

"Into the hand, into the mouth" is especially true for children under five years of age. Over 50 percent of all reported cases of poisoning involve children in this age group.

Children are naturally curious. Their curiosity takes them up onto tabletops and sinks and even into medicine cabinets. They see their parents consume drugs, and since youngsters are imitative, they wish to follow suit. Parents unwittingly encourage them when they call a flavored tablet "candy" or liquid medication "sweet syrup."

Actually, the number one cause of poisoning of children is well-meaning but careless adults. Many parents give their children aspirin at the first wheeze or sniffle. The first aspirin is quickly followed by a second, and a third, and before long, the child has been poisoned. Of course, aspirin is not the only drug given to

Drugs That Most Often Cause Poisoning

Drug Name	Symptoms
aspirin	Nausea, vomiting (may have blood in vomitus), fever, rapid breathing, weakness, confusion. May have white spots in the mouth.
Sedatives (barbiturates, Valium, Librium, etc.)	Drowsiness, dizziness, weakness, slow breathing, pinpoint pupils, May breathe with a "gurgling" sound.
cold medicines containing antihistamines	Drowsiness, dizziness, weakness, nervousness, dry mouth, fever, pounding in chest. (Children may experience excitement, increased pulse and breathing.)
narcotics (codeine, etc.)	Drowsiness, dizziness, weakness, pinpoint pupils, slow breathing. May breathe with a "gurgling" sound.
acetaminophen (Tylenol, Datril, etc.)	Nausea, vomiting, loss of color, weakness, difficult breathing. (Symptoms may disappear in four to eight hours, but it still is extremely important to call your doctor for help.)
antidepressants (Tofranil, Elavil, etc.)	Excitation, dry mouth, pounding in chest, nervousness. Respiration increases for first several hours then decreases.
vitamins and iron	Nausea, vomiting. vitamin A - above, plus loss of appetite, headache. vitamin D - above, plus twitching of muscles, nervousness. iron - above, plus diarrhea (may contain blood, or dark spots), drowsiness.

children, but it is the most common agent of drug poisoning of children.

Barbiturates and sleeping aids are the leading agents in adult drug poisoning. Other drugs commonly involved in poisonings are listed in the accompanying table.

WHAT TO DO

Most drug overdoses can be reversed by observing a few simple rules. Luckily, these rules can be used in the emergency treatment of overdoses from many drugs, and you need not follow a specific treatment for an overdose of a specific drug.

ACT FAST

After an adult or child has taken an overdose of a drug, your primary objective is to lessen the toxicity of the drug or to get rid of it as *quickly as possible.* Act fast! As soon as an overdose has been discovered, dilute the drug, induce vomiting, or administer activated charcoal to keep the drug from entering the bloodstream. Once you have administered emergency first aid, seek medical aid at once. Call your Poison Control Center, emergency medical unit, doctor, or pharmacist, or go directly to a hospital.

DILUTE THE POISON

Diluting the drug prevents it from damaging the lining of the stomach. Also, adding fluid to the stomach aids vomiting.

One cup of water may be given to a child, and two to three cups are suitable for an adult. Carbonated beverages (soda pop) should not be given. Carbonated beverages produce gas, which can distend the stomach wall and increase the chance of a stomach puncture. Besides water, fruit juice or milk is commonly used to dilute a drug. However, only water should be given until a doctor or pharmacist has been consulted regarding the use of milk or fruit juices.

INDUCE VOMITING—SOMETIMES

Vomiting (emesis) can be used to rid the body of any poison except an acid, a petroleum derivative, a corrosive such as lye, or a convulsive such as strychnine. These poisons can burn the throat as they are being vomited. Containers of these poisons have clearly marked labels, which warn against inducing vomiting. *Always check the label on the container of the poison that has been ingested before attempting to induce vomiting.*

Recommended Antidotes For Drug Poisoning

Syrup of Ipecac:
For children: 1 teaspoonful followed by 1 or 2 glasses of
water.
For adults: 1 tablespoonful followed by 2 or 3 glasses of
water.
(Dose may be repeated once, 15 to 20 minutes later.)

Activated Charcoal:
For children and adults: 2 heaping tablespoonsful (about 2
ounces) mixed with 1 cup of water to form a slurry.
(Dose may be repeated 30 to 60 minutes later, and again as
frequently as necessary.)

Drugs generally do not contain any such poisons. And inducing
vomiting in a child or adult who has taken a drug overdose
usually is safe as long as the victim is conscious. If the victim of
a drug overdose is unconscious, do not try to induce vomiting
because he may choke.

To induce vomiting, you may follow one of several methods.
You should know the benefits and risks of each.

Syrup of ipecac—Undoubtedly, syrup of ipecac is the emetic
of choice for home emergency treatment of drug poisoning. One
teaspoon of syrup of ipecac usually is given to a child, and one
tablespoonful to an adult. Make the victim drink water after the
syrup of ipecac is administered, if he has not drunk any before.
Vomiting should occur in about 15 minutes. If it does not, the
dose can be repeated once, 15 to 20 minutes after the first dose.
Syrup of ipecac is available in one-ounce bottles in first-aid kits
and it can be purchased from most pharmacies.

Mechanical stimulus—To induce vomiting by mechanical
stimulus, place the victim in a spanking position and gently stroke
the back of his tongue with your finger or a blunt object, such as
a spoon. Be careful if you stroke the back of the tongue with
your finger. The victim may bite down on it as he gags.

Mechanical stimulus is a common way to induce vomiting, but it
usually is not effective. In a study of 30 children who had
ingested a poison, only two vomited after this procedure was
followed, and the volume actually vomited was small, even though
the children had been given a cup of water. The time wasted
trying to induce vomiting by mechanical stimulus could be better
spent by administering an effective agent, such as syrup of
ipecac.

Mustard—Mustard powder (one or two teaspoonsful in a cup of water) has not been shown to effectively induce vomiting, even though its use has been advocated for years. Mustard powder is not available in most households, and the mustard used on hotdogs does not substitute for it.

Table salt—Table salt has long been thought to be a safe and effective agent for inducing vomiting but it is not. It should *never* be used to induce vomiting because the salt itself can be toxic and may be lethal. Unfortunately, many first-aid charts and package labels still recommend that it be used. Such recommendations should be disregarded. If you have any further questions, ask your doctor or pharmacist.

ACTIVATED CHARCOAL

In practically all cases of drug poisoning, activated charcoal can be used as an antidote. An ounce or two should be mixed as a slurry in a cup of water and drunk as soon as possible after poisoning. This dose is not absolute, and because activated charcoal is nontoxic, the victim of drug poisoning need not worry about consuming too much. To ensure complete removal of the drug, the dose of activated charcoal can be repeated once or twice at 30- to 60-minute intervals.

Activated charcoal prevents absorption of a drug into the bloodstream. Even though the benefits of activated charcoal in the treatment of drug overdoses have been known for years, many doctors and pharmacists largely have ignored it.

One reason for its rather poor acceptance is that charcoal has some disagreeable characteristics. It is black and stains the gums and mouth. It has a bitter taste and it creates a gritty sensation in the mouth.

When using activated charcoal to treat a drug overdose, you may want to remember a few "tricks of the trade." Mix a little cocoa powder with the charcoal solution or place a small amount of coca or powdered sugar directly on the victim's tongue before he drinks it. Mix the activated charcoal with water in an amber-colored container so that the victim cannot see the color of the mixture while drinking.

Prompt use of activated charcoal is effective for home emergency treatment of an overdose from a number of drugs. It is inexpensive, can be purchased in any quantity without a prescription, and is not irritating to the stomach.

One other thing to remember is that you should not use both syrup of ipecac and activated charcoal at the same time. Your doctor or pharmacist will help you decide which is better to use.

To be ready to take prompt action in the case of a drug overdose, get some syrup of ipecac and activated charcoal *now*.

Do not wait until you need them. Get them today and keep them handy. You may never need them, but do not take that chance.

WHAT COMES NEXT?

Home emergency treatment of a drug overdose is not enough. You must also seek professional care. If you live near a Poison Control Center, call for further instructions. Look up the Center's phone number and keep it handy in case of an emergency.

If you are not near a phone or a Poison Control Center, start for the hospital as soon as the antidote has been administered. Be sure to take the drug container and all remaining tablets, capsules, or liquid with you so an estimate of the amount of drug ingested can be made.

Take a sample of the vomit with you in a dish, or at least take an empty dish or pan to collect any material vomited on the way to the hospital. Your doctor may want to analyze it if the identity of the drug is not known.

By all means, stay calm. Note symptoms, and keep track of time. Your doctor will want to know how much time elapsed between swallowing the drug and the first symptoms.

Most cases of drug poisoning are not fatal. But survival depends on the drug, how much was taken, how soon the overdose was discovered, the age of the victim, and the emergency measures taken.

AVOIDING DRUG POISONINGS

Obviously, preventing drug poisoning is better than having to treat it. These tips may help you avoid a potential tragedy.

1. Store drugs out of the reach of children. Place drugs in a cabinet, closet, or trunk that can be locked.
2. Store medication intended for external use separate from drugs intended to be swallowed.
3. Use child-resistant drug containers if children live with you or visit often. Refasten the lid securely after use.
4. Read the label carefully, paying particular attention to warnings and precautions.
5. Do not take or give drugs in the dark—one bottle easily can be mistaken for another. Always turn on a light and check the label.
6. Do not keep unlabeled drugs in the house.
7. Do not take drugs when your children are nearby. They are apt to mimic you.
8. Do not refer to any drug (including vitamins) as "candy."

9. Do not leave medication within the reach of children. Take it with you or return it to its locked storage area if you are called to the telephone or the door.
10. Do not use drugs prescribed for someone else. They may be dangerous to you.
11. Keep handy the telephone numbers of your doctor, your pharmacist, and the local Poison Control Center.
12. Take no chances. If your child may have swallowed a drug (if you see him handling an open container or if there are particles of the drug in his mouth, for example), do not wait for symptoms of an overdose. Follow the procedures for emergency measures. Some drugs, such as aspirin, may not produce symptoms until several hours after poisoning.
13. Dispose of old drugs. Once a drug has served its purpose, discard it. Flush it down the toilet or pour it down the sink. Rinse the container and discard it.

The Right Way To Take Medications

WHEN YOUR DOCTOR prescribes a particular medication, you must follow his directions for taking it. To get the best results from the drugs you take, you must administer them properly. Following a few simple guidelines can help.

AEROSOL SPRAYS

Many topical agents (drugs that are used on the skin) are packaged as aerosol sprays. Generally, aerosols cost more than a cream or ointment, but the extra cost of these sprays is justified when they are used to apply medication to a tender area of the skin or to a part of the body on which creams or ointments cannot be applied easily (hair, for example).

Before using an aerosol, shake the can. Hold the can upright about four to six inches from the skin. Press the nozzle for a few seconds, then release.

An aerosol sprayed into the eyes or onto mucous membranes can cause pain and may damage the eyes. If your doctor tells you to apply the medication to part of your face, spray your hand, then rub the medication on your face.

An aerosol spray feels cold when it is applied. If you find this sensation uncomfortable, ask your doctor for another way of administering the drug.

TABLETS AND CAPSULES

Tablets may be chewed, placed under the tongue (sublingual), or swallowed. Be sure you know the type of tablet you have and how you should take it.

Chewable Tablets

Chewable tablets *must* be chewed to release the drug they

contain. Patients who have difficulty swallowing large tablets may prefer chewable ones, although they usually cost more.

Sublingual Tablets

Some drugs to relieve chest pain or an asthma attack are prepared as tablets that must be placed under the tongue. To take a sublingual tablet properly, place the tablet under your tongue, close your mouth, and hold the saliva in your mouth and under your tongue as long as you can before swallowing it. If you have a bitter taste in your mouth after five minutes, the drug has not been completely absorbed. Wait five more minutes before drinking water. Drinking water too soon may wash the medication into the stomach before it has been absorbed thoroughly.

Swallowing Capsules and Tablets

Many people cannot swallow a tablet or capsule without difficulty. If you're one of them, rinse your mouth with water before taking a tablet or capsule, or at least wet your mouth. Place the tablet or capsule on the back of your tongue, take a drink of water, and swallow.

If you cannot swallow a tablet or capsule because it is too large or because it "sticks" in your throat, empty the capsule or crush the tablet into a spoon and mix it with applesauce, soup, or even chocolate syrup. But be sure to check with your pharmacist first. Some tablets and capsules must be swallowed

The Following Drugs
Must Be Swallowed Whole

Aminodur Dura-Tabs	Isordil Tembids
Bendectin	Naldecon
Chlor-Trimeton Repetabs	Nebralin
Choledyl tablets	Polaramine Repetabs
Dimetane Extentabs	Pro-Banthine P.A.
Dimetapp Extentabs	Quinidex Extentabs
Disophrol Chronotabs	Slow-K
Donnatal Extentabs	Tagamet
Drixoral	Tenuate Dospan
E-Mycin	Tepanil Ten-tabs
Equanil Wyseals	Trilafon Repetabs

---

whole, and your pharmacist can tell you which ones they are.

If you have trouble swallowing a tablet or capsule and do not wish to mix the medication with food each time you take it, ask your doctor to prescribe a liquid drug preparation or a chewable tablet instead.

The Following Drugs Should Be Used Quickly (Within 12 Hours) If Crushed Or Opened

Combid Spansules	Phenergan
Compazine	Stelazine
Elavil	Sinequan
Eskatrol Spansules	Triavil
Etrafon	Tofranil
Haldol	Thorazine
Mellaril	

LIQUIDS

Liquids are used externally on the skin, instilled into the eye, ear, or nose, or they may be taken internally.

The first thing to do before taking or using any liquid medication is to look at the label for any specific directions, such as shaking the container before measuring the dose. Liquid medications that must be shaken before using include suspensions, mixtures, and emulsions. Solutions, tinctures, and elixirs do not have to be shaken. Those that must be shaken contain drugs that are insoluble, and in order to get a dose that contains the right amount of drug each time, the bottle must be shaken before the dose is removed.

Before opening the bottle, point it away from you since some liquid medications build up a pressure inside the bottle; the medication could spurt out quickly and stain your clothing.

If the medication is intended for application on the skin, pour a small quantity of it onto a cotton pledget or a piece of gauze. Do not use an excessively large piece of cotton or gauze as much liquid will be absorbed and wasted. If you must apply the liquid to a large area (such as a whole arm or leg), you should not place the liquid in your cupped hand because you are apt to spill some of it. If the liquid is to cover a small area, you may spread the medication with your finger. Never dip cotton-tipped applicators or pieces of cotton or gauze into the bottle as this might contaminate the liquid.

Liquid medications that are to be swallowed must be measured accurately. When your doctor prescribes one teaspoon of medication, he is thinking of a medical teaspoon which contains 5 cc. Teaspoons that most people have in their homes may contain anywhere from 2 cc to 10 cc. Thus, if you use a regular teaspoon to measure your liquid medication, you may get too little or too much with each dose. Consequently, you should ask your pharmacist for a medical teaspoon or for one of the other plastic devices that are available for accurately measuring liquid medications. Most of these cost only a few cents, but they are well worth their cost to ensure accurate dosages. These plastic measuring devices have another advantage. Many children will balk at medication taken from a teaspoon; they seem to enjoy taking it from the special measuring devices.

EARDROPS

Eardrops must be administered so they fill the ear canal. To administer eardrops properly, tilt your head to one side and turn the affected ear upward. Grasp the ear lobe and pull it upward and back to straighten the ear canal. When administering eardrops to a child, gently pull the child's ear lobe downward and back. Fill the dropper and place the prescribed number of drops (usually a dropperful) in the ear, but be careful to avoid touching the ear canal. The dropper can easily become contaminated if it comes into contact with the ear canal.

Keep your ear tilted upward for five to ten seconds, then gently insert a small piece of cotton into the ear to be sure the drops do not escape. Do not wash or wipe the dropper after use; replace it in the bottle and tightly close the bottle to keep out moisture.

You may warm the bottle of eardrops before administering the medication. The best way to warm eardrops is to roll the bottle back and forth between your hands to bring the solution to body temperature. Do not place the bottle in boiling water. The eardrops may become too hot and cause pain when placed in the ear. And boiling water can loosen or peel the label off the bottle.

EYEDROPS AND OINTMENTS

First, be sure the drops or ointment you are using are intended for the eye. Before administering eyedrops or ointments, wash your hands. Next, lie down or sit down and tilt your head back. Gently and carefully pull your lower eyelid down to form a pouch. To insert eyedrops, hold the dropper close to the eyelid but without touching it. Place the prescribed number of drops into the pouch. Do not place the drops directly on the eyeball; you probably will blink and lose the medication. Close your eye and keep it shut for a few moments. Do not wash or wipe the dropper before replacing it in the bottle. Tightly close the bottle to keep out moisture.

To administer an ointment to the eye, squeeze a one-quarter to one-half inch line of ointment into the pouch and close your eye. Roll your eye a few times to spread the ointment. As long as you do not squeeze the ointment directly onto the eyeball, you should feel no stinging or pain.

NOSE DROPS AND SPRAYS

Before using nose drops and sprays, gently blow your nose if you can. To administer nose drops, fill the dropper, tilt your head back, and place the prescribed number of drops in your nose without touching the dropper to the nasal membranes; this will prevent contamination of the medicine when the dropper is returned to the container. Keep your head tilted for five to ten seconds and sniff gently two or three times.

Do not tilt your head back when using a nasal spray. Insert the spray into the nose but try to avoid touching the inner nasal membranes. Sniff and squeeze the spray at the same time. Do not release your grip of the sprayer until you have withdrawn it from your nose to prevent nasal mucus and bacteria from entering the plastic bottle and contaminating its contents. After you have sprayed the prescribed number of times in one or both nostrils, sniff two or three times.

Unless your doctor has told you otherwise, nose drops and spray should not be used for more than two or three days at a time. If they have been prescribed for a longer period, do not administer nose drops or sprays from the same container for more than one week. Bacteria from your nose can enter the container easily and can contaminate the solution. If you must take medication for more than a week, purchase a new container. And, never allow someone else to use your nose drops or spray.

OINTMENTS AND CREAMS

Ointments and creams are topical medications that have local effects—that is, they affect only the area on which they are applied. Most creams and ointments are expensive (especially steroid hormones such as hydrocortisone, Aristocort A, Cordran, Kenalog, Lidex, Mycolog, Synalar, Valisone, Vioform with hydrocortisone) and should be applied to the skin as thinly as possible. Some steroid-containing creams and ointments can cause toxic side effects if applied too heavily. Also, a thin layer is as effective as a thick layer.

Before applying the ointment, moisten the skin by immersing it in water or by daubing the area with a clean, wet cloth. Blot the skin dry and apply the ointment as directed. Gently massage it into the skin until it has disappeared. You should feel no greasiness or wetness on the skin after applying a cream. After applying an ointment, the skin will feel slightly greasy.

If your doctor has not indicated whether you should receive a cream or an ointment, ask your pharmacist for a cream. Creams are greaseless and will not stain your clothing. Creams are best for use on the scalp or other hairy areas of the body.

If, however, your skin is dry, ask your pharmacist for an ointment. Ointments help keep skin soft for a longer period of time.

If your doctor tells you to place a wrap on top of the skin after the cream or ointment has been applied, you may use a piece of plastic wrap. A wrap of transparent plastic film will hold the medication close to the skin and help keep the skin moist so the drug can be absorbed. To use such a wrap correctly, apply the cream or ointment as directed, then wrap the area with a layer of transparent plastic wrap. Be careful to follow your doctor's directions. If he tells you to leave the wrap in place for a certain length of time, do not leave it in place longer. If you keep a wrap on the skin too long, too much of the drug may be absorbed, which may cause side effects.

POWDERS

Powders may be applied to any part of the body. They should be sprinkled evenly over the surface. Powders are used when the area is tender and should be kept dry, such as in fungal and bacterial infections. They can be applied without applying pressure to the area, and because they absorb moisture, they help keep the area dry. Whenever you use a powder on your feet—in the treatment of athlete's foot or other infections—sprinkle some of the powder in your socks and shoes. Also, regardless of the type of powder, avoid inhaling it. Even a small amount of powder used for skin infection may cause a respiratory problem if inhaled.

RECTAL SUPPOSITORIES

A rectal suppository may be used as a laxative (Dulcolax laxative, glycerin) or to relieve the itching, swelling and pain of hemorrhoids (Anusol-HC steroid hormone). Regardless of the reason for their use, all suppositories are inserted in the same way. If a suppository is wrapped in aluminum foil, remove it. In extremely hot weather, a suppository may become too soft to handle properly. If it does, place it inside the refrigerator or in a glass of cool water until firm.

Rubber finger coverings or disposable rubber gloves may be worn when inserting a suppository, but they are not necessary unless your fingernails are extremely long and sharp.

To insert a suppository, lie on your left side (if you are right-handed) and push the suppository, pointed end first, into the rectum as far as you can without experiencing discomfort. If you feel like defecating, lie still until the urge has passed. If you cannot insert a suppository, or if the process is painful, coat the suppository with a thin layer of Vaseline, mineral oil, or K-Y Jelly before trying to insert it.

Manufacturers of many suppositories that are used in the treatment of hemorrhoids suggest that the suppositories be stored in the refrigerator. Be sure to ask your pharmacist if the suppositories you have purchased should be stored in the refrigerator.

THROAT MEDICATION

Lozenges or Discs

Lozenges are made of crystalized sugar; discs are not. Both contain medication that is released in the mouth to soothe a sore throat, reduce coughing, or to treat laryngitis. Neither should be chewed; they should be allowed to dissolve in the mouth. After the lozenge or disc has dissolved, try not to swallow or drink any fluids for awhile.

Sprays

To administer throat spray, open your mouth wide and spray the medication as far back as possible. Try not to swallow but hold the spray in your mouth as long as you can and try not to drink any fluids for several minutes.

VAGINAL MEDICATIONS

Many women have questions concerning the proper administration of vaginal medications. Most products contain complete instructions. In fact, one manufacturer encloses with the product a short quiz the woman is asked to complete before administering the medication. But if a woman is not sure how to administer vaginal medication, she should ask her pharmacist.

Ointments and Creams

Before using any vaginal ointment or cream, read the directions. They probably will tell you to screw the applicator to the top of the tube and squeeze the tube from the bottom until the applicator plunger is completely filled. Lie on your back with your knees drawn up. Hold the applicator horizontally or pointed slightly downward and insert it into the vagina as far as it will go comfortably. Then, press the plunger down to empty the cream or ointment into the vagina. Withdraw the plunger and wash it in warm soapy water. Rinse it thoroughly and allow it to dry completely. Once it is dry, return the plunger to its package.

Tablets and Suppositories

Most vaginal tablets or suppositories have complete directions for their use. But you may wish to review some general instructions.

If a tablet or suppository is wrapped in foil, remove it. Place the tablet or suppository in the applicator that is provided. Lie on your back with your knees drawn up. Hold the applicator horizontally or tilted slightly downward and insert it into the vagina as far as it will go comfortably. Depress the plunger slowly to release the tablet or suppository into the vagina. Withdraw the applicator and wash it in warm, soapy water. Rinse it and let it dry completely. Once it is dry, return the applicator to its package.

Unless your doctor has told you otherwise, do not douche two to three weeks before or after you use vaginal tablets or suppositories. Be sure to ask your doctor for specific recommendations on douching.

Saving Money With Generic Drugs

ONE OF the best ways to save money on prescription medication is to buy generic drugs. But what is a generic drug?

DRUG NAMES

Drugs are composed of chemicals and therefore have a chemical name. Chemical names are complex; they describe the constituents of a drug precisely so scientists all over the world can recognize the drug immediately. Usually, use of chemical names of drugs is restricted to articles in professional journals and to papers presented at scientific meetings. Neither doctors, nor pharmacists, nor consumers use the chemical names of drugs because they are lengthy and difficult to remember. For example, the chemical name of a common antibiotic is 4-(dimethylamino)-1,4,4a,5,5a,6,11,12a-octahydro-3,6,10,12,12a-pentahydroxy-6-methyl-1-11,dioxo-2-naphthacenecarboxamide.

This antibiotic is also known as tetracycline. Tetracycline is the drug's generic name. Anyone may use the generic name of a drug to compare it with other drugs. Any manufacturer can use the generic name when marketing a drug. Thus, many manufacturers make a drug called tetracycline.

Generic names of drugs may be complicated, but they are easier to remember and use than chemical names. Although most American names are recognized in other countries, there are some exceptions. For example, the drug known as acetaminophen here is known as paracetamol in Europe.

Usually, a manufacturer uses a trade name as well as a generic name for a drug. A trade name is registered, and only the manufacturer who holds the trademark can use the trade name when marketing a drug. For example, only Lederle Laboratories can call their tetracycline product Achromycin, and only The Upjohn Company can use the trade name Panmycin for tetracycline. Most trade names are easy to remember, are capitalized in print, and usually include the register symbol ® after them. But trade names differ in other countries. If you know the trade name of a drug used in the United States, you may not be understood if you ask for it in another country.

You probably already know that you can often save money when buying products if you purchase a private-label rather than a brand-name product. If you insist on buying a brand-name product, however, you must pay the price charged for the product.

Your doctor can prescribe a drug by its trade (brand) name, its generic name, or its generic name plus the name of a manufacturer. By prescribing a drug by its trade name, he implicitly specifies the manufacturer as well as the drug, for example, Panmycin made by The Upjohn Company. And your pharmacist provides the drug made by this company. If your doctor uses the generic name of a drug, your pharmacist can dispense any brand of tetracycline, including Panmycin. However, if your doctor writes "tetracycline—Upjohn," your pharmacist knows that this is Panmycin because it is the brand of tetracycline made by The Upjohn Company.

In a report by the Federal Trade Commission dated January 1979, it was noted that about 90 percent of all prescriptions were written using trade names. The report stated that consumers could save more than *four hundred million dollars* a year if they would purchase generic drugs when possible.

ARE GENERIC DRUGS AS GOOD?

If several companies are marketing the same drug, are the drugs comparable? Is generic tetracycline as good as Panmycin? Is a generic drug as safe and as effective as the product with a trademark? In most instances, the answer to all three questions is yes! But that has not always been the case.

For many years, pharmacists could not be sure that generic drug products were as good as those with trademarks. In fact, most early reports indicated that they were not. Many doctors and most pharmacists can cite examples of generic drugs that were taken off the market because they did not have the pharmacologic activity advertised by their manufacturers. Sometimes, this lack of activity was because there was too much or too little drug in the dosage form. But more often, it happened because the drug present did not dissolve properly. It was assumed that if the drug was in the tablet, it would be absorbed. This assumption proved false. Doctors found that their patients did not respond to certain generic drugs the way they were supposed to and urged pharmacists to insist that manufacturers supply a complete chemical analysis of each generic drug. Thus, inadequate quality control measures tarnished the image of generic drugs.

But, within the last ten years, advanced methods of testing have made possible a quick and reliable determination of whether a generic drug provides the same pharmacologic activity as a drug with a trade name. Modern technology can measure the amount of a drug in the blood, which indicates the effectiveness of the drug. By relying on the results of such drug testing, doctors and pharmacists can be sure that generic drugs will benefit patients.

Bioequivalence

Bioequivalence (bio, body or action in a living body; equivalence, equal) simply means that two products have the same biologic effect. With drugs, bioequivalence means that two products are absorbed into the bloodstream at the same rate and have the same overall pharmacologic activity. If a generic drug and a drug with a trade name are bioequivalent, they are equally effective.

Much has been written about differences—real or imagined—in bioequivalence. Doctors and pharmacists have been told that the differences between drugs with trade names and generic drugs are major. But most of the reported differences are minor.

For example, differences in bioequivalence have been found

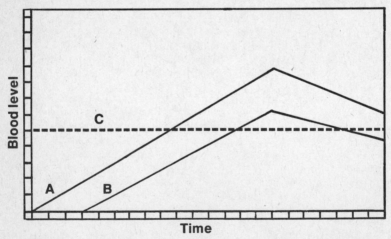

Sample curve of levels of a drug in the blood that might be provided by a drug manufacturer to sell his product. Line A is the manufacturer's trade-name product; Line B is the generic product; and Line C is the level needed for the drug to be effective.

among brands of the antibiotics oxytetracycline and chloramphenicol and the heart drug digoxin. But no differences in bioequivalence have been shown for many other drugs, including ampicillin and chloral hydrate.

Advertising puffery can be misleading. A drug manufacturer may provide a chart like the one illustrated here to point out that the product on line A provides higher levels of a drug in the blood than the generic product on line B. But line C shows the necessary level of the drug in the blood, and actually both drugs are effective. In fact, drug levels produced by the product on line A may be too high for a patient who is especially sensitive to the drug.

Reliability Of Generic Drugs

Many people think that drugs with trade names are made by large manufacturers and generic drugs are made by small manufacturers. But, in fact, a manufacturer may market large quantities of a drug under a trade name; the same manufacturer may sell the base chemical to another company, which produces the drug as its own generic brand. In this case, the base chemical for both the generic and the trademarked drugs came from the same company.

Some manufacturers produce a chemical and manufacture a drug that they sell under a trade name. These manufacturers may sell the same base chemical to other companies, who then produce their own products with their own trade names. For example, Mallinckrodt, Inc., produces the chemical diphenoxylate and combines it with atropine and markets it under the name Colonil. Mallinckrodt, Inc., also sells diphenoxylate to Searle Laboratories, which transforms it into Lomotil. And because Searle Laboratories has the better known product, it charges pharmacists $11.66 for 100 Lomotil tablets. In contrast, 100 Colonil tablets cost $7.86.* And who pays the difference? You do, of course.

A manufacturer may buy a chemical from a wholesale chemical company and produce a drug with a trade name. The wholesale company may sell the same chemical to other drug companies, which make drugs under their own trade names. One drug company, for example, reported that it produced its antibiotics in the United States. But, actually, it produces only oral antibiotics in the United States. The company's injectables (or at least some of them) are made by another manufacturer in Italy.

In many cases, drugs with trade names and their generic

---

* Prices quoted from Drug Topics Redbook, 1979, published by the Medical Economics Company, Oradell, NJ, 07649.

equivalents are produced by the same manufacturer—sometimes even in the same batch. For example, the antibiotic ampicillin is the base for 220 different products. However, all ampicillin is produced by only 24 drug companies. About 215 different brands of the female hormone conjugated estrogens are available, but the hormone is manufactured by only 45 companies.

Chloral hydrate, for example, is marketed by E.R. Squibb and Sons as Noctec and wholesales for $5.52 per 100 capsules. E.R. Squibb and Sons buys chloral hydrate from its manufacturer, the R.P. Scherer Company, which also sells chloral hydrate to at least 51 other companies. These other companies sell the same item for as little as $1.55 per 100 capsules.* Again, you the consumer pay for the "privilege" of receiving the trade-named item, Noctec.

The question is how can you—the consumer—be assured that generic drugs meet certain standards of quality control.

Your assurance comes directly from the Food and Drug Administration. The FDA has the responsibility for assuring the public that generic drugs meet all the standards set for them.

If a drug company wishes to market a generic drug, it must receive approval from the FDA to do so. The FDA imposes rules to which all drug manufacturers must adhere. The FDA's Bureau of Drugs actually tests drug samples and makes recommendations to the FDA. And, after all the confusion of the past, the FDA has recently stated that there are no serious differences between most trade-name drugs and their generic equivalents.

WHY ARE GENERIC DRUGS LESS POPULAR?

With such support from the FDA, why do some doctors and pharmacists oppose the widespread use of generic drugs?

Surely, advertising campaigns conducted by the manufacturers of drugs with trade names have been a major reason. Some manufacturers spend millions of dollars to advertise a drug. Drug advertising, which appears in medical and pharmaceutical journals and on such items as pens and desk blotters, encourages doctors to prescribe, and pharmacists to dispense, a drug by its trade name. Doctors and pharmacists are not resistant to drug advertising. Most advertising campaigns for drugs are first-rate and effective.

Pharmacists and doctors do not have the time to assess all

---

*Prices quoted from Drug Topics Redbook, 1979, published by the Medical Economics Company, Oradell, NJ, 07649.

the claims made by a drug company in its advertising. And they may come to believe drug ads, never realizing that most generic drugs are as good as their trademarked counterparts.

One reason Bayer aspirin costs two to three times more than St. Joseph aspirin is the immense cost of promoting the Bayer brand. The same holds for prescription-only trade-name drugs versus generic products. Manufacturers of most generic drugs do not advertise their products extensively and can charge less for them.

Doctors and pharmacists are scientists. They know that the manufacturers of drugs with trademarks have invested large sums of money in the development of their drugs. They may believe that if these manufacturers do not make a profit on their products, new drug development may be slowed down. Then, too, many doctors simply do not realize how expensive many trade-named items really are. In one recent study, doctors were asked to state their knowledge on drug prices. Over 32 percent admitted that they knew very little about the prices of commonly prescribed drugs. The other two thirds admitted to being entirely uninformed.

Some doctors and pharmacists probably prefer drugs with trade names for many reasons. If your doctor or pharmacist does insist, ask why. You should get an honest, professional answer which includes information about bioequivalence and relative price. A small number of drugs should not be replaced by generic brands; pay attention to the answer and if your prescription appears to be one of those, accept the advice. But if you are not satisfied with his answer, tell your doctor or pharmacist that you do not wish to pay for a drug with a trade name when you can get its equivalent for less money.

DRUG SUBSTITUTION LAWS

Many pharmacy organizations have joined with consumer groups to repeal the outmoded laws that prevent pharmacists from substituting a generic equivalent for a drug with a trade name prescribed by a physician.

The movement to repeal the so-called antisubstitution laws began only about five years ago. Yet all but five states (Alabama, Texas, Louisiana, Indiana, and Hawaii) and the District of Columbia have now repealed the antisubstitution law. And, each of these five has considered repealing the law. If you live in one of the states that hasn't yet repealed this law, contact your state senator or representative and express your opinion. Until the law is repealed, you can save a substantial amount of money if you ask your doctor to prescribe drugs by generic name.

Remember, for the law to work for you, you must take advantage of it. Talk with your doctor or pharmacist.

In states where substitution is allowed, your pharmacist may automatically substitute a generic product for a trade-name drug; it is possible that your pharmacist may neglect to tell you that a substitution has been made. So, when you bring in your prescription, be sure to ask if the drug prescribed is a trade-name or generic product. If the drug prescribed is a trade-name product and you do not wish to have a substitution made, you must advise your pharmacist of your wishes.

HOW MUCH CAN YOU SAVE?

How much you save depends on the drug. One hundred capsules of Darvon Compound-65 can cost $10 to $12; the generic equivalent can cost as little as $3 for 100 capsules. One hundred capsules of Pavabid Plateau Caps may cost $12 to $15; the generic equivalent may cost only $5 for 100 capsules.

But do not expect to save as much as $7 or $10 on every prescription drug you buy. First, not all drugs have generic equivalents. Many commonly prescribed drugs are protected by patents. And the prices of many drugs with trade names are almost as low as the prices of their generic equivalents.

Drug Categories

IN PREVIOUS chapters, you have read about what drugs are, where they come from, and how to take them correctly. Now, you will read about their classifications.

CARDIOVASCULAR DRUGS

Adrenergics

Adrenalin is produced in the body and is secreted in small amounts when one must flee from danger or resist attack (the "flight or fight syndrome"). Adrenalin increases the amount of sugar in the blood, accelerates the heartbeat, and dilates the lungs. Adrenalin and drugs like it are called *adrenergic agents.* An adrenergic agent may be used in the treatment of many diseases, such as low blood pressure, asthma, and even glaucoma.

Antiarrhythmics

Some drugs depress the heart or reduce its activity. If the heart does not beat rhythmically or smoothly (arrhythmia) because of excessive adrenalin or a heart attack, its rate of contraction must be slowed. *Antiarrhythmic drugs*—including Inderal, lidocaine, Pronestyl, and quinidine—prevent or alleviate cardiac arrhythmia. Dilantin anticonvulsant is used in the treatment of epilepsy and also acts as an antiarrhythmic agent.

Antihypertensives

Drugs that reduce high blood pressure can effectively prolong a hypertensive patient's life. However, many patients do not take these drugs correctly or do not take them at all. They fail to realize that they may be able to prevent other cardiovascular diseases by controlling hypertension.

Drugs that lower blood pressure (*antihypertensives*) include Aldomet, Aldoril, Apresoline, Catapres, Diupres, Hydropres, Minipress, Rauzide, reserpine, Salutensin, and Ser-Ap-Es.

Diuretics

Diuretic drugs—such as Aldactazide, Aldactone, Diamox, Diuril, Dyazide, Enduron, Esidrix, hydrochlorothiazide, HydroDIURIL, Hygroton, Lasix, and Regroton—lower blood pressure by increasing the width of blood vessels. Diuretics, or water pills, also affect the kidneys.

Thiazide diuretics are the most popular water pills available today. They rarely become toxic and can be taken once or twice a day. Thiazide diuretics are effective all day—they do not act only in the morning. And since patients do not develop a tolerance for the antihypertensive effect, they can be taken for long periods. Diuril was the first thiazide diuretic. Thiazide diuretics go by many names, but their action is the same.

Other drugs act much like thiazide diuretics. One of them, Hygroton diuretic, lasts longer than Diuril diuretic and may still be an effective antihypertensive if taken only once every other day.

Thiazide diuretics often deplete potassium. Many people take a potassium supplement, such as K-Lor or Kaochlor, along with their diuretic. Others eat or drink potassium-rich foods and liquids, such as bananas, apricots, or orange juice. Salt substitutes, such as Neocurtasal or Co-Salt, are other sources of potassium.

Loop diuretics, including Edecrin and Lasix, act more vigorously than thiazide diuretics. They promote more water loss but also deplete more potassium. Thiazide diuretics tend to be more effective in the treatment of high blood pressure.

To remove excess water from the body but retain its store of potassium, manufacturers developed *potassium-sparing diuretics*. Currently, two potassium-sparing diuretics are on the market—Aldactone and Dyrenium. They are effective in the treatment of potassium loss, heart failure, and hypertension. Other types of diuretics are available, but are much less widely used.

Digitalis

Drugs from digitalis—for example, Lanoxin—depress the heart but are not strictly antiarrhythmics. Digitalis slows the rate of the heart but increases the force of contraction. Digitalis acts as a depressant as well as a stimulant, and may be used to regulate erratic heart rhythm or to increase the output of the heart in heart failure.

Anticoagulants

Drugs that thin the blood are called *anticoagulants*. Anticoagulant drugs fall into one of two categories.

The first category contains only one drug—heparin. Heparin must be given by injection, and its use is restricted to patients hospitalized with a heart attack or stroke.

The second category includes oral anticoagulants that are derivatives of the drug warfarin. Warfarin and heparin may be used to treat many of the same conditions. Use of warfarin after a heart attack, however, is controversial. Some physicians believe that anticoagulants are not helpful beyond the first month or two following a heart attack.

Patients taking warfarin must avoid using many other drugs for fear of causing internal bleeding, and they must have blood samples checked frequently by their physician.

Antilipidemics

Drugs used to treat atherosclerosis act to reduce the cholesterol and triglycerides (fats) that form plaques on the walls of the arteries. Among the drugs that reduce the amount of fat in the blood are the antilipidemics Atromid-S and Choloxin.

Vasodilators

Vasodilators are often used in the treatment of stroke. Two vasodilators are Hydergine and Pavabid. Neither has been shown to be effective, and both are expensive.

Hydergine vasodilator is derived from ergot. Drugs derived from ergot are adrenergic blockers, although not exactly like Inderal antiarrhythmic, which was mentioned before. Inderal antiarrhythmic blocks adrenergic nerves in the heart, while ergot blocks similar nerves elsewhere in the body. Many ergot drugs, for example, the drug Methergine, cause the uterus to contract, but only when a woman is about to deliver.

DRUGS FOR THE EARS

Many eardrops that could be purchased over the counter in the past now require a prescription—even those that contain the mild pain-killer benzocaine. Eardrops require a prescription because pain-relieving eardrops may lead someone to delay treatment of a serious infection, and that delay could result in hearing impairment.

For an ear infection, a physician usually prescribes an antibiotic and a steroid—for example, Cortisporin ophthalmic suspension. The antibiotic attacks infecting bacteria, and the steroid reduces inflammation and pain. Often, a local anesthetic, such as benzocaine or lidocaine, may be prescribed to relieve pain.

When earwax becomes impacted, it must be removed or

dissolved. Auralgan and Cerumenex eardrops commonly are used to dissolve earwax. After the drops have dissolved the wax, the wax can be removed by gently rinsing out the ear with a rubber-tipped syringe.

A condition called "swimmer's ear" arises when infecting organisms multiply in the ear while it is still damp after swimming. The infecting organisms cause an earache. Swimmer's ear can be treated effectively by drying the ear canal. Over-the-counter medications contain alcohol, which dries the ear canal. Often, simply drying the ear canal will improve the condition. Prescription drugs that are used to treat this condition include antibiotics to fight the infection and steroids to reduce pain and inflammation.

DRUGS FOR THE EYES

Almost all drugs that are used to treat eye problems can be used to treat disorders of other parts of the body as well.

Glaucoma is one of the major disorders of the eye—especially for people over age 40. It is caused by increased pressure within the eyeball. Although sometimes treated surgically, glaucoma often can be resolved by using eyedrops regularly, and blindness should not occur. Two drops frequently used are epinephrine and pilocarpine. Pilocarpine is a *cholinergic drug*. Cholinergic drugs act by stimulating the body's parasympathetic nerve endings. These are nerve endings that assist in the control of the heart, lungs, bowels, and eyes. Some cholinergic drugs are similar to certain insecticides—phospholine iodide is much like the organophosphate insecticides, for example. The action of this type of cholinergic lasts much longer, but these drugs also are much more toxic. Oral cholinergic drugs may be used in the treatment of the muscular disorder myasthenia gravis.

Antibiotics usually resolve eye infections. Steroids can be used to treat eye inflammations as long as they are not used for too long. Pharmacists carefully monitor requests for eyedrop refills, particularly drops that contain steroids, and may refuse to refill such medication.

GASTROINTESTINAL DRUGS

Antinauseants

One of the major causes of nausea is motion sickness, which apparently occurs when the eyes tell the brain one thing but the sense of balance in the middle ear tells it another. The antinauseants Dramamine and Marezine prevent nausea from motion sickness.

Another is "morning sickness." The morning sickness that occurs in the first few months of pregnancy can be relieved by Bendectin antinauseant. Expectant mothers take Bendectin antinauseant at bedtime so it can take action the following morning.

Oral drugs also may cause nausea. To avoid nausea, a drug can be taken with food or administered by a rectal suppository or given by injection.

Perhaps the most effective antinauseant is a *phenothiazine derivative* such as Compazine. Compazine antinauseant is often administered rectally and usually alleviates acute nausea and vomiting within a few minutes or an hour. Compazine antinauseant may be used for short periods of time or on a long-term basis.

Antacids

Antacids relieve the pain of ulcers but probably have no effect on the underlying disease.

They fall into one of two groups—the systemics (sodium bicarbonate or baking soda) or the nonabsorbable antacids (Amphojel and Maalox, for example). Efforts to make antacids more tasty and less likely to cause constipation have not been successful.

Liquid antacids are more effective than tablets. Liquids contain smaller particles of the active drug and neutralize stomach acid more quickly.

Anticholinergics

Anticholinergic drugs have the opposite effect of cholinergics. Anticholinergic drugs—atropine, Librax, Pro-Banthine, and Robinul—slow the action of the bowel and reduce the amount of stomach acid. However, these drugs must be taken in large doses and can cause decreased saliva, blurred vision, and decreased sweating.

Histamine Blocker

The only currently available gastrointestinal *histamine blocker* is Tagamet, which stops the production of stomach acid.

Laxatives

Many laxatives, or cathartics, are available, and none requires a prescription. In the past, a cathartic was considered to be stronger than a laxative, but today the terms *laxative* and *cathartic* may be used interchangeably.

Saline laxatives increase water in the bowel. The bowel fills with water to dilute the salt contained in the laxative. Citrate of magnesia, epsom salts, and milk of magnesia are saline laxatives.

Chemicals in a *bulk-forming laxative*, such as Metamucil, absorb water and swell within the bowel.

A *stimulant laxative*, such as Ex-Lax, activates the nerves that cause the bowel to act.

Finally, a *lubricant*, such as mineral oil, adds oil to the bowel.

Antidiarrheals

Diarrhea may be caused by many conditions—including influenza, ulcerative colitis—and can occur as a side effect to drug therapy. It can be stopped by using Kaopectate antidiarrheal, which absorbs fluid in the bowel.

Narcotics (for example, paregoric) and anticholinergics (for example, atropine) are also used to treat diarrhea. Narcotics and anticholinergics slow the action of the bowel to check diarrhea. A medication such as Lomotil antidiarrheal combines a narcotic with an anticholinergic.

HORMONES

Thyroid Drugs

The thyroid hormone was one of the first to be produced synthetically. Originally, thyroid preparations were made by drying the thyroid glands of animals and pulverizing them into tablets. Such preparations often are used today. However, synthetic thyroid hormone, in Cytomel and Synthroid, as well as purified extracts of thyroid, in Proloid, are available.

Drugs, such as propylthiouracil, and radioactive-iodine therapy are used to slow down thyroid hormone products in patients who have excessive amounts.

Diabetic Drugs

Insulin, which is secreted by the pancreas, regulates the level of sugar in the blood and the metabolism of carbohydrates and fats.

Insulin's counterpart *glucagon* stimulates the liver to produce glucose, or sugar. Both insulin and glucagon must be present in the right amounts to maintain a proper blood sugar level.

Treatment of diabetes may involve an adjustment of diet or the administration of insulin. Glucagon is given only in emergencies (for example, insulin shock when the blood sugar must be raised quickly).

Oral *sulfonylurea* drugs—including Diabinese, Dymelor, Orinase, and Tolinase—induce the pancreas to secrete more insulin. The drugs act on small groups of cells within the pancreas called beta cells, which make and store insulin.

Diabetics who cannot follow a diet program or do not wish to use insulin may be able to take sulfonylureas.

Steroids

The pituitary gland secretes *adrenocorticotropic hormone* (ACTH), which directs the adrenal glands to produce glucocorticoids such as hydrocortisone and other steroids. Steroids help us fight inflammation, and ACTH may be injected to treat inflammatory diseases.

Oral steroid preparations—Aristocort, Decadron, Kenacort, Medrol, and prednisone—may also be used to treat inflammatory diseases such as arthritis or to treat poison ivy, hay fever, or insect bites.

Steroid preparations also may be applied to the skin. Cordran, Kenalog, Lidex, Mycolog, Synalar, Valisone, and Vioform hydrocortisone steroid hormones are available as creams or ointments.

But steroids can cause side effects. They may cause fluid retention (edema), weight gain, or changes in the metabolism of carbohydrates and fats. These side effects can be reduced, however, by taking the entire daily dose of steroids once every day, or even taking the entire two-day supply once every second day.

Adrenal glands also secrete *mineralocorticoids.* One mineralocorticoid is *aldosterone,* which helps retain water in the body.

A few drugs mimic the action of aldosterone, but they are used rarely. One drug—the diuretic Aldactone—blocks the action of aldosterone.

Sex Hormones

Although the adrenal glands secrete small amounts of sex hormones, these hormones are produced mainly by the sex glands. *Estrogens* are the female hormones responsible for secondary sex characteristics such as development of the breasts, maintenance of the lining of the uterus, and enlargement of the hips at puberty. *Testosterone* (also called androgen) is the corresponding male hormone. It is responsible for secondary sex characteristics such as beards and muscles. *Progesterone* is produced in females and prepares the uterus for pregnancy.

Testosterone causes retention of protein in the body and therefore larger muscles. Athletes sometimes take drugs called anabolic steroids, similar to testosterone, but this use of the hormone may be dangerous. Anabolic steroids can adversely affect the heart, nervous system, and kidneys.

Most *oral contraceptives* or birth control pills combine estrogen and progesterone, but some contain only progesterone.

The estrogen in birth control pills prevents the production of the egg. Progesterone, or rather, its cessation at the end of the 21-day cycle, brings on menstruation. The hormones in birth control pills may have other contraceptive action. For example, these hormones may thicken vaginal secretions to prevent sperm from reaching the egg. Oral contraceptives, while still used regularly, have many side effects (both minor and major), and their use appears to be declining. Popular oral contraceptive products include Demulen, Norinyl, Norlestrin, and Ortho-Novum.

Premarin estrogen hormone is used to treat symptoms of menopause. Provera progesterone hormone is used for uterine bleeding and menstrual problems.

ANTI-INFECTIVES

Antibiotics

Antibiotics are used to treat many bacterial infections. Antibiotics are produced by microorganisms, and they have the ability to destroy or inhibit the growth of other microorganisms.

Antibiotics were introduced in 1940 and quickly grew to prominence. They changed the way drugs were used and the way hospital care was provided in the United States: They helped shorten hospital stays by preventing post-operative infection and by responding to complications. They stemmed the great white plague known as tuberculosis. With the introduction of antibiotics, patients could be treated on an out-patient basis, and many of the isolated tuberculosis sanatoriums were closed.

Usually, use of antibiotics is effective. Occasionally, however, they are used excessively or improperly. For example, antibiotics do not counteract viruses. And to adequately treat an infection, they must be taken regularly for a specific period of time. If a patient does not take an antibiotic for the prescribed period, the infection may not be resolved, and microorganisms resistant to the antibiotic may appear. Antibiotics are potent, at times life-saving, drugs that must be used appropriately. They include aminoglycosides, cephalosporins, erythromycins, penicillins, and tetracyclines.

Chemotherapeutics

Another group of drugs may be used to treat infection. This group—the *chemotherapeutics*—includes synthetically produced drugs, such as sulfonamides (Gantrisin), nitrofurantoins (Furadantin, Macrodantin) and others (NegGram).

Some chemotherapeutic agents are used in the treatment of cancer. These *antineoplastics* are, without exception, extremely toxic. They cause serious side effects, but many cancer victims are willing to take that risk.

Malignant cells differ from normal cells only in the rate of growth: Malignant cells grow far more rapidly. Because the difference is slight, antineoplastic drugs may attack normal cells as well as malignant ones. But in the hands of physicians who specialize in the treatment of cancer (oncologists), these drugs—the chemotherapeutics Alkeran, Fluorouracil, Cytoxan, methotrexate, Purinethol, Thiotepa, and Uracil Mustard Capsules, for example—can stall the spread of cancer.

Vaccines

Vaccines were used long before antibiotics. A vaccine contains weakened or dead disease-causing microorganisms. Microorganisms activate the body's defense mechanisms to produce a natural immunity against disease. A vaccine may be used to alleviate or treat infectious disease, but, most commonly, it is used to prevent a specific disease. Probably the most famous was the Salk vaccine.

Other vaccines greatly reduced the incidence of diphtheria, pertussis, tetanus, measles, mumps, and smallpox. Some vaccines have been so successful, they are no longer kept in most pharmacies. For example, in the United States today, children no longer receive smallpox vaccinations. Vaccination and other health measures have made smallpox almost unheard of in this country.

Antiseptics

Antiseptics kill germs on contact. Despite television commercials to the contrary, killing germs in the mouth is useless; as soon as the mouth is opened, germs enter. Antiseptics are used to clean medical equipment or sterilize hospital operating areas. They also may be applied to a body surface.

TOPICAL DRUGS

Dry skin is a very common complaint. The most effective treatment of dry skin is to increase moisture in the air. The skin also may become infected or inflamed. Antibiotics treat skin infections; steroids treat inflammations.

Another common dermatologic problem is acne. Acne can be—and often is—treated with over-the-counter drugs, but it sometimes requires prescription medications. Over-the-counter drugs often contain benzoyl peroxide to open the pores. Oral prescription antibiotics such as the tetracyclines prevent pimple formation, and steroids prevent inflammation.

CENTRAL NERVOUS SYSTEM DRUGS

Sedatives

All drugs used in the treatment of anxiety or insomnia selectively reduce activity in the central nervous system. Drugs that have a calming effect include Atarax, barbiturates, Equanil, Librium, Miltown, Serax, Sinequan, Tranxene, and Valium. Drugs to induce sleep in insomniacs include chloral hydrate, Dalmane, Doriden, Nembutal, Noludar, Placidyl, Quaalude, and Seconal. All these drugs have similar action, but those used to induce sleep are more potent.

Tranquilizers

Psychotics usually receive *major tranquilizers,* which calm part of the brain but permit the rest of the brain to function normally. These drugs act as a screen that allows transmission of some nerve impulses but restricts others. Reserpine was the first major tranquilizer to be introduced. It is rarely prescribed to treat psychosis today, however, because it has been a factor in some suicides.

The drugs most frequently used are *phenothiazines*—Mellaril, Stelazine, Thorazine, and Trilafon. Haldol, a butyrophenone, has the same effect as Thorazine.

Psychotic patients sometimes become depressed. They may receive an *antidepressant,* such as Elavil, or a *monoamine oxidase inhibitor*, such as Parnate.

Antidepressants may produce dangerous side effects or interact with other drugs. In fact, monoamine oxidase inhibitors may be taken off the market soon because they greatly increase blood pressure when taken with certain kinds of cheese or other foods.

Anorectics

Anorectics are drugs that reduce appetite and are useful in the treatment of obesity. Amphetamines are anorectics. Amphetamines quiet the part of the brain that causes hunger. But they also keep people awake, speed up the heart, and raise blood pressure. And after two or three weeks, they lose their effectiveness. Besides amphetamines, the anorectics Biphetamine, Eskatrol, Fastin, Ionamin, Sanorex, and Tenuate are used to treat obesity.

Amphetamines stimulate most people, but they have the opposite effect on a special group of people—hyperkinetic children. Hyperkinesis is difficult to diagnose or define and requires a specialist to treat. Hyperkinetic children appear normal but they are highly overactive. When they take amphetamine or the adrenergic Ritalin properly, their activity slows down. Why amphetamines affect hyperkinetic children is unknown. But most likely, they quiet these youngsters by selectively stimulating parts of the brain that ordinarily cause sedation and thereby counterbalance hyperactivity.

Antiepileptics

Drugs such as Dilantin and phenobarbital can effectively control most symptoms of epilepsy. They act selectively on the parts of the brain that send out too many impulses.

Anti-Parkinson Agents

Parkinson's disease is progressive, and it is due to a chemical imbalance in the brain. Victims of Parkinson's disease have uncontrollable tremors, develop a characteristic stoop, and eventually are unable to walk. Drugs such as Artane anticholinergic or levodopa sometimes correct the chemical imbalance and relieve the symptoms of the disease.

Analgesics

Pain, of course, is not a disease but a symptom. Drugs used to relieve pain are called *analgesics.*

The analgesic drugs form a rather diffuse group. Whether they all act in the brain or whether some act outside the brain is not known. Nor is their mechanism of action completely understood: Do they actually relieve pain, or do they merely make patients feel better so they do not care about the pain?

Analgesics may be *narcotic* or *non-narcotic.*

Narcotics are derived from the opium poppy. They act on the brain to cause deep analgesia and often drowsiness. They also cause difficulty in breathing, constipation, and constricted pupils of the eyes. Narcotics relieve coughing spasms and are used in many cough syrups.

Narcotics relieve pain but also give the patient a feeling of well-being. They also are addictive. Manufacturers have attempted to produce nonaddictive synthetic narcotic derivatives. Demerol, for example, is a synthetic narcotic analgesic. When first introduced, it was thought to be nonaddictive, but later studies showed that it was addictive.

Another synthetic narcotic analgesic is Talwin, or pentazocine. And it, too, can be abused, at least to some extent. Synthetic narcotic analgesics relieve pain, but many professionals believe that they are not able to do so as well as the natural opium derivative, morphine.

Many *non-narcotic* pain relievers are commonly used. *Salicylates* are the most commonly used pain relievers in the United States today. And the most widely used salicylate is aspirin. While aspirin does not require a prescription, many doctors may prescribe it to treat such diseases as arthritis.

The aspirin substitute acetaminophen (Tylenol, Datril) may be used in place of aspirin. It, however, cannot relieve inflammation caused by arthritis, and it is much more toxic.

A number of analgesics contain codeine or other narcotics as well as analgesics such as aspirin or acetaminophen—for example, Empirin Compound with Codeine Phosphate, Fiorinal with Codeine, Percodan, Phenaphen with Codeine, Synalgos-DC, and Tylenol with Codeine. These analgesics are not as potent as pure narcotics, but frequently they are as effective. While they may be abused, they are not as addictive as pure narcotics.

The analgesic Darvon is much less addictive than the narcotics. As an analgesic, it is as effective as aspirin, perhaps more. And it does not interfere with blood clotting, as aspirin does. Darvon is used widely and may be combined with aspirin and called Darvon Compound. A newer drug, Darvon-N, is similar to Darvon and has the same effects. Darvocet is a combination of Darvon and acetaminophen.

Anti-inflammatory Drugs

Inflammation, or swelling, is the body's response to injury and causes pain, fever, redness, and itching.

Both aspirin and acetaminophen relieve pain, but aspirin also reduces inflammation.

Other drugs—Butazolidin, Indocin, Motrin, Nalfon, Naprosyn,

Tandearil, and Tolectin—relieve inflammation, but none is more effective than aspirin.

Gout, however, is an inflammatory disease that can be treated more effectively with other agents, such as Benemid uricosoric, colchicine antigout remedy, or Zyloprim antigout remedy. Gout is due to excessive uric acid, which causes swelling and pain in the toes and joints. Benemid stimulates excretion of the uric acid in urine; colchicine prevents swelling; and Zyloprim decreases the production of uric acid. Both Benemid and Zyloprim guard against attacks of gout. They do not relieve the pain of an attack as does colchicine.

When sore muscles tense up, they cause pain and inflammation. And *skeletal muscle relaxants*—Equagesic, Norgesic, Parafon Forte, Robaxin, Robaxisal, and Soma Compound—can relieve the symptoms. Skeletal muscle relaxants often are given with an anti-inflammatory drug such as aspirin. Some doctors believe that aspirin and rest alleviate the pain and inflammation of muscle strain more than skeletal muscle relaxants.

Local Anesthetics

Other pain-relieving drugs are *local anesthetics.* Local anesthetics are applied directly to a painful area and relieve such localized pain as a toothache. Local anesthetics do not relieve major, generalized pain, and many people are allergic to them. Some local anesthetics, such as lidocaine, are also useful in the treatment of heart disease when given by intravenous or intramuscular injection because they restore the heartbeat to normal.

RESPIRATORY DRUGS

Antitussives

Antitussives control coughs. Dextro-methorphan is a non-narcotic that controls the cough from a cold. Another drug is the narcotic codeine. Most cough drops and syrups must be absorbed into the blood and circulate through the brain before they act on a cough; they do not "coat" the throat and should be taken with a glass of water.

Expectorants

Expectorants also are cough control agents. Expectorants increase the amount of mucus produced. However, most expectorants are no better than water. In other words, drinking water or using a vaporizer or humidifier effectively increases mucus. Popular expectorant products include Ambenyl, Novahistine Expectorant, Phenegran Expectorant, and Robitussin.

Decongestants

Decongestants constrict the blood vessels in the nose and sinuses to open up the airway. Decongestants can be taken by mouth or as nose drops. Ephedrine sulfate, Sudafed, and others are oral decongestants. They do not interfere with the production of mucus or the movement of the cilia but increase blood pressure. Nose drops such as Neo-Synephrine or Afrin do not increase blood pressure as much as oral decongestants, but they do slow the movements of the cilia. People who use nose drops may also develop a tolerance for them. Consequently, they should not be used for more than a few days.

Epinephrine and Isuprel adrenergic are commonly used to relieve the symptoms of asthma and pulmonary emphysema. Usually, epinephrine is injected to reverse acute symptoms. Isuprel may be inhaled or taken as a sublingual tablet. Patients with severe asthma may receive steroids. Aminophylline is often given to patients with pulmonary emphysema.

Antihistamines

The use of *antihistamines* in the treatment of a cold is controversial. A cold is a viral infection—not an allergy—and antihistamines counteract the symptoms of an allergy. For mild respiratory allergies, such as hay fever, antihistamines like Benadryl can be used. Benadryl and other antihistamines are slow acting, however, and are not potent. For severe allergies, injectable epinephrine, a decongestant, often will be prescribed. Epinephrine is fast acting and potent.

VITAMINS AND MINERALS

Vitamins and minerals are chemicals, and they often are taken by people who do not need them. Some people have vitamin deficiencies, but their number is small. And most people get enough vitamins and minerals in their diet. Even fast food often is nutritionally balanced and contains sufficient amounts of vitamins and minerals and protein.

Popular vitamin-mineral supplements, such as Mi-Cebrin, Sigtab Tablets and Theragran-M, contain vitamins and minerals from A to zinc.

Serious nutritional deficiencies such as pellagra and beri-beri must be treated by a physician. But many vitamin and mineral deficiencies can be prevented by eating a well-balanced diet.

Is The Cure Worse Than The Disease?

HOW SAFE are the drugs you take? The Federal Government tests drugs for safety, and you should know about the government safeguards against unsafe or ineffective drugs. But you should also know when to be wary of using drugs.

GOVERNMENT REGULATIONS

USP and NF Drugs

Often, the letters USP *(United States Pharmacopoeia)* or NF *(National Formulary)* appear on the label of a prescription drug. The *United States Pharmacopoeia* and *National Formulary* are books that list drugs that have passed federal government standards. Whenever the label on a drug container has the letters USP or NF, you can use the drug with confidence because it was manufactured according to strict government regulations. The *National Formulary* and *United States Pharmacopoeia* will be combined in 1980 and called USP XX-NFXV. But until then, to assure the purity of the drugs you use, look for "USP" or "NF" on the label.

The FDA

Since 1931, the Food and Drug Administration (FDA) has tried to protect Americans against health hazards from food or drugs. The FDA approves all new prescription drugs out on the market and requires continual testing of new drugs to be sure they are safe and effective. If a drug or chemical has not met government standards, the FDA can remove it from the market. The FDA safeguards against drugs that are poorly made or mislabeled, drugs that are nothing more than quackery, and drugs that are ineffective.

Each year, the FDA inspects thousands of drugs and foods to be sure that they are manufactured or processed within set standards. If a food or drug is found to be unfit or unsafe, the FDA orders the manufacturer to stop marketing it. Most manufacturers obey the FDA's orders voluntarily, but some have sued the FDA—and lost.

SPECIFIC CONCERNS

Serious, as well as minor, side effects will be discussed in detail in the next chapter. In this chapter, the focus is on possible devastating, long-term consequences of drug use.

Birth Defects

Would-be parents often wonder whether the drugs they take can cause birth defects. Expectant mothers worry about taking drugs during pregnancy. Indeed, the current rate of birth defects from all causes, about 2 percent of all live births, seems high, and some birth defects may be caused by drug use.

Drug manufacturers must prove that their products, both old and new, do not cause birth defects and can be used safely by pregnant women. But until 1962, testing a drug to determine if it caused birth defects was just another routine step in the process of getting the drug on the market. Manufacturers injected the drug or chemical into a pregnant mouse or rat or into a fertilized chicken egg and looked for abnormalities in the offspring.

What happened in 1962? Thalidomide. Thalidomide was commonly used as a sleeping aid in Europe, particularly in Germany and Great Britain, and the drug was thought to be so safe, it was sold without a prescription. However, the drug caused severe birth defects of the skeletal system. By 1962, more than 8,000 malformed infants had been delivered to mothers who had taken thalidomide early in their pregnancies.

At the time scientists were becoming aware of the drug's effects, thalidomide was being investigated for sale in the United States. Thanks to Frances Kelsey, MD, of the FDA, who kept the drug from the United States market, thalidomide was not marketed in this country.

Nevertheless, the severity of the birth defects due to thalidomide use prompted a widespread effort in this country to determine whether other drugs could cause birth defects.

What do these findings mean to an expectant mother who may need to take drugs during pregnancy? Expectant mothers should try not to take medication—including tobacco, alcohol, and marijuana. Sometimes, of course, they must, but they should

Drugs That May Be Dangerous If Taken During Some Period of Pregnancy*

anabolic hormones (Dianabol, Maxibolin, etc.)
androgen hormones (testosterone, etc.)
anticoagulants (Coumadin, etc.)
busulfan (Myleran)
chlorambucil (Leukeran)
chlorpropamide (Diabinese)
corticosteroids (hydrocortisone, Decadron, prednisone, etc.)
cyclizine (Marezine)
cyclophosphamide (Cytoxan)
dextroamphetamine (Dexedrine, etc.)
dienestrol
diethylstilbestrol
ergot alkaloids
ethionamide (Trecator-SC)
iodides
lithium carbonate (Eskalith, Lithane, etc.)
meclizine (Antivert, etc.)
methotrexate
opiates (codeine, morphine, etc.)
penicillamine (Cuprimine)
phenmetrazine (Preludin)
phenothiazines (Stelazine, Thorazine, etc.)
phenytoin (Dilantin, etc.)
phytonadione (vitamin K)
progestins (oral contraceptives)
propylthiouracil
reserpine (Serpasil, etc.)
streptomycin
sulfonamides (Gantrisin, etc.)
tetracyclines (Achromycin, Panmycin, Sumycin, etc.)
thyroid hormone
vaccines for measles, mumps, smallpox
vitamin A
vitamin D

Only the more common drugs are listed. Not included are items, such as thalidomide, that are not available in the United States and the general anesthetics, which people don't administer to themselves.

avoid the use of drugs if they can.

A fetus is more susceptible to birth defects from drugs during the first trimester, or first three months, of pregnancy. Generally after the fourth month, the chances of causing damage to the unborn child are reduced. However, the infant may still be affected. For example, tetracycline taken during the last three months of pregnancy may cause discoloration of the child's teeth. A thyroid hormone taken during the last trimester may cause a thyroid disorder in the infant. A child's teeth discolored by tetracycline will not whiten completely, but a thyroid disorder caused by thyroid hormone can be corrected by proper treatment. If a woman is addicted to narcotics during pregnancy, the baby may go into withdrawal at birth. Drug withdrawal can be treated, and the infant may survive without any permanent damage. Of course, it makes little difference to the parent or damaged infant whether the damage occurred during the first three months or the last three months of pregnancy. The point is, it did happen.

By the time a woman discovers she is pregnant, the damage may have already been done. Usually, a fetus is not affected until the 20th day after conception. If a woman misses a period, she may continue taking drugs after the 20th day following conception and unwittingly endanger the fetus. If for any reason a woman believes she may be pregnant, she should see her doctor at once. He probably will advise her to stop taking medication. A drug manufacturer's instructions for use of a drug usually warn against taking the drug during pregnancy. The statement, "Safety for use of this product during pregnancy has not been established," does not mean that the drug causes birth defects. It simply means that not enough studies have been done to demonstrate safe use of the drug during pregnancy. The key is to use extreme caution. If there is even a slight chance that you may be pregnant, or that you could become pregnant, do not take any drug without consulting your doctor first.

CANCER

Chemicals in the environment—in drinking water, food, and air—can cause cancer. But what about drugs?

Very careful measurements of cancer rates have begun to show that some drugs might also be linked with cancer. Among the drugs under investigation are some of the very drugs used to treat the disease. These appear to be "double-edged" swords. Many other drugs, including reserpine, isoniazid, and methapyrilene, are also being tested.

Studies have shown that diethylstilbestrol (DES) causes cancer in women whose mothers took the hormone while pregnant. DES may also cause underdeveloped organs in males whose mothers took it during pregnancy. But, as yet, use of diethylstilbestrol during pregnancy has not been shown to cause cancer in male offspring.

Oral contraceptives contain estrogen, which can increase the risk of cancer. In fact, one report noted that chances of developing cancer are seven times greater in woman taking oral contraceptives.

Does this mean that you will get cancer if you take one of these drugs. No, but your risk of getting cancer *may* be increased. What you must do is weigh the risk of cancer against the benefit of taking the drug in question.

Common Side Effects

DRUGS have certain desirable effects—that's why they are taken. The desirable effects of a drug are known as the drug's activity. Most drugs, however, have undesirable effects as well. Undesirable effects are called side effects, adverse reactions, or, in some cases, lethal effects. A side effect is any undesirable effect of a drug—even a minor one that is not dangerous. An adverse reaction is serious and may outweigh the desirable effects of the drug. A lethal effect is one capable of causing death. Often, the terms "side effect" and "adverse reaction" are used interchangeably. They have different meanings, however. Although all adverse reactions are side effects, not all side effects are adverse reactions.

Some side effects are expected and unavoidable, but others may surprise the doctor as well as the patient. Unexpected reactions may be due to one of the factors discussed in the chapter, "What Went Wrong," or to variations among patients (what doctors call an idiosyncratic response) or to drug allergies.

Side effects and adverse reactions fall into one of two major groups—those that cause obvious symptoms and those that cannot be detected without laboratory testing. We think the discussion of a drug should not be restricted to its easily recognized side effects; other, less obvious, side effects may also be harmful.

If you know a particular side effect is expected from a particular drug, you can relax a little. Most expected side effects are temporary and need not cause alarm. You may merely experience discomfort or inconvenience for a few minutes, hours, or days. For example, you may be drowsy after taking an antihistamine or have a stuffy nose after taking reserpine or other drugs that lower blood pressure. Of course, if you find minor side effects especially bothersome, you should discuss them with your doctor. He may be able to prescribe another drug, or at least assure you that the benefits of the drug far outweigh its side effects.

Many symptoms, however, signal a serious—perhaps dangerous—problem. And when these symptoms appear, you should consult your doctor immediately.

The following discussion should help you decide which symptoms call for patience and which require immediate attention from your physician.

OBVIOUS SYMPTOMS

Symptoms of an adverse reaction may arise in any part of the body, but certain organs and body systems commonly are

---

Common Minor Side Effects

Side Effect	Management
Blurred vision	Avoid operating machinery
Decreased sweating	Avoid work or exercise in the sun
Diarrhea	Drink lots of water; if diarrhea lasts longer than 3 days, call your doctor
Dizziness	Avoid operating machinery
Drowsiness	Avoid operating machinery
Dry mouth	Suck on candy or ice chips, or chew gum
Dry nose and throat	Use a humidifier or vaporizer
Fluid retention	Avoid adding salt to foods
Headache	Remain quiet; take aspirin or acetaminophen
Insomnia	Take last dose earlier in the day; drink a glass of warm milk at bedtime; ask your doctor about an exercise program
Itching	Take frequent baths or showers
Nasal congestion	If necessary, use nose drops
Palpitations (mild)	Rest often; avoid tension; do not drink coffee, tea, or cola; stop smoking
Potassium loss	Eat a banana or dried fruit such as apricots or figs, or drink a glass of orange juice, every day
Upset stomach	Take the drug with milk or food

Drugs That May Cause Blurred Vision

Actifed	Minipres
Ambenyl	Narcotics
antibiotics	Nitro-Bid
anticonvulsants	Nitrostat
antihistamines	Norpace
antihypertensives	oral antidiabetics
Ativan	peptic ulcer drugs
Bendectin	quinidine sulfate
cancer-treating drugs	Robaxin
Clinoril	Sinequan
Darvon	sleeping aids
Digoxin	Talwin
Dimetane	tranquilizers
diuretics	Triavil
Haldol	Tussionex
hormones	Tylenol products
Inderal	Valium
Indocin	

associated with symptoms of an adverse reaction. And if you are alert, you may discover the first indications of an adverse reaction.

Ear

A few drugs may cause loss of hearing if taken in large quantities, but such a reaction is uncommon. Drugs that are used to treat problems of the ear may cause dizziness. And many drugs produce tinnitus, or ringing in the ears. If your doctor or pharmacist tells you the drug you will be taking may cause tinnitus, you may not necessarily hear a true "ringing" sound. Many people hear buzzing or thumping or merely have a feeling of hollowness in the ear. Nevertheless, discuss with your doctor any hearing or ear problem if it persists for more than three days.

Eye

Blurred vision is a common side effect of many drugs. Drugs such as digitalis may cause the patient to see a "halo" around a lighted object (a television screen or a traffic light), and other drugs may cause night blindness. Indocin anti-inflammatory (used in the treatment of arthritis) may cause blindness. Atropine anticholinergic and Librax sedative make it difficult to accurately judge distance while driving and make the eyes sensitive to sunlight. While the effects on the eye caused by digitalis and Indocin are dangerous signs of toxicity, the effects caused by atropine and Librax sedative are to be expected. In any case, if you have difficulty seeing while taking drugs, contact your doctor.

Gastrointestinal System

The gastrointestinal system includes the mouth, esophagus, stomach, small and large intestines, and rectum. Side effects from drugs commonly affect the gastrointestinal system, and a gastrointestinal symptom can be expected from almost any drug. Many drugs affect the gastrointestinal system by producing a dry mouth, mouth sores, difficulty in swallowing, heartburn, nausea,

Drugs That May Cause Dry Mouth

Actifed	Dyazide
Aldomet	Flagyl
Aldoril	Haldol
Atarax	Mellaril
Benadryl	Minipres
Bendectin	Naldecon
Bentyl	Norpace
Catapres	Ornade
chlorpheniramine maleate	Pro-Banthine
Combid Spansules	Quaalude
Compazine	Sinequan
Demerol	Stelazine
Dimetane	Thorazine
Dimetapp Extentabs	Triavil
Donnatal	Valium

Drugs That May Cause Ulcers

Aristocort	Norpace
Butazolidin	oral contraceptives
Clinoril	prednisone
Medrol	Tandearil
nicotinic acid	

vomiting, diarrhea, constipation, loss of appetite, or abnormal cramping. Other drugs cause bloating and gas, and some cause rectal itching.

Diarrhea can be expected after taking many drugs. Drugs are chemicals and can create localized reactions in intestinal tissue—usually a more rapid rate of contraction, which leads to diarrhea. Diarrhea caused by most drugs is temporary.

But diarrhea may signal a problem. For example, Cleocin antibiotic may cause severe diarrhea. When diarrhea is severe, the intestine may become ulcerated and begin bleeding. If you develop diarrhea while taking Cleocin antibiotic, or any other antibiotic, contact your doctor.

Drugs That May Cause Diarrhea

Actifed
Aldactone
Aldactazide
Aldomet
Aldoril
Ambenyl
Apresoline
Atromid-S
Benadryl
Bendectin
Butazolidin
chlorpheniramine maleate
Clinoril
Combid Spansules
Compazine
Coumadin
Dalmane
Darvon
Diamox
Digoxin
Dimetane
Dimetapp Extentabs
Diuril
Dyazide
Enduron
erythromycin
Flagyl
Haldol
Inderal

Indocin
K-Lyte
Keflex
Mellaril
meprobamate
Minipres
Minocin
Motrin
Norpace
oral antidiabetics
oral contraceptives
Ornade
Pavabid
penicillins
Proloid
Pronestyl
Quaalude
Rauzide
reserpine
Stelazine
sulfa drugs
Tagamet
Talwin
tetracycline
Thorazine
Tofranil
Tussionex
Zyloprim

Drugs That May Cause Constipation

Actifed	Flagyl
Aldomet	Haldol
Aldoril	Inderal
Ambenyl	Librax
Benadryl	Librium
Bentyl	Mellaril
Catapres	Minipres
Clinoril	Pavabid
Combid Spansules	Percodan
Compazine	Pro-Banthine
Dalmane	Sinequan
Darvon	Stelazine
Demerol	Talwin
Diamox	Thorazine
Dilantin	Tussionex
Dimetane	Valium
Dyazide	

Diarrhea produced by a drug should be self-limiting, that is, it should stop within three days. During this time, do not take any medication such as Kaopectate diarrhea remedy; drink liquids to replace the fluid you are losing. If diarrhea lasts more than three days, call your doctor.

As a side effect of drug use, constipation is less serious and more common than diarrhea. It occurs when a drug slows down the activity of the bowel. Drugs such as atropine and Pro-Banthine anticholinergic slow down bowel activity, and the constipation they produce lasts a few days to a week. Constipation occurs when drugs, such as Questran and Colestid cholesterol reducers, adsorb moisture in the bowel. And it may occur if a drug acts on the nervous system and decreases nerve impulses to the intestine—for example, a drug such as Aldomet antihypertensive. Constipation produced by a drug may last several days, and you may help relieve it by drinking at least eight glasses of water a day. If constipation continues, call your doctor.

Heart and Circulatory System

Drugs may speed up or slow down the heartbeat. If a drug slows the heartbeat, you may feel drowsy and tired or even dizzy. If a drug accelerates the heartbeat, you probably will experience

75

Drugs That May Cause Fluid Retention*

Apresoline	Nalfon
Aristocort	Naprosyn
Butazolidin	Norpace
Clinoril	oral contraceptives
Combid Spansules	prednisone
Compazine	Premarin
Elavil	Stelazine
Eskatrol Extentabs	sulfa drugs
Librax	Tandearil
Librium	Thorazine
Medrol	Tolectin
Mellaril	Tolinase
Motrin	Triavil

Indicated by a weight gain of two or more pounds a week.

palpitations (thumping in the chest). You may feel as though your heart is skipping a beat occasionally, and you may have a headache. For most people, none of these symptoms indicates a serious problem. If, however, they bother you, consult your doctor. He may adjust the dosage of the drug or prescribe other medication.

Some drugs cause edema (fluid retention). When edema forms, fluid from the blood collects outside the blood vessels. Ordinarily, edema is not serious. But if you are steadily gaining weight or have gained more than two or three pounds a week, talk to your doctor.

Drugs may increase or decrease blood pressure. When blood pressure decreases, you may feel drowsy and tired. Or, you may become dizzy and even faint, especially when you rise suddenly from a reclining position. When blood pressure increases, you may feel dizzy, have a headache or blurred vision, or hear ringing or buzzing in your ears. If you develop any of these symptoms, call your doctor.

Nervous System

Drugs that act on the nervous system may cause drowsiness or stimulation. If you are drowsy, you may become dizzy, or your coordination may be impaired. If a drug causes stimulation, you may become nervous or have insomnia or tremors. Neither drowsiness nor stimulation is cause for concern for most people.

Drugs That May Cause Dizziness

Actifed	Flagyl
Aldactone	Keflex
Aldactazide	Lomotil
Aldomet	Medrol
Ambenyl	meprobamate
Antivert	Minipres
Aristocort	Nitro-Bid
Ativan	Nitrostat
Atromid-S	Norpace
Benadryl	oral antidiabetics
Bendectin	oral contraceptives
Benemid	Ornade
Bentyl	Pavabid
chlorpheniramine maleate	Rauzide
Clinoril	reserpine
Dalmane	Robaxin
Darvon	Tagamet
Digoxin	Talwin
Dimetane	Tofranil
Dimetapp Extentabs	Triavil
Diuril	Tussionex
Enduron	Vasodilan

When you are drowsy, however, you should be careful around machinery and avoid driving. Some drugs cause throbbing headaches, and others produce tingling in the fingers or toes. These symptoms are expected and should disappear in a few days or a week.

Respiratory System

Side effects common to the respiratory system include stuffy nose, dry throat, shortness of breath, and slowed breathing. A stuffy nose and dry throat usually disappear within days, but you may use nose drops or throat lozenges or gargle with warm saltwater to relieve them. Shortness of breath is a characteristic side effect of some drugs (for example, Inderal antiarrhythmic). Shortness of breath may continue, but it is not usually serious. Barbiturates or drugs that promote sleep retard respiration. Slowed breathing is expected, and you should not be concerned as long as your doctor knows about it.

Drugs That May Cause Headache

Actifed
Aldactazide
Aldoril
Ambenyl
Apresoline
Aristocort
Ativan
Atromid-S
Benadryl
Brethine
Dilantin
Dimetane
Diuril
Dyazide
Enduron
Flagyl
Isordil
Keflex
Lomotil
Medrol

meprobamate
Minipres
Nitro-Bid
Nitrostat
Norpace
oral antidiabetics
Ornade
Pavabid
Pro-Banthine
Quaalude
Rauzide
reserpine
Robaxin
Serax
Talwin
Tofranil
Triavil
Tussionex
Valium

Skin

Skin reactions include rash, swelling, itching, and sweating.
Itching, swelling, and rash frequently indicate a drug allergy. Only
a few drugs usually produce an allergic skin reaction. Penicillin
and sulfa drugs are examples. However, you should not continue
to take a drug if you have developed an allergy to it. See your
doctor if symptoms of an allergic reaction appear and intensify
while you are taking medication or if they fail to go away after
two days. Also, if you have an allergic reaction to a drug, you
may have difficulty breathing or seem to have fluid in your
lungs—and you should see your doctor immediately.

Some drugs increase sweating; others decrease it. Drugs that
decrease sweating may cause problems in hot weather when the
body must sweat to reduce body temperature.

Another type of skin reaction that requires consultation with
your doctor is photosensitivity (or phototoxicity or sun
toxicity)—that is, unusual sensitivity to the sun. Tetracyclines, such
as Declomycin antibiotic can cause photosensitivity. If, after taking
Declomycin antibiotic, you remain exposed to the sun for a brief
period of time, say 10 or 15 minutes, you may receive a severe

Drugs That May Cause A Mild Rash

Actifed
Aldactone
Aldactazide
Aldoril
Ambenyl
Ativan
Atromid-S
Benadryl
Bendectin
Benemid
Butazolidin
Catapres
chlorpheniramine maleate
Clinoril
Combid Spansules
Compazine
Demerol
Dilantin
Dimetane
Dimetapp Extentabs
Diuril
Dyazide
Elavil
Enduron
Haldol

Indocin
Keflex
Librax
Librium
Lomotil
Minipres
Minocin
Nembutal
Norpace
Ornade
Pronestyl
Quaalude
Rauzide
reserpine
Robaxin
Stelazine
sulfa drugs
Tagamet
tetracycline
Thorazine
Tofranil
Triavil
Tussionex
Valium
Zyloprim

Drugs That May Cause Photosensitivity

antimalarial drugs
barbiturates
Benadryl
Butazolidin
Compazine
Dilantin
Dimetane
Diuril
Enduron
Haldol

HydroDIURIL
Librium
oral antidiabetics
Phenergan
quinine sulfate
sulfa drugs
tetracycline
Thorazine
Tofranil

sunburn. You do not have to stay indoors while taking this drug. But you should be fully clothed while outside, and you should not remain in the sun too long. Since Declomycin antibiotic may be present in the bloodstream after you stop taking it, you should continue to take these precautions for two days.

If you have a minor skin reaction that does not indicate an allergy or photosensitivity, ask your pharmacist for a soothing cream. He may also suggest frequent bathing and dusting the area with a suitable powder.

SUBTLE SYMPTOMS

Some side effects are difficult to detect. You may not have any symptoms at all or only slight ones. And laboratory testing is necessary to confirm the existence of some side effects or adverse drug reactions.

Blood

A great many drugs affect the blood and the circulatory system but do not produce symptoms for some time. If a drug lowers the level of sugar in the blood, for example, you probably will not have any symptoms for several minutes to an hour. If symptoms develop, they may include tiredness, muscular weakness, and perhaps palpitations or tinnitus.

Drugs That May Cause Blood Diseases*

Actifed-C	Phenergan products
Aldactazide	Rauzide
Apresoline	Regroton
Atarax	reserpine
Benadryl	Stelazine
Butazolidin	sulfa drugs
Dimetane	Tagamet
Dyazide	Tandearil
Elavil	Thorazine
Hygroton	Tofranil
Lasix	Tolinase
Mellaril	Triavil
Minocin	Tussionex
oral contraceptives	Zyloprim
Orinase	

*Indicated by a sore throat that doesn't go away in one or two days.

Low blood levels of potassium produce similar symptoms. But you may also become slightly nauseated. All you may notice is that breakfast seems less appealing.

Some drugs decrease the number of red blood cells, which carry oxygen and nutrients throughout the body. If the number of red blood cells is too low, you have anemia, and you may feel tired, weak, and perhaps hungry.

Some drugs decrease the number of white blood cells, which combat bacteria. Too few white blood cells increase susceptibility to infection and may prolong illness. If a sore throat or a fever begins after taking the drug and continues for a few days, you may have an infection and not enough white blood cells to fight it.

Kidney

If a drug reduces the kidney's ability to remove chemicals and other substances from the blood, they begin to collect. Over a period of time, this buildup may cause vague symptoms such as nausea, headache, or weakness. Obvious symptoms, especially pain, are rare.

Liver

Drug-induced liver damage may be due to an accumulation of fat. Usually, however, liver damage occurs because the drug increases or decreases the number of enzymes that enable the liver to metabolize drugs. Liver damage may be quite advanced before it produces any symptoms.

Psychological Changes

Some drugs cause psychological changes even though they do not act primarily on the brain or nervous system. For example, women taking oral contraceptives often become depressed and people taking antihistamines may feel restless or confused. Consult your doctor if such side effects become troublesome.

Superinfection

Antibiotics and sulfa drugs may cause superinfection. Superinfection occurs when a drug kills or inhibits the growth of some bacteria needed by the body while others flourish.

The body needs bacteria to digest food, synthesize vitamins, and carry out other vital functions. Infecting bacteria are also present in the body, but they usually are held in check by the other bacteria and the body's defense system. As long as the infecting bacteria must compete with the other bacteria, the body maintains a system of checks and balances.

When you take an antibiotic or a sulfa drug, it begins to attack some kinds of the infecting bacteria. After several doses, the drug may also attack the bacteria the body needs. Other infecting organisms may multiply (even in the presence of the drug) and cause symptoms. The most common symptoms of superinfection in the gastrointestinal tract are diarrhea, sores in the mouth, and rectal itching. If the superinfection is located in the lungs, you may develop a sore throat and a cough. If it is located in the kidneys or urinary tract, you may urinate more frequently and notice itching.

Superinfection usually poses no problem as long as it is recognized early. If you are taking an antibiotic or a sulfa drug and detect any of these symptoms, call your doctor immediately. He most likely will tell you to stop taking the drug and that the symptoms will disappear in a few days.

Summary

Watch for symptoms and side effects whenever you are taking a drug. Know why you are having them and why you need not worry about them. In the case of potentially hazardous side effects, promptly inform your doctor when you spot something that is wrong. Side effects and adverse reactions associated with specific drugs are listed in "Drug Profiles."

What Went Wrong

WHAT HAPPENED? You've taken a drug and expect certain effects. You're supposed to feel better, but you don't. In fact, you feel worse. You watched for certain side effects but didn't have any. Worse yet, you had other effects.

If prescription drugs are tested, shouldn't everyone receive the same effect from the same drug? This assumption seems logical. Millions of dollars are spent on drugs to make sure they do what they are supposed to do. Thousands, or perhaps millions, of doses of certain drugs have been taken, and they have reliably produced the same results. What went wrong in your case?

Many factors influence the way a drug works in the body. These factors may modify the effect of a drug or cause the drug to have an opposite effect. The way a drug is made can influence the way it affects a patient.

But other factors also play a role. These factors are well known to doctors and pharmacists, but you should know about them, too, to understand why your doctor increases or decreases the dose of your medication or why he prescribes another one for you.

AGE

Age can affect the way a person responds to drugs. In general, doctors abide by different rules when they prescribe medication for the very young and the very old. Doctors carefully select the drugs and the dosage they give to children under two or three years of age and adults over age 60. Doctors carefully select drugs and their dosages for such patients mainly because of the way drugs are metabolized and excreted from the body.

A drug enters the bloodstream from the stomach or intestine and circulates throughout the body. When it reaches certain parts of the body, it begins to act: to stimulate the heart, increase urination, improve blurred vision, induce sleep, or attack infecting bacteria.

After the drug acts, the liver metabolizes (detoxifies) the drug to render it inactive, and the kidneys excrete it.

However, until a child is about two years old, the liver does not develop enough to detoxify most drugs—nor is kidney development and function sufficient to excrete a drug. Because of incompletely developed organs, babies and children under this age cannot take some drugs routinely prescribed for adults. But they can take many other drugs as long as the dosage is calculated carefully.

A drug that is much more deadly to children than to adults is the antibiotic chloramphenicol (Chloromycetin). For many years, this drug was given to newborns in the hospital nursery to prevent infection. Some doctors, however, suspected the drug had a toxic effect on babies' blood. Research in the 1960s disclosed that many infants could not metabolize chloramphenicol properly. The active drug remained in the bloodstream longer, and, as the infants received more doses of chloramphenicol, drug levels in the blood rose higher and eventually caused death.

Drug metabolism and excretion also differ in the elderly. The liver and kidneys of many adults over age 60 may not function efficiently, and the elderly may develop toxic reactions to some drugs.

For example, digoxin is excreted almost entirely by the kidneys. Some patients may begin taking digoxin at age 50 at a dosage calculated on the basis of how well the drug works and how efficiently the kidneys function in a patient of that age.

If the same patients continue the drug at the same dosage without a regular assessment of their kidney function, they may begin to feel sick and lazy and have blurred vision and palpitations. They are suffering from an overdose of digoxin. Because their kidneys are not excreting the drug properly, drug levels in the blood rise higher with each daily dose.

DIET

Food in the stomach may hamper the absorption of orally administered drugs. Food "covers" the drug and keeps it away from the stomach wall, where it is absorbed into the bloodstream.

Dairy products or foods with a high calcium content—milk, cheese, and yogurt—may retard the absorption of tetracycline. Calcium chemically combines with the tetracycline and prevents absorption of the drug. If tetracycline is not absorbed properly, drug levels in the blood will be low, and the action of the drug will diminish.

Some foods actually enhance the absorption of drugs. For example, the antibiotic griseofulvin should be taken with a meal rich in fat, a piece of bread with butter, or at least a glassful of milk.

Mineral oil may decrease the absorption of fat-soluble vitamins A, D, E, and K from the intestine, eventually resulting in a vitamin deficiency.

Vitamin B_6 (pyridoxine) inhibits the effects of levodopa (a drug used in the treatment of Parkinson's disease). In fact, the effects from levodopa may be negated completely by taking more than 10 mg of vitamin B_6 at the same time.

Monoamine oxidase inhibitors—drugs used by patients with high blood pressure or by sufferers of severe mental depression—may become toxic when taken with certain aged cheeses (especially New York cheddar), some alcoholic beverages (wines), pickled herring, chicken livers, or broad-pod beans. Such drugs prevent detoxification of a chemical present in these foods. If the chemical is not detoxified, blood pressure will rise, causing a stroke or even death.

Unless your doctor tells you otherwise, do not take drugs with soda pop, which can affect drug absorption. Diets rich in leafy green vegetables may interfere with anticoagulant drugs. Natural licorice may counteract the action of medication to control high blood pressure. Acidic fruit or vegetable juices may inhibit the action of sulfa drugs. Be sure to ask your doctor or your pharmacist if the drug you are taking may interact with certain foods.

DISEASE

In general, diseases of the gastrointestinal system, liver, kidneys, and blood are expected to modify the effects of drugs. For example, many diseases of the stomach or intestine decrease the rate of absorption of drugs and reduce drug levels in the blood.

Malnutrition that is not caused by a stomach or intestinal problem may promote greater-than-expected drug activity. The liver needs protein to produce the enzymes that metabolize drugs. If a person does not get sufficient protein in the diet, the liver may not be able to produce enzymes. Consequently, a drug will not be metabolized rapidly and drug levels in the blood will remain high for a longer period of time.

Kidney or liver disease may prolong drug action because the drug cannot be excreted quickly.

Hypoproteinemia, a disease of the blood characterized by insufficient protein, may also produce greater-than-expected drug activity. Many drugs are attached to protein in the blood. As long as a drug remains attached, it cannot act. As soon as the drug is released—at the site in the body of its intended activity—it can.

With hypoproteinemia, the protein concentration in the blood is low. Some of the drug attaches to the protein, but much of the drug is left unattached, or free to circulate throughout the body in the blood and cause a greater effect. Drugs such as Butazolidin anti-inflammatory, Coumadin anticoagulant, Indocin anti-inflammatory, methotrexate, and Orinase oral antidiabetic can cause toxic effects in patients with hypoproteinemia.

OCCUPATION

Most jobs have no effect on people's response to drugs. Several years ago, however, people who worked with chlorophenothane (DDT) were shown to have reduced responses to the prescription drugs they took. Later, men who worked in factories that produced highly volatile organic chemicals showed similar responses to drugs. After some detective work, researchers found that DDT and highly volatile organic chemicals affected the liver. The liver was stimulated by the chemicals these workers inhaled during the day and overreacted to drugs, that is, the liver metabolized the drugs too soon. Therefore, these workers required larger doses of prescription drugs. There may be other occupations that affect a drug's action.

SEX

"Women react more strongly to drugs than men." This statement is false. Studies done on rats have shown different responses to drugs between males and females, but most studies on humans have not.

However, women may respond more noticeably to drugs because they weigh less than men. Generally, women are smaller, and their total circulating blood volume is also less. When men and women take the same dose of a drug, the drug is absorbed and distributed throughout the body in the blood. But the blood concentration of the drug is higher in women because they are lighter and have a lesser blood volume than men. The effect is much like putting a drop of food coloring in a pint of water and in a quart; the pint will be darker because it has less volume. With a higher concentration of drug in the blood, women have a slightly more potent effect from it.

Nevertheless, the more potent effect arises from size—not sex. The effect of a drug may be increased in small men who take the same dose of a drug as larger men.

SMOKING

Several studies have shown that smokers require greater amounts of some drugs to produce expected effects. The nicotine in tobacco stimulates the liver to metabolize drugs. Drugs are reduced to their inactive form more readily, and the overall effect is reduced. Consequently, smokers require higher doses.

TEMPERATURE

The response to a drug decreases as the air temperature decreases. In cold weather, a drug may not be absorbed as quickly, or it may not be distributed throughout the body as efficiently. On the other hand, after a drug begins to act, its effects may last longer. The liver and kidneys do not function as well in cold weather; so they do not remove the drug from the body as quickly.

But taking drugs in hot weather poses certain risks. One of the side effects of drugs used to treat the symptoms of peptic ulcer—atropine, Pro-Banthine anticholinergic, or Librax sedative—is decreased sweating. And, when sweating is decreased, working or exercising in the hot sun may cause heat exhaustion.

TIME OF DAY

Researchers are beginning to discover that many drugs are more potent and produce fewer side effects when they are taken at a specific time during the day. For example, drugs like cortisone (prednisone, Aristocort steroid hormone) produce the greatest activity when taken about 8:00 A.M. The activity of these drugs is related to the physiological response to cortisone. Blood levels of the body's cortisone are highest at 8:00 A.M. Taking drugs like cortisone at that time mimics the body's own production of cortisone and therefore enhances the effects of the drug. Many doctors now recommend taking the total daily dose of such drugs at one time in the early morning (for example, four tablets at 8:00 A.M.)

Sleeping aids are taken in the evening, and stimulants usually are taken in the morning or early to mid-afternoon. The effectiveness of these drugs probably is related to people's physiologic and psychologic readiness to go to sleep at night and be awakened in the morning, regardless of work shifts.

Each person supposedly has a "natural clock," which biologists call "biologic rhythm" (biorhythm or circadian rhythm). This biologic rhythm regulates emotions, attitudes, and actions and may be one reason why the effects of drugs are greater when they are taken at certain times of the day.

COMPLIANCE

Another important factor—perhaps the most vital one of all—is compliance. Compliance is adherence to a doctor's or pharmacist's directions regarding the use of drugs.

Compliance to drug therapy may be difficult for some people.

People with high blood pressure, for example, must take medication regularly. Many people who do not take medication properly or on time say that they "forgot." Probably they forgot because they do not have any noticeable effects from the medication, or have unpleasant side effects. Yet, unless people with high blood pressure take their medication at prescribed times, they are in danger of heart failure or kidney malfunction.

Compliance to drug therapy for even minor diseases is important; for, if drugs are not taken properly, they will not produce the desired effects.

DRUG INTERACTIONS

Two drugs taken at the same time may produce dangerous side effects. Perhaps the best example is the alcohol and sleeping pills combination. Many "suicides" probably are due to accidentally taking alcohol and sleeping pills together. Both are depressants, and together they can cause unconsciousness and death.

When two drugs are taken at the same time, one may interfere with the action of the other. The antibiotic Lincocin causes diarrhea in a great many people, but taking Kaopectate antidiarrheal remedy will prevent the absorption of Lincocin. Similarly, iron tablets inhibit the absorption of tetracycline.

Not all drug interactions are adverse. Bactrim antibacterial contains two antibacterial drugs, and each intensifies the action of the other. The two together are more effective than either alone.

But because drug interactions may be adverse, your doctor and your pharmacist should have a complete record of the medication you take (including over-the-counter drugs such as aspirin or a laxative) as well as tobacco, marijuana, and alcohol.

Examples of Potentially Serious Drug Interactions*

If you take	And then start taking	The result may be
Aldactone or Dyrenium	potassium products such as potassium chloride, K-Lyte	overdose of potassium
Antabuse	alcohol	flushing, fall in blood pressure, vomiting
antidiabetic drugs	alcohol	loss of control of blood sugar

Examples of Potentially Serious Drug Interactions*

If you take	And then start taking	The result may be
antidiabetic drugs	Butazolidin; Dicumarol; Parnate or other monoamine oxidase inhibitors	fall in blood sugar
antidiabetic drugs	Inderal	rise in blood pressure, loss of control of blood sugar
antihypertensive drugs	amphetamine, anorectics, oral decongestants	rise in blood pressure
Anturane or Benemid	aspirin	worsening of gout
Coumadin	a barbiturate or Doriden	hemorrhage if latter medication is stopped
Coumadin	Dianabol	hemorrhage
Dilantin	Antabuse or isoniazid	clumsiness
Inderal	decongestants	lessened effect of both
Ismelin	tricyclic antidepressants	rise in blood pressure
levodopa	pyridoxine (vitamin B_6)	worsening of Parkinson's disease
Lincocin	Kaopectate	lessened effectiveness of Lincocin
Mandelamine	Diamox	lessened effectiveness of Mandelamine; worsening of infection

Examples of Potentially Serious Drug Interactions*		
If you take	**And then start taking**	**The result may be**
methotrexate	aspirin	increase in toxicity of methotrexate
methotrexate	vaccinations	infection develops
Parnate or other monoamine oxidase inhibitors	antidepressants	high temperature, excitement
Parnate or other monoamine oxidase inhibitors	amphetamines or anorectics, ephedrine, Neo-Synephrine, Propadrine, Sudafed, some foods (including cheese, broad-pod beans, chicken livers, herring, wines)	rise in blood pressure, stroke, possible death
sedatives	any other sedative	increased sedation (especially when alcohol is used with any other sedative)
tetracycline antibiotics	antacids or dairy products	lessened effectiveness of tetracycline; worsening of infection
Zyloprim	Azathioprine or mercaptopurine	increase in toxicity of Azathioprine or mercaptopurine

*Your doctor may decide that you need both drugs despite these possible interactions. He will regulate the dosages you take or tell you to take the drugs several hours apart to reduce the chance of interactions. Follow these instructions very carefully.

Drug Profiles

This chapter outlines the most frequently prescribed drugs in the United States. By studying a drug profile, you learn what to expect from your medication, when to be concerned about possible side effects or drug interactions, and how to take the drug to achieve its maximum benefit. The information for each drug profile is divided appropriately into several sections:

Name: Most of the drugs in this chapter are listed by trade name. Some drugs, however, are prescribed generically because they are better known by their generic name and because many manufacturers produce the same drug. For example, tetracycline is a generic drug. (Note that generic drugs, unless they appear at the beginning of a sentence, are denoted by lower case letters.) The most commonly known trade names for tetracycline are listed under "Equivalent Products," and these entries are cross-referenced. Thus, if you wish to find information on Achromycin V antibiotic (a trade name for tetracycline), you will be referred to the drug profile for "tetracycline hydrochloride antibiotic." The chemical or pharmacological class is listed for each drug after its name.

Generic Name: The generic (or chemical) components of each trademarked drug are itemized. Many drugs contain several chemical components, and all are included in this category.

Equivalent Products: This category includes other trademarked drugs that are chemically equivalent to the one profiled. Trade-name drugs in this category represent the most commonly known equivalents. Each entry in this category is followed by the manufacturer's name.

Dosage Forms: The most common forms (i.e., tablets, capsules, liquid, injectables, suppositories) of each profiled drug are listed, along with the color of the tablets or capsules. Colors for liquids, injectables, and suppositories are not included. Strengths are given for tablets, capsules, and liquid forms.

Use: This category includes the most important and most common clinical uses for each profiled drug. Your doctor may prescribe a drug for a reason that does not appear in this category. This exclusion does not mean that your doctor has made an error. But if the use for which you are taking a drug does not appear in this category, and if you have any questions concerning the reason for which the drug was prescribed, consult your doctor.

Minor Side Effects: The most common and least serious reactions to a drug are found in this category. Most of these side effects, *if they occur,* disappear in a day or two. *Do not expect* to experience these minor side effects, *but if they occur and are particularly annoying,* do not hesitate to seek medical advice. Your doctor may wish to try an alternative drug.

Major Side Effects: *Should they occur,* the reactions listed in this category are signs that the drug is not working properly for one reason or another. Drug dosage may require adjustment, you may have an allergy that interferes with the drug's action within the body, or perhaps you should not be taking the drug at all. Major side effects are less common than minor side effects, and you will probably never experience them. If you do, call your doctor immediately.

Contraindications: Some drugs are counterproductive in people with certain conditions, i.e., they should not be taken by people with these conditions. These conditions are outlined under "Contraindications." If the profiled drug has been prescribed for you and if you have a condition listed in this category, consult your doctor.

During the first trimester of pregnancy, almost all drugs are contraindicated. If you have any doubts about taking a drug during this period, consult your doctor at once.

Warnings and Precautions: This category indicates when the profiled drug should be used with caution. For example, a close monitor is usually necessary if a drug is prescribed for people with liver or kidney disease. Many drugs, especially those containing narcotics, barbiturates, or hypnotic components, have the potential for abuse because tolerance (or decreased sensitivity) to the drug can develop. "Warnings and Precautions" will guide you concerning the possible dangers of using the profiled drug. Heed them and consult your doctor if you have any of the conditions listed.

Interacts With: Certain drugs are perfectly safe when used alone but may cause serious reactions when taken with other drugs or chemicals. The drugs listed in this category may intensify or diminish the action of the profiled drug. Alcohol, for example, should never be taken with narcotics, barbiturates, or hypnotic compounds; a serious reaction may result. Avoid taking drugs with compounds shown in this section. If you are not certain whether you are taking one of these compounds, consult your doctor or pharmacist.

Comments: Both vital and general information concerning the

92

profiled drug are presented under "Comments." Paragraphs include such information as whether to take the drug at mealtime or before or after meals; whether the drug is habit-forming and should be taken with caution; whether the drug can cause an allergic reaction when taken with another drug. They also describe what to do if dizziness or light-headedness occurs; when a drug can mask some symptoms; how long the profiled drug takes to work; when to expect some side effects and which ones; and under what circumstances, if any, the patient should be monitored with blood tests or x-rays. You will find this information helpful, especially if your doctor or pharmacist has failed to relate all the facts you should have.

The entries in the "Comments" section, combined with the other information included in the drug profiles, should guide you as to what to expect from the drug you are taking and when to seek medical advice. Never be reluctant to ask your doctor or pharmacist for further information about any drug you are taking.

Achromycin V antibiotic (Lederle Laboratories), see tetracycline hydrochloride antibiotic.

Actifed adrenergic and antihistamine

Manufacturer: Burroughs Wellcome Co.
Generic Name: pseudoephedrine hydrochloride, triprolidine hydrochloride
Equivalent Products: Corphed adrenergic and antihistamine (Bell Pharmacal Corp.); Eldefed adrenergic and antihistamine (Elder Pharmaceuticals); Sherafed adrenergic and antihistamine (Sheraton Laboratories, Inc.)
Dosage Forms: Liquid (content per 5 ml): pseudoephedrine hydrochloride, 30 mg; triprolidine hydrochloride, 1.25 mg). Tablets: pseudoephedrine hydrochloride, 60 mg; triprolidine hydrochloride, 2.5 mg (white)
Use: Relief of hay fever symptoms, respiratory congestion, middle ear congestion
Minor Side Effects: Diarrhea, dizziness, drowsiness, dry mouth, headache, heartburn, difficult urination, loss of appetite, nausea, rash, restlessness, vomiting, weakness, blurred vision, confusion, constipation, insomnia, nasal congestion, palpitations, reduced sweating
Major Side Effects: Low blood pressure, severe abdominal pain, sore throat, high blood pressure, chest pain
Contraindications: Asthma, some glaucomas, certain ulcers, enlarged prostate, obstructed bladder, obstructed intestine, pregnancy, severe heart disease
Warnings and Precautions: Diabetes, high blood pressure, thyroid disease, liver and kidney diseases

Interacts With: guanethidine, monoamine oxidase inhibitors

Comments: Although Actifed adrenergic and antihistamine is frequently prescribed for the prevention and treatment of the common cold, a government panel of experts has concluded that the product may not be effective for this use.

While taking Actifed adrenergic and antihistamine, do not take any nonprescription item for cough, cold, or sinus problems without first checking with your doctor.

Actifed adrenergic and antihistamine may cause dryness of the mouth. To reduce this feeling, chew gum or suck on a piece of hard candy.

Actifed adrenergic and antihistamine reduces sweating; avoid excessive work or exercise in hot weather.

Actifed adrenergic and antihistamine may cause drowsiness; to prevent oversedation avoid the use of other sedative drugs or alcohol.

Products equivalent to Actifed adrenergic and antihistamine are available. Consult your doctor and pharmacist.

Actifed-C expectorant

Manufacturer: Burroughs Wellcome Co.

Generic Name: codeine phosphate, triprolidine hydrochloride, guaifenesin, pseudoephedrine hydrochloride

Equivalent Products: Sherafed-C expectorant (Sheraton Laboratories, Inc.)

Dosage Form: Liquid (content per 5 ml): pseudoephedrine hydrochloride, 30 mg; triprolidine hydrochloride 2 mg; codeine phosphate, 10 mg; guaifenesin, 100 mg

Use: Cough suppressant; symptomatic relief of cough in conditions such as common cold, acute bronchitis, allergic asthma, bronchiolitis, croup, emphysema, tracheobronchitis

Minor Side Effects: Diarrhea, dizziness, drowsiness, dry mouth, headache, heartburn, difficult urination, loss of appetite, nausea, rash, restlessness, vomiting, weakness, blurred vision, confusion, constipation, insomnia, nasal congestion, palpitations, reduced sweating

Major Side Effects: Low blood pressure, severe abdominal pain, sore throat, high blood pressure, chest pain

Contraindications: Asthma, some glaucomas, certain ulcers, enlarged prostate, obstructed bladder, obstructed intestine, pregnancy, severe heart disease

Warnings and Precautions: Diabetes, high blood pressure, thyroid disease, liver and kidney diseases, potential for abuse

Interacts With: guanethidine, monoamine oxidase inhibitors, phenothiazines, antidepressants

Comments: Although Actifed-C expectorant is frequently prescribed for the prevention and treatment of the common cold, a government panel of experts has concluded that the product may not be effective for this use.

If you need an expectorant, you need more moisture in your environment. Drink nine to 10 glasses of water each day. The use of a vaporizer or humidifier may also be beneficial. Consult your doctor.

While taking Actifed-C expectorant, do not take any nonprescription item for cough, cold, or sinus problems without first checking with your doctor.

Actifed-C expectorant may cause dryness of the mouth. To reduce this feeling, chew gum or suck on a piece of hard candy.

Actifed-C expectorant reduces sweating; avoid excessive work or exercise in hot weather.

Actifed-C expectorant may cause drowsiness; to prevent oversedation avoid the use of other sedative drugs or alcohol.

Products containing narcotics (e.g., codeine) are usually not used for more than seven to 10 days.

Actifed-C expectorant has the potential for abuse and must be used with caution. Tolerance may develop quickly; *do not* increase the dose of this drug without first consulting your doctor. An overdose usually sedates an adult but may cause excitation leading to convulsions and death in a child.

Products equivalent to Actifed-C expectorant are available and vary widely in cost. Ask your doctor to prescribe a generic preparation; then ask your pharmacist to fill it with the least expensive brand.

Adapin antidepressant (Pennwalt Prescription Products), see Sinequan antidepressant.

Adipex-8 anorectic (Lemmon Pharmacal Company), see Fastin anorectic.

Adsorbocarpine ophthalmic solution (Burton, Parsons & Company, Inc.), see Isopto Carpine ophthalmic solution.

Aldactazide diuretic and antihypertensive

Manufacturer: Searle & Co.
Generic Name: spironolactone with hydrochlorothiazide
Equivalent Products: None
Dosage Form: Tablets: spironolactone, 25 mg; hydrochlorothiazide, 25 mg (ivory)
Use: Treatment of high blood pressure, removal of fluid from the tissues, congestive heart failure, cirrhosis of the liver accompanied by edema or ascites or both
Minor Side Effects: Diarrhea, dizziness, drowsiness, headache, increased urination, nausea, rash, restlessness, vomiting, tingling in the fingers and toes
Major Side Effects: Confusion, elevated blood sugar, elevated uric acid, impotence, enlargement of breasts (in both sexes), muscle spasm, sore throat, weakness, blurred vision, difficulty in achieving an erection
Contraindications: Allergy to sulfa drugs, severe kidney disease, hyperkalemia (high blood levels of potassium), pregnancy
Warnings and Precautions: Bronchial asthma, diabetes, gout, certain liver and kidney diseases
Interacts With: colestipol hydrochloride, digitalis, lithium carbonate, oral antidiabetics, potassium salts, steroids
Comments: Unlike many diuretics, Aldactazide diuretic and antihypertensive does not cause potassium loss. Hence, the relatively high price of this drug is justified for persons with low potassium levels. Do not take potassium supplements while taking Aldactazide.

Aldactazide diuretic and antihypertensive causes frequent urination. Expect this effect; it should not alarm you.

While taking this product (as with many drugs that lower blood pressure), you should limit your consumption of alcoholic beverages in order to prevent dizziness or light-headedness.

If dizziness or light-headedness occurs when you stand up, place your legs on the floor and "pump" the muscles for a few moments before rising.

Persons taking this product and digitalis should watch carefully for symptoms of increased toxicity (e.g., nausea, blurred vision, palpitations).

If you have high blood pressure, do not take any nonprescription item for cough, cold, or sinus problems without first checking with your doctor.

Spironolactone causes cancer in rats, but it has not yet been shown to cause cancer in people.

A doctor probably should not prescribe Aldactazide diuretic and antihypertensive or other "fixed dose" products as the first choice in the treatment of high blood pressure. The patient should receive each of the individual ingredients singly, and if the response is adequate to the fixed dose contained in Aldactazide diuretic and antihypertensive, this product can then be substituted. The advantage of a combination product such as Aldactazide diuretic and antihypertensive is based on increased convenience to the patient.

Aldactone diuretic and antihypertensive

Manufacturer: Searle & Co.
Generic Name: spironolactone
Equivalent Products: None
Dosage Forms: Tablets: 25 mg (light tan)
Use: Treatment of high blood pressure, removal of fluid from the tissues, hypokalemia (low blood levels of potassium)
Minor Side Effects: Diarrhea, dizziness, drowsiness, nausea, rash, restlessness, vomiting, weakness
Major Side Effects: Confusion, enlarged breasts (in both sexes), impotence, difficulty in achieving an erection
Contraindications: Anuria (no urination), acute renal insufficiency, significant impairment of renal function, hyperkalemia (high blood levels of potassium), pregnancy
Warnings and Precautions: Liver or kidney diseases
Interacts With: potassium salts
Comments: Unlike many diuretics, Aldactone diuretic and antihypertensive does not cause potassium loss. Hence, the relatively high price of this drug is justified for persons with low potassium levels. Do not take potassium supplements while taking Aldactone diuretic and antihypertensive.

Aldactone diuretic and antihypertensive causes frequenty urination. Expect this effect; it should not alarm you.

While taking this product (as with many drugs that lower blood pressure), you should limit your consumption of alcoholic beverages in order to prevent dizziness or light-headedness.

If dizziness or light-headedness occurs when you stand up, place your legs on the floor and "pump" the muscles for a few moments before rising.

If you have high blood pressure, do not take any nonprescription item for cough, cold, or sinus problems without first checking with your doctor. Spironolactone causes cancer in rats, but it has not yet been shown to cause cancer in people.

Aldomet antihypertensive

Manufacturer: Merck Sharp & Dohme
Generic Name: methyldopa
Equivalent Products: None
Dosage Forms: Tablets: 125 mg (light yellow), 250 mg (medium yellow), 500 mg (dark yellow)
Use: Treatment of high blood pressure
Minor Side Effects: Constipation, diarrhea, dizziness, dry mouth, headache, inflamed salivary glands, light-headedness, nasal congestion, nausea, sedation, vomiting
Major Side Effects: Chest pain, anemia
Contraindications: Active liver disease (e.g., acute hepatitis or active cirrhosis), pregnancy
Warnings and Precautions: Certain liver or kidney diseases
Interacts With: amphetamine, decongestants
Comments: Mild side effects (e.g., nasal congestion) are most noticeable during the first two weeks of therapy and become less bothersome after this period.
   While taking Aldomet antihypertensive, do not take any nonprescription item for cough, cold, or sinus problems without first checking with your doctor.
   While taking this product (as with many drugs that lower blood pressure), you should limit your consumption of alcoholic beverages in order to prevent dizziness or light-headedness.
   If dizziness or light-headedness occurs when you stand up, place your legs on the floor and "pump" the muscles for a few moments before rising.
   Remind your doctor if you have or are being treated for gout if he prescribes Aldomet antihypertensive. Aldomet antihypertensive may interfere with the measurement of blood uric acid. Also, many patients react positively to the Coombs' test. The positive reaction usually indicates an allergy or destruction of red blood cells. Often, however, the test is false positive, and no disease is present. Have periodic blood tests as long as you take Aldomet antihypertensive.

Aldoril antihypertensive and diuretic

Manufacturer: Merck Sharp & Dohme
Generic Name: methyldopa, hydrochlorothiazide
Equivalent Products: None
Dosage Forms: Aldoril-15 tablets: methyldopa, 250 mg; hydrochlorothiazide, 15 mg (salmon). Aldoril-25 tablets: methyldopa, 250 mg; hydrochlorothiazide, 25 mg (white)
Use: Treatment of high blood pressure
Minor Side Effects: Constipation, diarrhea, dizziness, dry mouth, headache, increased urination, inflamed salivary glands, light-headedness, loss of appetite, nasal congestion, nausea, rash, sedation, vomiting, weakness,

tingling in the fingers and toes

Major Side Effects: Chest pain, elevated blood sugar, hyperuricemia, (elevated uric acid in the blood), muscle spasm, sore throat, hypokalemia, weakness, blurred vision

Contraindications: Active liver disease (e.g., acute hepatitis or active cirrhosis), allergy to sulfa drugs, severe kidney disease, pregnancy

Warnings and Precautions: Certain liver or kidney diseases, bronchial asthma, diabetes, gout

Interacts With: amphetamine, colestipol hydrochloride, decongestants, digitalis, lithium carbonate, oral antidiabetics, steroids

Comments: While taking Aldoril antihypertensive and diuretic, do not take any nonprescription item for cough, cold, or sinus problems without first checking with your doctor.

Mild side effects (e.g., nasal congestion) are most noticeable during the first two weeks of therapy and become less bothersome after this period.

While taking this product (as with many drugs that lower blood pressure), you should limit your consumption of alcoholic beverages in order to prevent dizziness or light-headedness.

If dizziness or light-headedness occurs when you stand up, place your legs on the floor and "pump" the muscles for a few moments before rising.

Aldoril antihypertensive and diuretic can cause potassium loss. To avoid potassium loss, take Aldoril antihypertensive and diuretic with a glass of fresh or frozen orange juice. You may also eat a banana each day. The use of Diasal or Co-Salt salt substitutes helps prevent potassium loss.

Persons taking this product and digitalis should watch carefully for symptoms of increased toxicity (e.g., nausea, blurred vision, palpitations).

Remind your doctor if you have or are being treated for gout if he prescribes Aldoril antihypertensive and diuretic. Aldoril antihypertensive and diuretic may interfere with the measurement of blood uric acid. Also, many patients react positively to the Coombs' test. The positive reaction usually indicates an allergy or destruction of red blood cells. Often, however, the test is false positive, and no disease is present. Have periodic blood tests as long as you take Aldoril antihypertensive and diuretic.

If you are allergic to a sulfa drug, you may likewise be allergic to Aldoril antihypertensive and diuretic.

A doctor probably should not prescribe Aldoril antihypertensive and diuretic or other "fixed dose" products as the first choice in the treatment of high blood pressure. The patient should receive each ingredient singly; and if the response is adequate to the fixed dose contained in this product, it can then be substituted. The advantage of a combination product is increased convenience.

Allernade cold remedy (Rugby Laboratories), see Ornade antihistamine, anticholinergic, and adrenergic.

Almocarpine ophthalmic solution (Ayerst Laboratories), see Isopto Carpine opthalmic solution.

Ambenyl expectorant

Manufacturer: Marion Laboratories

Generic Name: bromodiphenhydramine hydrochloride, diphenhydramine hydrochloride, potassium guaiacolsulfonate, ammonium chloride, codeine sulfate

Equivalent Products: None
Dosage Forms: Liquid (content per 5 ml): diphenhydramine hydrochloride, 8.75 mg; bromodiphenyhydramine hydrochloride, 3.75 mg; codeine sulfate, 10 mg; potassium guaiacolsulfonate, 80 mg; ammonium chloride, 80 mg
Use: Relief of coughing
Minor Side Effects: Blurred vision, confusion, constipation, diarrhea, difficult urination, dizziness, drowsiness, headache, insomnia, nasal congestion, nausea, nervousness, palpitations, rash, restlessness, vomiting, dry mouth, loss of appetite, weakness, reduced sweating
Major Side Effects: Low blood pressure, rash from exposure to sunlight, severe abdominal pain, sore throat
Contraindications: Asthma attacks, certain types of glaucoma, certain types of peptic ulcer, enlarged prostate, obstructed bladder, obstructed intestine, pregnancy
Warnings and Precautions: Liver or kidney disease, potential for abuse
Interacts With: phenothiazine
Comments: If you need an expectorant, you need more moisture in your environment. Drink nine to 10 glasses of water each day. The use of a vaporizer or humidifier may also be beneficial. Consult your doctor.

While taking Ambenyl expectorant, do not take any nonprescription item for cough, cold, or sinus problems without first checking with your doctor.

Ambenyl expectorant may cause dryness of the mouth. To reduce this feeling, chew gum or suck on a piece of hard candy.

Ambenyl expectorant reduces sweating; avoid excessive work or exercise in hot weather.

Ambenyl expectorant may cause drowsiness; to prevent oversedation, avoid the use of other sedative drugs or alcohol.

Products containing narcotics (e.g., codeine) are usually not used for more than seven to 10 days.

Ambenyl expectorant has the potential for abuse and must be used with caution. Tolerance may develop quickly; *do not* increase the dose of this drug without first consulting your doctor. An overdose usually sedates an adult but may cause excitation leading to convulsions and death in a child.

Amcill antibiotic (Parke, Davis & Company), see ampicillin antibiotic.

Amen progesterone hormone (Carnrick Laboratories), see Provera progesterone hormone.

Ameri-EZP antibacterial and analgesic (W.E. Hauck, Inc.), see Azo Gantrisin antibacterial and analgesic.

Aminodur Dura-Tabs bronchodilator (Cooper Laboratories, Inc.), see aminophylline bronchodilator.

aminophylline bronchodilator

Aminophylline is a generic drug.
Equivalent Products: aminophylline (various manufacturers); Aminodur Dura-Tabs bronchodilator (Cooper Laboratories, Inc.); Somophyllin bronchodilator (Fisons Corporation)

Dosage Forms: aminophylline (various manufacturers). Liquid (content per 15 ml): 270 mg. Suppositories (content per suppository): 99 mg [pediatric]; 190 mg; 277 mg; 395 mg. Tablets: 100 mg; 200 mg (various colors). Aminodur Dura-Tabs sustained release tablets: 300 mg (tan). Somophyllin capsules: 100 mg; 200 mg; 250 mg (all white)

Use: Relief of bronchial asthma, pulmonary emphysema and other lung diseases

Minor Side Effects: Gastrointestinal disturbances (stomach pain, vomiting), nervousness or restlessness

Major Side Effects: Convulsions, palpitations, difficult breathing

Contraindications: Pregnancy

Warnings and Precautions: Peptic ulcer, heart disease, liver and kidney disease

Interacts With: lithium carbonate, propranolol

Comments: If you have gastrointestinal distress, take an over-the-counter product like Maalox or Gelusil antacids.

Take aminophylline with food or milk.

Brands of aminophylline vary widely in cost. Ask your pharmacist to fill your prescription with the least expensive brand.

Call your doctor if you have severe pain, vomiting, or restlessness because aminophylline may aggravate an ulcer.

Be sure to take your dose at exactly the right time.

Avoid drinking tea, cocoa, or other beverages that contain "xanthines" while taking aminophylline. Consult your pharmacist.

Do not use nonprescription items for asthma unless your doctor has told you to do so.

Amitril antidepressant (Warner/Chilcott), see Elavil antidepressant.

amoxicillin antibiotic

Amoxicillin is a generic drug.

Equivalent Products: amoxcillin antibiotic (various manufacturers); Amoxil antibiotic (Beecham Laboratories); Larotid antibiotic (Roche Products Inc.); Polymox antibiotic (Bristol Laboratories); Robamox antibiotic (A.H. Robins Company); Sumox antibiotic (Reid-Provident Laboratories, Inc.)

Dosage Forms: Liquid (content per 5 ml): 125 mg, 250 mg; capsules: 250 mg and 500 mg (various colors). Amoxil capsules: 250 mg, 500 mg (red/blue); Larotid capsules: 250 mg (brown/tan), 500 mg (white); Polymox capsules: 250 mg, 500 mg (red/pink); Sumox capsules: 250 mg, 500 mg (yellow/white)

Use: Treatment of a wide variety of bacterial infections

Minor Side Effects: Diarrhea, nausea, vomiting

Major Side Effects: Superinfection, vaginal and rectal itching, cough, severe diarrhea, irritation of the mouth, "black tongue," rash

Contraindications: Allergy to penicillin or ampicillin, pregnancy

Warnings and Precautions: Asthma. liver and kidney diseases, significant allergies

Interacts With: chloramphenicol, erythromycin, tetracycline
Comments: The pharmacology and toxicology of amoxicillin are almost identical to those of penicillin. A severe allergic reaction (indicated by a drop in blood pressure and breathing difficulties) has been reported, but it is rare when the drug is taken orally.

Amoxicillin may cause allergic reactions and should not be taken by persons with asthma, severe hay fever, or other allergies unless the doctor is aware of these conditions.

Amoxicillin should be taken for at least 10 full days, even if symptoms have disappeared.

The liquid form of amoxicillin should be stored in the refrigerator.

Diabetics using Clinitest urine test may get a false high sugar reading. Change to Clinistix or Tes-Tape urine tests to avoid this problem.

Brands of amoxicillin vary widely in cost. Ask your pharmacist to fill your prescription with the least expensive brand.

Amoxil antibiotic (Beecham Laboratories), see amoxicillin antibiotic.

ampicillin antibiotic

Ampicillin is a generic drug.
Equivalent Products: ampicillin antibiotic (various manufacturers); Amcill antibiotic (Parke, Davis & Company); Omnipen antibiotic (Wyeth Laboratories); Penbritin-S antibiotic (Ayerst Laboratories); Polycillin antibiotic (Bristol Laboratories); Principen antibiotic (E.R. Squibb & Sons); Totacillin antibiotic (Beecham Laboratories)
Dosage Forms: Liquid (content per 5 ml): 100 mg, 125 mg, 250 mg, 500 mg; capsules: 250 mg, 500 mg (various colors). Amcill capsules: 250 mg, 500 mg (blue/gray); Omnipen capsules: 250 mg, 500 mg (purple/pink); Penbritin-S capsules: 250 mg, 500 mg (red/black); Polycillin capsules: 250 mg, 500 mg (gray/crimson); Principen capsules: 250 mg, 500 mg (dark/light gray); Totacillin capsules: 250 mg, 500 mg (orange/brown)
Use: Treatment of a wide variety of bacterial infections
Minor Side Effects: Diarrhea, nausea, vomiting
Major Side Effects: Superinfection, vaginal and rectal itching, cough, severe diarrhea, irritation of the mouth, "black tongue," rash
Contraindications: Allergy to penicillin, pregnancy
Warnings and Precautions: Asthma, liver and kidney diseases, significant allergies
Interacts With: chloramphenicol, erythromycin, tetracycline
Comments: The pharmacology and toxicology of ampicillin are almost identical to those of penicillin. A severe allergic reaction (indicated by a drop in blood pressure and breathing difficulties) has been reported, but it is rare when the drug is taken orally.

Ampicillin may cause allergic reactions and should not be taken by persons with asthma, severe hay fever, or other allergies unless the doctor is aware of these conditions.

Take ampicillin on an empty stomach (one hour before or two hours after a meal).

Ampicillin should be taken for at least 10 full days, even if symptoms have disappeared.

The liquid forms of ampicillin should be stored in the refrigerator.

Diabetics using Clinitest urine test may get a false high sugar reading. Change to Clinistix or Tes-Tape urine test to avoid this problem.

Brands of ampicillin vary widely in cost. Ask your pharmacist to fill your prescription with the least expensive brand.

Antivert antinauseant

Manufacturer: Roerig
Generic Name: meclizine hydrochloride
Equivalent Products: Eldezine antinauseant (Paul B. Elder Co.); Bonine antinauseant (Pfizer Laboratories Division)
Dosage Forms: Chewable tablets: 25 mg (pink); tablets: 12.5 mg (blue/white), 25 mg (yellow/white)
Use: Dizziness due to ear diseases, dizziness and nausea due to motion sickness
Minor Side Effects: Blurred vision, drowsiness, dry mouth
Major Side Effects: No major side effects
Contraindications: Pregnancy
Warnings and Precautions: Liver or kidney diseases
Interacts With: central nervous system depressants
Comments: Because of a high association of birth defects in experimental studies in rats, women who are pregnant or who may become pregnant are especially warned not to take Antivert antinauseant.

When used for motion sickness, take Antivert antinauseant one hour before leaving, then one dose every 24 hours during travel.

Antivert antinauseant may cause drowsiness; to prevent oversedation, avoid the use of other sedative drugs or alcohol and tasks that require alertness.

Anusol-HC steroid-hormone-containing anorectal product

Manufacturer: Warner/Chilcott
Generic Name: hydrocortisone acetate, bismuth subgallate, bismuth resorcin compound, benzyl benzoate, Peruvian balsam, zinc oxide
Equivalent Products: None
Dosage Forms: Rectal suppository; cream
Use: Relief of pain and itching of hemorrhoids and anorectal tissues
Minor Side Effects: Burning sensation on application
Major Side Effects: No major side effects when used for short time only
Contraindications: Viral or fungal infections of the rectum
Warnings and Precautions: No major warnings or precautions
Interacts With: No significant drug interactions
Comments: See the chapter "The Right Way To Take Medications."

Anusol-HC suppositories should not be used for longer than seven consecutive days, unless your doctor specifically says to do so.

Apresoline antihypertensive

Manufacturer: CIBA Pharmaceutical Company
Generic Name: hydralazine hydrochloride
Equivalent Products: hydralazine hydrochloride (various manufacturers); Dralzine antihypertensive (Lemmon Pharmacal Company); Rolazine antihypertensive (Robinson Laboratory, Inc.)
Dosage Forms: Tablets: 10 mg (yellow), 25 mg (deep blue), 50 mg (dark blue), 100 mg (peach)
Use: Treatment of high blood pressure
Minor Side Effects: Diarrhea, headache, loss of appetite, nasal congestion, nausea, numbness or tingling in fingers and toes, palpitations, vomiting
Major Side Effects: Fluid retention, rash, sore throat, tenderness in joints
Contraindications: Coronary heart disease, mitral valvular rheumatic heart disease, pregnancy
Warnings and Precautions: Suspected coronary heart disease
Interacts With: amphetamine, decongestants
Comments: The effects of Apresoline antihypertensive therapy may not be apparent for at least two weeks.

Mild side effects (e.g., nasal congestion) are most noticeable during the first two weeks of therapy and become less bothersome after this period.

While taking Apresoline antihypertensive, do not take any nonprescription item for cough, cold, or sinus problems without first checking with your doctor.

While taking this product (as with many drugs that lower blood pressure), you should limit your consumption of alcoholic beverages in order to prevent dizziness or light-headedness.

If dizziness or light-headedness occurs when you stand up, place your legs on the floor and "pump" the muscles for a few moments before rising.

Products equivalent to Apresoline antihypertensive are available and vary widely in cost. Ask your doctor to prescribe a generic preparation; then ask your pharmacist to fill it with the least expensive brand.

If you experience numbness or tingling in your fingers or toes when taking Apresoline antihypertensive, your doctor may recommend that you take vitamin B_6 (pyridoxine) to relieve the symptoms.

Aquatensen diuretic (Mallinckrodt, Inc.), see Enduron diuretic.

Aristocort steroid hormone

Manufacturer: Lederle Laboratories
Generic Name: triamcinolone
Equivalent Products: Kenacort steroid hormone (E.R. Squibb & Sons); Rocinolone steroid hormone (Robinson Laboratory, Inc.); SK-Triamcinolone steroid hormone (Smith Kline & French Laboratories)
Dosage Forms: Tablets: 1 mg (yellow), 2 mg (pink), 4 mg (white), 8 mg (yellow), 16 mg (white); syrup (content per 5 ml): 2 mg; cream; ointment
Use: Treatment of inflammations such as arthritis, dermatitis, poison ivy, endocrine and rheumatic disorders, asthma, blood diseases, certain cancers and gastrointestinal disturbances such as ulcerative colitis
Minor Side Effects: Dizziness, headache, increased sweating, menstrual irregularities

103

Major Side Effects: Abdominal distension, fluid retention, glaucoma, growth impairment in children, high blood pressure, impaired healing of wounds, peptic ulcer, potassium loss, weakness, cataracts

Contraindications: Systemic fungal infections

Warnings and Precautions: Peptic ulcer, pregnancy, tuberculosis, diabetes

Interacts With: aspirin, barbiturates, diuretics, estrogens, indomethacin, oral anticoagulants, antidiabetics, phenytoin

Comments: Aristocort steroid hormone is often taken on a decreasing-dosage schedule (four times a day for several days, then three times a day, etc.). Aristo-Pak steroid hormone (Lederle Laboratories) contains 4-mg tablets arranged in this way. It is convenient but more expensive than buying loose tablets.

For long-term treatment, taking the drug every other day (16 mg every other day rather than 8 mg each day, for example) is preferred. Generally, taking the entire dose at one time (about 8:00 A.M.) gives the best results. Ask your doctor about alternate-day dosing and the best hour of the day to take Aristocort steroid hormone.

Blood pressure and body weight should be checked at regular intervals. Stomach x-rays are desirable for persons with suspected or known peptic ulcers.

Products equivalent to Aristocort are available and vary widely in cost. Ask your doctor to prescribe a generic preparation; then ask your pharmacist to fill it with the least expensive brand.

Do not stop taking this drug without your doctor's knowledge.

If you are taking Aristocort steroid hormone chronically, you should carry with you a notice that you are taking a steroid.

Asma-lief antiasthmatic (Columbia Medical Co.), see Tedral antiasthmatic.

Atarax sedative

Manufacturer: Roerig

Generic Name: hydroxyzine hydrochloride

Equivalent Products: Vistaril sedative (Pfizer Laboratories Division)

Dosage Forms: Tablets: 10 mg (orange), 25 mg (green), 50 mg (yellow), 100 mg (red); liquid (content per 5 ml): 10 mg

Use: Relief of anxiety, tension, withdrawal from alcohol addiction

Minor Side Effects: Drowsiness, dry mouth

Major Side Effects: Convulsions, tremors

Contraindications: Pregnancy

Warnings and Precautions: Liver or kidney disease

Interacts With: alcohol and central nervous system depressants

Comments: Atarax sedative interacts with other sedatives and alcohol. Avoid the use of other sedatives and alcohol while taking this product.

Ativan sedative and hypnotic

Manufacturer: Wyeth Laboratories

Generic Name: lorazepam

Equivalent Products: None
Dosage Forms: Tablets: 0.5 mg (white); 1.0 mg (scored white); 2.0 mg (scored white)
Use: Relief of anxiety or tension, insomnia
Minor Side Effects: Sedation, dizziness, weakness, unsteadiness, depression, nausea, headache, rash
Major Side Effects: Eye function disturbance
Contraindications: Certain types of glaucoma, pregnancy
Warnings and Precautions: Liver and kidney disease, potential for abuse. Elderly people should not take more than 2 mg per day to start
Interacts With: alcohol, other central nervous system depressants
Comments: Ativan sedative and hypnotic is currently used by many people to relieve nervousness. It is effective for this purpose, but it is important to try to remove the cause of the anxiety as well. Phenobarbital is also effective for this purpose, and it is less expensive. Consult your doctor.

Ativan sedative and hypnotic has the potential for abuse and must be used with caution. Tolerance may develop quickly; *do not* increase the dose without first consulting your doctor.

Ativan sedative and hypnotic is a safe drug when used alone. When it is combined with other sedative drugs or alcohol, serious adverse reactions may develop.

Ativan sedative and hypnotic may cause drowsiness, and people taking it should be careful about driving.

Atromid-S antilipidemic

Manufacturer: Ayerst Laboratories
Generic Name: clofibrate
Equivalent Products: None
Dosage Forms: Capsules: 500 mg (orange-red)
Use: Reduction of fat or cholesterol in the blood in atherosclerosis (arteriosclerosis), hardening of the arteries, and certain kinds of skin lesions caused by excessive fat levels in the blood
Minor Side Effects: Abdominal cramps, diarrhea, dizziness, dry and falling hair, fatigue, flu-like symptoms, gas, headache, muscle cramps, nausea, palpitations, rash, vomiting, weakness, impotence
Major Side Effects: chest pains, blood clots, enlarged liver
Contraindications: Severe liver and kidney disease
Warnings and Precautions: Peptic ulcer, certain types of heart arrhythmias, pregnancy
Interacts With: coumarin, furosemide
Comments: Atromid-S antilipidemic effectively lowers cholesterol and fats in the blood, but whether this drug actually prevents a heart attack or other diseases associated with hardening of the arteries is not known.

Before taking any nonprescription item to treat the aches of a cold, check with your doctor. Your aches may be a side effect of Atromid-S antilipidemic.

Before taking Atromid-S antilipidemic, your doctor should attempt to reduce your blood fat and cholesterol levels by controlling your diet.

If you are taking a ''blood thinner'' (anticoagulant), such as coumarin, be sure your doctor is aware of it.

Auralgan otic solution

Manufacturer: Ayerst Laboratories
Generic Name: antipyrine, benzocaine, dehydrated glycerin
Equivalent Products: None
Dosage Forms: Drops
Use: Relief of pain and swelling due to middle ear infections, "swimmer's ear," removal of earwax
Minor Side Effects: No minor side effects
Major Side Effects: No major side effects
Contraindications: No major documented contraindications to this drug
Warnings and Precautions: No major warnings or precautions
Interacts With: No significant drug interactions
Comments: Water greatly reduces the effectiveness of Auralgan otic solution, so keep the bottle tigtly closed and do not rinse the dropper after use.

Discard any remaining medicine after treatment has been completed. Middle ear disorders are serious and should be treated only according to a doctor's advice.

See "The Right Way to Take Medications."

AVC anti-infective

Manufacturer: Merrell-National Laboratories
Generic Name: sulfanilamide, aminacrine hydrochloride, allantoin
Equivalent Products: None
Dosage Forms: Cream; vaginal suppositories (yellow)
Use: Treatment of vaginal infections
Minor Side Effects: Itching, mild rash
Major Side Effects: No major side effects
Contraindications: No major documented contraindications to this drug
Warnings and Precautions: Allergy to sulfa drugs
Interacts With: No significant drug interactions
Comments: See "The Right Way To Take Medications."

Use until the prescribed amount of medication is gone.

Call your doctor if you develop burning or itching.

Refrain from sexual intercourse, or ask your sexual partner to use a condom until treatment is finished, to avoid reinfection.

Azo Gantanol antibacterial and analgesic

Manufacturer: Roche Products Inc.
Generic Name: sulfamethoxazole, phenazopyridine hydrochloride
Equivalent Products: None
Dosage Forms: Tablets: sulfamethoxazole, 0.5 g; phenazopyridine hydrochloride, 100 mg (dark red)
Use: Treatment of a variety of painful bacterial infections of the urinary tract
Minor Side Effects: Abdominal pain, change in urine color, depression, diarrhea, headache, nausea, vomiting
Major Side Effects: Fluid retention, hallucinations, itching, jaundice, rash, ringing in the ears, sore throat
Contraindications: Pregnancy
Warnings and Precautions: Bronchial asthma, severe hay fever, liver and kidney diseases

Interacts With: barbiturates, methenamine hippurate, methenamine mandelate, methotrexate, oral antidiabetics, oxacillin, para-aminobenzoic acid, phenytoin

Comments: Azo Gantanol antibacterial and analgesic may cause allergic reactions and should not be taken by persons with asthma; severe hay fever, or other allergies unless the doctor is aware of these conditions.

Take Azo Gantanol antibacterial and analgesic with at least a full glass of water. Drink at least nine to 10 glasses of water each day.

Azo Gantanol antibacterial and analgesic contains phenazopyridine hydrochloride which is used to treat burning and pain of urination.

Azo Gantrisin antibacterial and analgesic

Manufacturer: Roche Products Inc.

Generic Name: sulfisoxazole, phenazopyridine hydrochloride

Equivalent Products: Ameri-EZP antibacterial and analgesic (W.E. Hauck, Inc.); Azo-Soxazole antibacterial and analgesic (Columbia Medical Co.); Azosul antibacterial and analgesic (Reid-Provident Laboratories, Inc.); Suldiazo antibacterial and analgesic (Kay Pharmacal Company, Inc.)

Dosage Form: Tablets: sulfisoxazole, 0.5 g; phenazopyridine hydrochloride, 50 mg (red)

Use: Treatment of a variety of painful bacterial infections of the urinary tract

Minor Side Effects: Abdominal pain, change in urine color, depression, diarrhea, headache, nausea, vomiting

Major Side Effects: Fluid retention, hallucinations, itching, jaundice, rash, ringing in the ears, sore throat

Contraindications: Pregnancy

Warnings and Precautions: Bronchial asthma, significant allergies

Interacts With: barbiturates, methenamine hippurate, methenamine mandelate, methotrexate, oral antidiabetics, oxacillin, para-aminobenzoic acid, phenytoin

Comments: Azo Gantrisin antibacterial and analgesic may cause allergic reactions and should not be taken by persons with asthma, severe hay fever, or other allergies unless the doctor is aware of these conditions.

Take Azo Gantrisin antibacterial and analgesic with at least a full glass of water. Drink at least nine to ten glasses of water each day.

Products equivalent to Azo Gantrisin antibacterial and analgesic are available and vary widely in cost. Ask your doctor to prescribe a generic preparation; then ask your pharmacist to fill it with the least expensive brand.

Azo Gantrisin antibacterial and analgesic contains phenazopyridine hydrochloride which is used to treat burning and pain of urination.

Azolid anti-inflammatory (USV [P.R.] Development Corp.), see Butazolidin anti-inflammatory.

Azo-Soxazole antibacterial and analgesic (Columbia Medical Co.), see Azo Gantrisin antibacterial and analgesic.

Azo-Standard analgesic (Webcon Pharmaceuticals), see Pyridium analgesic.

Azo-Stat analgesic (O'Neal, Jones & Feldman), see Pyridium analgesic.

Azosul antibacterial (Reid-Provident Laboratories, Inc.), see Azo Gantrisin antibacterial and analgesic.

Bactrim antibacterial

Manufacturer: Roche Products Inc.
Generic Name: trimethoprim, sulfamethoxazole
Equivalent Product: Septra antibacterial (Burroughs Wellcome Co.)
Dosage Forms: Liquid (content per 5 ml): trimethoprim, 40 mg; sulfamethoxazole, 200 mg. Tablets: trimethoprim, 80 mg; sulfamethoxazole, 400 mg (yellowish green). Double-strength tablets: trimethoprim, 160 mg; sulfamethoxazole, 800 mg (white)
Use: Treatment of chronic urinary tract infections, certain respiratory infections, middle ear infections
Minor Side Effects: Abdominal pain, depression, diarrhea, headache, nausea, vomiting
Major Side Effects: Fluid retention, hallucinations, itching, rash, ringing in the ears, sore throat, jaundice
Contraindications: Allergy to sulfonamides
Warnings and Precautions: Bronchial asthma, pregnancy, liver and kidney diseases, significant allergies
Interacts With: barbiturates, methenamine hippurate, local anesthetics, methenamine mandelate, methotrexate, oral antidiabetics, oxacillin, para-aminobenzoic acid, phenytoin
Comments: Bactrim antibacterial should be taken for at least 10 full days, even if symptoms have disappeared.

Take Bactrim antibacterial with at least a full glass of water. Drink at least nine to 10 glasses of water each day.

Bactrim antibacterial may cause allergic reaction and should not be taken by persons with asthma, severe hay fever, or other allergies unless the doctor is aware of these conditions.

If you are allergic to a sulfa drug, you may likewise be allergic to Bactrim antibacterial.

Benadryl antihistamine

Manufacturer: Parke, Davis & Company
Generic Name: diphenhydramine hydrochloride
Equivalent Products: Benylin cough syrup (Parke, Davis & Company); Fenylhist antihistamine (Mallard Incorporated); Valdrene antihistamine (The Vale Chemical Co., Inc.)
Dosage Forms: Liquid (content per 5 ml): 12.5 mg. Capsules: 25 mg, 50 mg (both pink/white)
Use: Treatment of itching and swelling due to allergy, motion sickness, Parkinson's disease, insomnia, cough
Minor Side Effects: Blurred vision, confusion, constipation, diarrhea, difficult urination, dizziness, drowsiness, headache, insomnia, nasal congestion, nausea, nervousness, palpitations, rash, restlessness, vomiting, dry mouth, loss of appetite, weakness, reduced sweating
Major Side Effects: Low blood pressure, rash from exposure to sunlight, severe abdominal pain, sore throat
Contraindications: Asthma attacks, certain types of glaucoma, certain types of peptic ulcer, enlarged prostate, obstructed bladder, obstructed intestine, pregnancy
Warnings and Precautions: Liver or kidney diseases

Interacts With: alcohol, other central nervous system depressants

Comments: Although Benadryl antihistamine is frequently prescribed for the prevention and treatment of the common cold, a government panel of experts has concluded that the product may not be effective for this use.

Benadryl antihistamine may cause drowsiness; to prevent oversedation avoid the use of other sedative drugs or alcohol.

While taking Benadryl antihistamine, do not take any nonprescription item for cough, cold, or sinus problems without first checking with your doctor.

Benadryl antihistamine may cause dryness of the mouth. To reduce this feeling, chew gum or suck on a piece of hard candy.

Benadryl antihistamine reduces sweating; avoid excessive work or exercise in hot weather.

Products equivalent to Benadryl antihistamine are available and vary widely in cost. Ask your doctor to prescribe a generic preparation; then ask your pharmacist to fill it with the least expensive brand.

Bendectin antinauseant

Manufacturer: Merrell-National Laboratories
Generic Names: doxylamine succinate, pyridoxine hydrochloride
Equivalent Products: None
Dosage Forms: Tablets: doxylamine succinate, 10 mg; pyridoxine hydrochloride, 10 mg (white)
Use: Treatment of nausea and vomiting due to pregnancy ("morning sickness")
Minor Side Effects: Blurred vision, confusion, constipation, diarrhea, dizziness, nausea, nervousness, palpitations, rash, restlessness, vomiting
Major Side Effects: Low blood pressure, rash from exposure to sunlight, severe abdominal pain, sore throat
Contraindications: Asthma attacks, certain types of glaucoma, certain types of peptic ulcer, obstructed bladder, obstructed intestine
Warnings and Precautions: Liver and kidney diseases
Interacts With: alcohol and other central nervous system depressants
Comments: Bendectin antinauseant should not be chewed or crushed, but swallowed whole.

Bendectin antinauseant has sustained action; never take it more frequently than your doctor prescribes. A serious overdose may result.

There is no scientific proof that pyridoxine hydrochloride (vitamin B_6) works to reduce nausea of pregnancy. Consult your doctor.

Benemid uricosuric

Manufacturer: Merck Sharp & Dohme
Generic Name: probenecid
Equivalent Products: probenecid (various manufacturers)
Dosage Forms: Tablets: 500 mg (yellow, capsule-shaped)
Use: Prevention of gout attacks, used with penicillin to prolong blood levels of penicillin
Minor Side Effects: Dizziness, headache, loss of appetite, nausea, rash, vomiting
Major Side Effects: Fatigue, flushing, paleness, kidney disease

Contraindications: Kidney stones, peptic ulcer, pregnancy
Warnings and Precautions: Liver or kidney disease
Interacts With: indomethacin, para-aminosalicylic acid, salicylates (such as aspirin), sulfinpyrazone, methotrexate
Comments: The effects of Benemid uricosuric therapy may not be apparent for at least two weeks.

Do not begin Benemid uricosuric therapy during an acute attack of gout. At the beginning of therapy, attacks may increase in number and severity, and your doctor may prescribe colchicine. A combination of probenecid and colchicine is available. Called ColBENEMID uricosuric, it is useful during the initial treatment of gout and later as well. If you are taking both colchicine and Benemid uricosuric, ask your doctor about taking the combination product. You may save some money.

Take Benemid uricosuric with at least a full glass of water. Drink at least nine to 10 glasses of water each day.

Do not take aspirin while taking Benemid uricosuric without first consulting your doctor.

Diabetics using Clinitest urine test may get a false high reading of sugar. Change to Clinistix or Tes-Tape urine test to avoid this problem.

Bentyl antispasmodic

Manufacturer: Merrell-National Laboratories
Generic Name: dicyclomine hydrochloride
Equivalent Products: Dibent antispasmodic (W.E. Hauck, Inc.); dicyclomine hydrochloride (various manufacturers)
Dosage Forms: Liquid (content per 5 ml): 10 mg. Capsules: 10 mg (blue). Tablets: 20 mg (blue)
Use: Treatment of gastrointestinal disorders, including peptic ulcer, irritable colon, mucous colitis, acute enterocolitis, and neurogenic colon
Minor Side Effects: Blurred vision, constipation, difficult urination, dizziness, dry mouth, increased sensitivity to light, headache, insomnia, loss of taste, reduced sweating, nervousness, palpitations
Major Side Effects: Rapid heartbeat, impotence, rash
Contraindications: Enlarged prostate, obstructed intestine, certain types of glaucoma, asthma, bladder obstruction, certain heart diseases, porphyria
Warnings and Precautions: Certain kinds of heart disease, pregnancy, liver and kidney diseases
Interacts With: amantadine, haloperidol, antacids, phenothiazine
Comments: Bentyl antispasmodic is best taken one-half to one hour before meals.

The drug does not *cure* ulcers but may help them to improve.

Bentyl antispasmodic always produces certain side effects. These include dry mouth, blurred vision, reduced sweating, difficult urination, constipation, increased sensitivity to light, and palpitations. To reduce dryness of the mouth, chew gum or suck on a piece of hard candy. Avoid excessive work in hot weather.

A product combining Bentyl antispasmodic with phenobarbital is available for persons who are especially nervous or anxious. Despite the phenobarbital content, Bentyl antispasmodic with phenobarbital has not been shown to have high potential for abuse.

Call your doctor if you notice a rash, flushing, or pain in the eye.

Benylin cough syrup (Parke, Davis & Company), see Benadryl antihistamine.

Bonine antinauseant (Pfizer Laboratories Division), see Antivert antinauseant.

Brethine bronchodilator

Manufacturer: Geigy Pharmaceuticals
Generic Name: terbutaline sulfate
Equivalent Products: Bricanyl Sulfate bronchodilator (Astra Pharmaceutical Products)
Dosage Forms: Tablets: 2.5 mg; 5 mg (white)
Use: Relief of bronchial asthma and bronchospasm associated with bronchitis and emphysema
Minor Side Effects: Nervousness, tremor, headache, nausea, vomiting, sweating, muscle cramps, increased heart rate, palpitations
Major Side Effects: No major side effects
Contraindications: Pregnancy, allergy to any sympathomimetic amine drug
Warnings and Precautions: Diabetes, high blood pressure, hyperthyroidism, epilepsy: not recommended for children under age 12
Interacts With: guanethidine, monoamine oxidase inhibitors
Comments: While taking Brethine bronchodilator, do not take any nonprescription item for cough, cold, or sinus problems without first checking with your doctor.
   Although an equivalent product is available, purchasing it will not result in significant savings.
   Do not take any other drug containing a sympathomimetic amine without consulting your doctor.

Brevicon oral contraceptive (Syntex Laboratories, Inc.), see oral contraceptives.

Bromatane antihistamine (Henry Schein, Inc.), see Dimetane antihistamine.

Brometapp cold remedy (Henry Schein, Inc.), see Dimetapp cold remedy.

Bronkodyl bronchodilator (Breon Laboratories, Inc.) see Elixophyllin bronchodilator.

Bu-Lax Plus laxative (Ulmer Pharmacal Company), see Peri-Colace laxative.

Butazolidin anti-inflammatory

Manufacturer: Geigy Pharmaceuticals
Generic Name: phenylbutazone
Equivalent Products: Azolid anti-inflammatory (USV [P.R.] Development Corp.)
Dosage Forms: Tablets: 100 mg (red)
Use: Reduction of pain, redness, and swelling due to arthritis or thrombophlebitis
Minor Side Effects: Diarrhea, nausea, rash, vomiting

Major Side Effects: Allergic reactions, blood in urine or stools, blurred vision, fatigue, hearing difficulty, itching, jaundice, severe abdominal pain, sore throat, swelling, weight gain (more than two pounds a week), ulcer, heart disease

Contraindications: Anemia and other blood problems; chronic stomach problems; high blood pressure; thyroid disorders; ulcers; water retention; pregnancy; kidney, liver, or heart diseases; not recommended for children under age 12

Warning and Precautions: Persons over age 40, blood diseases, blurred vision

Interacts With: anticoagulants, cancer drugs, oral antidiabetics, sulfonamides

Comments: Butazolidin anti-inflammatory is remarkably effective and also one of the most toxic drugs on the market. It should never be used for trivial aches or pains. The doctor's directions should be followed exactly. Blood checks should be done at least every two weeks, and you should request them even if your doctor does not order them. Report any symptoms of sore throat to the doctor at once, since sore throat is a first sign of Butazolidin-induced blood disorders. Persons over age 40 should be doubly careful when taking this product.

When first beginning Butazolidin therapy, the manufacturer recommends that the drug should be tried for not more than one week. If no relief has been obtained, the drug should be discontinued.

Take Butazolidin with food or milk.

Do not take aspirin while taking Butazolidin without first consulting your doctor.

If you are also taking an anticoagulant ("blood thinner"), remind your doctor.

Tandearil and Oxalid anti-inflammatories (USV [P.R.] Development Corp.) (oxyphenbutazone is the generic name) have the same uses, side effects, contraindications, warnings and precautions and comments as Butazolidin anti-inflammatory.

Another product, Butazolidin Alka anti-inflammatory capsules, is available for people who experience excessive stomachaches or pains when taking Butazolidin anti-inflammatory.

Butisol Sodium sedative and hypnotic (McNeil Laboratories), see Nembutal sedative and hypnotic.

Candex antifungal cream or lotion (Dome Laboratories), see Mycostatin antifungal.

Capade cold remedy (Spencer-Mead Inc.), see Ornade Spansule capsules cold remedy.

Cardabid antianginal (Saron Pharmacal Corp.), see Nitro-Bid Plateau Caps antianginal.

Catapres antihypertensive

Manufacturer: Boehringer Ingelheim Ltd.
Generic Name: clonidine hydrochloride
Equivalent Products: None
Dosage Forms: Tablets: 0.1 mg (tan), 0.2 mg (orange)
Use: Treatment of high blood pressure

Minor Side Effects: Constipation, dizziness, drowsiness, dry mouth, fatigue, headache, increased sensitivity to alcohol, insomnia, nasal congestion, nausea, rash, vomiting

Major Side Effects: Breathing difficulty, enlarged breasts (in both sexes), hair loss, impotence, jaundice, pain, urine retention, weight gain

Contraindications: Pregnancy

Warnings and Precautions: Liver or kidney diseases

Interacts With: alcohol, barbiturates, sedatives

Comments: Take Catapres antihypertensive with food or milk.

Mild side effects (e.g., nasal congestion) are most noticeable during the first two weeks of therapy and become less bothersome after this period.

Have your eyes checked frequently while taking Catapres antihypertensive. Although there is no documented evidence of such an effect in humans, some research animals being given clonidine hydrochloride have suffered retinal degradation.

Because Catapres antihypertensive may cause drowsiness, avoid other sedatives and alcohol and driving or working with machinery.

If dizziness or light-headedness occurs when you stand up, place your legs on the floor and "pump" the muscles for a few moments before rising.

While taking Catapres antihypertensive, do not take any nonprescription item for cough, cold, or sinus problems without first checking with your doctor.

Never stop taking Catapres antihypertensive abruptly. Rather, you should decrease consumption over a period of two to four days.

Cerebid smooth muscle relaxant (Saron Pharmacal Corp.), see Pavabid Plateau Caps smooth muscle relaxant.

Cerespan smooth muscle relaxant (USV [P.R.] Development Corp.), see Pavabid Plateau Caps smooth muscle relaxant.

Cerylin expectorant and smooth muscle relaxant (Spencer-Mead Inc.), see Quibron expectorant and smooth muscle relaxant.

Chlordiazachel sedative and hypnotic (Rachelle Laboratories, Inc.) see Librium sedative and hypnotic.

chlorpheniramine maleate antihistamine

Chlorpheniramine maleate is a generic drug.

Equivalent Products: chlorpheniramine maleate antihistamine (various manufacturers); Chlor-Trimeton antihistamine (Schering Corporation); Teldrin Spansule antihistamine capsules (Smith Kline & French Laboratories)

Dosage Forms: Chlor-Trimeton syrup (content per 5 ml): 2 mg; Chlor-Trimeton tablets: 4 mg (yellow); Chlor-Trimeton Repetabs: 8 mg (gold), 12 mg (orange); Teldrin Spansule capsules: 8 mg, 12 mg (green/clear with pellets)

Use: Symptomatic relief of allergies and hay fever

Minor Side Effects: Diarrhea, dizziness, drowsiness, dry mouth, headache, heartburn, difficult urination, loss of appetite, nausea, nervousness, rash, restlessness, vomiting, weakness, blurred vision, confusion, insomnia, nasal congestion, palpitations

Major Side Effects: Low blood pressure, rash from exposure to sunlight, severe abdominal pain, sore throat

Contraindications: Asthma, certain types of glaucoma, certain types of peptic ulcer, enlarged prostate, obstructed intestine, pregnancy
Warnings and Precautions: Liver or kidney diseases
Interacts With: alcohol, other central nervous system depressants
Comments: All chlorpheniramine maleate antihistamine products, except the 12 mg Chlor-Trimeton Repetab tablets, are available over-the-counter.

Take only the prescribed amount. An overdose usually sedates an adult but can cause excitation leading to convulsions and death in a child.

Although chlorpheniramine antihistamine is frequently prescribed for the prevention and treatment of the common cold, a government panel of experts has concluded that the product may not be effective for this use.

Chlorpheniramine antihistamine may cause dryness of the mouth. To reduce this feeling, chew gum or suck on a piece of hard candy.

While taking chlorpheniramine antihistamine do not take any additional nonprescription item for cough, cold, or sinus problems without first checking with your doctor.

Chlorpheniramine antihistamine may cause drowsiness; to prevent oversedation, avoid the use of other sedative drugs or alcohol.

Brands of chlorpheniramine antihistamine vary widely in cost. Ask your pharmacist to fill your 'prescription with the least expensive brand.

Chlor-PZ phenothiazine (USV [P.R.] Development Corporation), see Thorazine phenothiazine.

Chlor-Trimeton Repetabs antihistamine (Schering Corporation), see chlorpheniramine maleate antihistamine.

Choledyl bronchodilator

Manufacturer: Warner/Chilcott
Generic Name: oxytriphylline
Equivalent Products: None
Dosage Forms: Liquid (content per 5 ml) 100 mg; tablets: 100 mg (red); 200 mg (yellow)
Use: Relief of bronchial asthma and bronchospasm associated with bronchitis and emphysema
Minor Side Effects: Gastric distress, central nervous system stimulation
Major Side Effects: Convulsions, palpitations, difficult breathing
Contraindications: Pregnancy
Warnings and Precautions: Peptic ulcer, heart disease, liver and kidney disease
Interacts With: lithium carbonate, propranolol
Comments: If you have mild gastrointestinal distress while taking Choledyl bronchodilator, take an over-the-counter product like Maalox or Gelusil antacid.

Take Choledyl bronchodilator with food or milk.

Call your doctor if you have severe stomach pain, vomiting, or restlessness.

Be sure to take your dosage at exactly the right time. Do not crush Choledyl bronchodilator tablets.

Avoid drinking tea, cocoa, or other beverages that contain "xanthines" while taking Choledyl bronchodilator. Consult your pharmacist.

Do not use over-the-counter items for asthma while taking Choledyl bronchodilator unless your doctor has told you to do so.

Chronotab tablets cough and cold remedy (Schering Corporation), see Drixoral cough and cold remedy.

Cin-Quin antiarrhythmic (Rowell Laboratories, Inc.), see quinidine sulfate antiarrhythmic.

Circanol vasodilator (Riker Laboratories, Inc.), see Hydergine vasodilator.

Clinoril anti-inflammatory

Manufacturer: Merck Sharp & Dohme
Generic Name: sulindac
Equivalent Products: None
Dosage Forms: Tablets: 150 mg, 200 mg (hexagon-shaped/yellow)
Use: Reduction of pain, redness, and swelling due to arthritis
Minor Side Effects: Abdominal pain, dyspepsia, nausea, vomiting, diarrhea, constipation, gas, loss of appetite, rash, itching
Major Side Effects: Headache, dizziness, ringing in ears, edema and weight gain, gastrointestinal bleeding, high blood pressure, numbness in fingers and toes, nerve damage, visual disturbance, nosebleed, depression
Contraindications: Allergy to aspirin or other nonsteroidal anti-inflammatory agents, pregnancy
Warnings and Precautions: Peptic ulcer, certain blood diseases or blood-clotting disorders, liver and kidney diseases, certain types of heart disease
Interacts With: aspirin, oral anticoagulants, probenecid, steroids
Comments: Clinoril anti-inflammatory is a potent pain-killing drug and is not intended for general aches and pains.

Regular checkups by the doctor, including blood tests and eye examinations, are required by persons taking Clinoril anti-inflammatory.

Clinoril anti-inflammatory must be taken with food or milk. Never take this product on an empty stomach or with aspirin, and never take more than directed.

If you are taking an anticoagulant ("blood thinner"), remind your doctor.

Coastaldyne analgesic and narcotic (Coastal), see Tylenol with Codeine analgesic and narcotic.

Co-Estrol estrogen hormone (Robinson Laboratory, Inc.), see Premarin estrogen hormone.

ColBENEMID uricosuric and anti-inflammatory (Merck Sharp & Dohme), see Benemid uricosuric.

Col-Decon adrenergic and antihistamine (Columbia Medical Co.), see Naldecon adrenergic and antihistamine.

Colonil anticholinergic and antispasmodic (Mallinckrodt, Inc.), see Lomotil anticholinergic and antispasmodic.

Combid anticholinergic and phenothiazine

Manufacturer: Smith Kline & French Laboratories
Generic Name: isopropamide iodide, prochlorperazine maleate
Equivalent Products: Com-Pro-Span anticholinergic and phenothiazine (Columbia Medical)
Dosage Forms: Capsules: isopropamide iodide, 5 mg; prochlorperazine, 10 mg (yellow/clear with multicolored pellets).
Use: Treatment of intestinal or stomach disorders, including peptic ulcer
Minor Side Effects: Blurred vision, change in urine color, constipation, diarrhea, difficult urination, drooling, drowsiness, dry mouth, headache, jitteriness, insomnia, loss of the sense of taste, menstrual irregularities, nasal congestion, nausea, nervousness, rash, restlessness, reduced sweating, uncoordinated movements, vomiting, increased sensitivity to light, palpitations
Major Side Effects: Difficult ejaculation; impotence; difficult swallowing; enlarged breasts (in both sexes); fluid retention; involuntary movements of the face, tongue, mouth, or jaw; muscle stiffness; sore throat; tremors; jaundice; rise in blood pressure
Contraindications: Coma, drug-induced depression, shock, blood disease, Parkinson's disease, liver damage, jaundice, severe kidney disease, stroke, heart disease, certain types of glaucoma, enlarged prostate, obstructed intestine, asthma, bladder obstruction, certain heart diseases, porphyria
Warnings and Precautions: Asthma and other respiratory disorders, epilepsy, exposure to extreme heat, pregnancy, severe heart disease, liver and kidney diseases
Interacts With: amantadine, haloperidol, antacids, phenothiazines, alcohol, other anticholinergics, depressants
Comments: The effects of Combid anticholinergic and phenothiazine therapy may not be apparent for at least two weeks.

Combid anticholinergic and phenothiazine has sustained action; never take it more frequently than your doctor prescribes. A serious overdose may result.

Combid anticholinergic and phenothiazine may cause drowsiness; to prevent oversedation, avoid the use of other sedative drugs or alcohol.

While taking Combid anticholinergic and phenothiazine, do not take any nonprescription item for cough, cold, or sinus problems without first checking with your doctor.

Combid anticholinergic and phenothiazine is best taken one-half to one hour before meals.

The drug does not *cure* ulcers but may help them to improve.

Combid anticholinergic and phenothiazine always produces certain side effects. These include dry mouth, blurred vision, reduced sweating, difficult urination, constipation, increased sensitivity to light, and palpitations. To reduce dryness of the mouth, chew gum or suck on a piece of hard candy. Avoid excessive work in hot weather.

Call your doctor if you notice a rash, flushing, or pain in the eye.

If you are scheduled for a thyroid function test, tell your doctor that you are taking Combid anticholinergic and phenothiazine, because the drug may influence the results of the test.

If dizziness and light-headedness occur when you stand up, place your legs on the floor and "pump" the muscles for a few moments before rising.

As with any other drug that has antivomiting activity, symptoms of severe disease or toxicity due to overdose of other drugs may be masked by Combid anticholinergic and phenothiazine.

Products equivalent to Combid anticholinergic and phenothiazine are available and vary widely in cost. Ask your doctor to prescribe a generic preparation; Then ask your pharmacist to fill your prescription with the least expensive brand.

Comfolax Plus laxative (Searle Laboratories), see Peri-Colace laxative.

Compazine phenothiazine

Manufacturer: Smith Kline & French Laboratories
Generic Name: prochlorperazine maleate
Equivalent Products: None
Dosage Forms: Syrup (content per 5 ml) 5 mg; suppositories; concentrate; capsules: 10 mg, 15 mg, 30 mg (all are black/clear with yellow and white beads); tablets: 5 mg, 10 mg, 25 mg (all are yellow)
Use: Control of severe nausea and vomiting, relief of certain kinds of anxiety, tension, agitation, psychiatric disorders
Minor Side Effects: Blurred vision, constipation, diarrhea, drooling, drowsiness, dry mouth, jitteriness, menstrual irregularities, nasal congestion, nausea, rash, restlessness, uncoordinated movements, vomiting, change in urine color, reduced sweating
Major Side Effects: Difficulty in swallowing; enlarged or painful breasts (in both sexes); fluid retention; impotence; involuntary movements of the face, mouth, tongue, or jaw; muscle stiffness; sore throat; tremors; jaundice; rise in blood pressure
Contraindications: Coma, drug-induced depression, shock, blood disease, Parkinson's disease, liver damage, jaundice, kidney disease, stroke, pregnancy
Warnings and Precautions: Asthma and other respiratory disorders, epilepsy, exposure to extreme heat or certain insecticides
Interacts With: alcohol, oral antacids, anticholinergics, depressants
Comments: The effects of Compazine phenothiazine therapy may not be apparent for at least two weeks.

Compazine phenothiazine has sustained action; never take it more frequently than your doctor prescribes. A serious overdose may result.

While taking Compazine phenothiazine, do not take any nonprescription item for cough, cold, or sinus problems without first checking with your doctor.

Compazine phenothiazine interacts with alcohol or other sedative drugs; avoid them while taking this product.

Compazine phenothiazine may cause dryness of the mouth. To reduce this feeling, chew gum or suck on a piece of hard candy.

Compazine phenothiazine reduces sweating; therefore avoid excessive work or exercise in hot weather.

If dizziness or light-headedness occurs when you stand up, place the legs on the floor and "pump" the muscles for a few moments before rising.

As with any other drug that has antivomiting activity, symptoms of severe disease or toxicity due to overdose of other drugs may be masked by Compazine phenothiazine.

Com-Pro-Span anticholinergic and phenothiazine (Columbia Medical), see Combid anticholinergic and phenothiazine.

Conest estrogen hormone (Century Pharmaceuticals), see Premarin estrogen hormone.

Cordran steroid hormone

Manufacturer: Dista Products Company
Generic Name: flurandrenolide
Equivalent Products: None
Dosage Forms: Cream; lotion; ointment; tape
Use: Relief of pruritis and inflammations of the skin such as eczema and poison ivy
Minor Side Effects: Burning sensation, dryness, irritation, itching, rash
Major Side Effects: Secondary infection
Contraindications: No absolute contraindications
Warnings and Precautions: Bacterial or viral infections of the skin, diseases causing severe impairment of blood circulation
Interacts With: No significant drug interactions
Comments: If the affected area of the skin is extremely dry or is scaling, the skin may be moistened before applying the medication by soaking in water or by applying water with a clean cloth. The ointment form is probably better for dry skin.

Do not use Cordran steroid hormone with an occlusive wrap unless instructed to do so by your doctor. See: "The Right Way to Take Medications."

Corphed adrenergic and antihistamine (Bell Pharmacal Corp.), see Actifed adrenergic and antihistamine.

Cortin steroid hormone and anti-infective (C & M Pharmacal, Inc.), see Vioform-Hydrocortisone steroid hormone and anti-infective.

Cortisporin ophthalmic suspension

Manufacturer: Burroughs Wellcome Co.
Generic Name: hydrocortisone, neomycin sulfate, polymyxin B sulfate
Equivalent Products: None
Dosage Form: Drops
Use: Short-term treatment of bacterial infections of the eye
Minor Side Effects: Burning, stinging
Major Side Effects: Perception of a "halo" effect around lights, worsening of the condition
Contraindications: Fungal infections, pus in the eye
Warnings and Precautions: No major warnings or precautions.
Interacts With: No significant drug interactions
Comments: As with all eyedrops, Cortisporin ophthalmic suspension may cause minor, transitory clouding or blurring of vision when first applied.

When used for an extended period of time, Cortisporin ophthalmic suspension may cause serious eye damage. Discard any unused portion of the drug, and consult your doctor if symptoms reappear.

Be careful about the contamination of medications used for the eyes. See: "The Right Way to Take Medications."

Cortisporin otic solution/suspension

Manufacturer: Burroughs Wellcome Co.
Generic Name: polymyxin B sulfate, neomycin sulfate, hydrocortisone
Equivalent Products: Otobione otic suspension (Schering Corporation)
Dosage Forms: Solution; suspension
Use: Anti-inflammatory steroid hormone, antibacterial for the treatment of superficial bacterial infections of the outer ear
Minor Side Effects: Burning sensation, hives, itching
Major Side Effects: No major side effects
Contraindications: Perforated eardrum, tuberculosis
Warnings and Precautions: No major warnings or precautions
Interacts With: No significant drug interactions
Comments: Discard any unused portion of the drug when therapy is complete.
Middle ear infections are serious and should be treated only according to a doctor's advice.
See: "The Right Way to Take Medications."

Coumadin anticoagulant

Manufacturer: Endo Laboratories, Inc.
Generic Name: sodium warfarin
Equivalent Products: Panwarfin anticoagulant (Abbott Laboratories)
Dosage Form: Tablets: 2 mg (lavender), 2.5 mg (orange), 5 mg (peach), 7.5 mg (yellow), 10 mg (white), 25 mg (red)
Use: Prevention of blood clot formation in conditions such as heart disease and pulmonary embolism
Minor Side Effects: Change in urine color, diarrhea, nausea
Major Side Effects: Black stools, bleeding, fever, rash, red urine
Contraindications: Any disease that causes bleeding (such as ulcers), pregnancy
Warnings and Precautions: Liver and kidney diseases
Interacts With: alcohol, allopurinol, anabolic steroids, antipyrine, barbiturates, chloral hydrate, chloramphenicol, cholestyramine, clofibrate, dextrothyroxine, diazoxide, disulfiram, ethacrynic acid, ethchlorvynol, glucagon, glutethimide, griseofulvin, indomethacin, mefenamic acid, neomycin, oral antidiabetics, oral contraceptives, oxyphenbutazone, phenylbutazone, phenytoin, quinidine, rifampin, salicylates, steroids, thyroid, triclofos, antidepressants
Comments: Coumadin anticoagulant interacts with many other drugs; do not start or stop taking another medication, including aspirin, without checking with your doctor.
If clots fail to form over cuts and bruises or if purple or brown spots appear under bruised skin, call your doctor immediately.
Regular prothrombin time determinations are essential while taking Coumadin anticoagulant.

A change in urine color may or may not be serious; if you notice a change, contact your doctor or pharmacist.

cyclandelate vasodilator (various manufacturers), see Cyclospasmol vasodilator.

Cyclanfor vasodilator (Forest Laboratories, Inc.), see Cyclospasmol vasodilator.

Cyclospasmol vasodilator

Manufacturer: Ives Laboratories, Inc.
Generic Name: cyclandelate
Equivalent Products: cyclandelate vasodilator (various manufacturers); Cyclanfor vasodilator (Forest Laboratories, Inc.); Cydel vasodilator (W.E. Hauck, Inc.)
Dosage Forms: Capsules: 200 mg (blue), 400 mg (blue/red); tablets: 100 mg (orange)
Use: Dilation of blood vessels
Minor Side Effects: Flushing, headache, stomach distress
Major Side Effects: Palpitations, weakness
Contraindications: Pregnancy
Warnings and Precautions: Glaucoma, severe hardening of the arteries, heart disease, liver and kidney diseases
Interacts With: No significant drug interactions
Comments: While Cyclospasmol vasodilator dilates blood vessels, a government panel of experts has determined that the drug is only "possibly" effective in the treatment of hardening of the arteries, leg cramps, and in the prevention of stroke.

While taking Cyclospasmol vasodilator, do not take any nonprescription item for cough, cold, or sinus problems without first checking with your doctor.

Stomach distress is usually mild and can be avoided by taking the drug with food or an antacid.

Mild side effects (e.g., flushing) are most noticeable during the first two weeks of therapy and become less bothersome after this period.

Products equivalent to Cyclospasmol vasodilator are available and vary widely in cost. Ask your doctor to prescribe a generic preparation; then ask your pharmacist to fill it with the least expensive brand.

Cydel vasodilator (W.E. Hauck, Inc.), see Cyclospasmol vasodilator.

Dalmane hypnotic

Manufacturer: Roche Products, Inc.
Generic Name: flurazepam hydrochloride
Equivalent Products: None
Dosage Form: Capsules: 15 mg (orange/ivory), 30 mg (red/ivory)

Use: Sleeping aid
Minor Side Effects: Confusion, constipation, depression, difficult urination, dizziness, drowsiness, dry mouth, fatigue, headache, nausea, rash, slurred speech, uncoordinated movements
Major Side Effects: Blurred vision, decreased sexual drive, double vision, jaundice, low blood pressure, stimulation, tremors
Contraindications: Certain types of glaucoma
Warnings and Precautions: Pregnancy, suicidal tendencies, liver and kidney diseases, potential for abuse
Interacts With: central nervous system depressants
Comments: Dalmane hypnotic currently is the most widely used drug for inducing sleep. It is effective, but eliminating the cause of insomnia is also important. Phenobarbital is also an effective sleep-inducer, and it is cheaper. Consult your doctor.

Take Dalmane hypnotic 30 to 60 minutes before retiring, and avoid other sedatives and alcohol to prevent oversedation.

Dalmane hypnotic has the potential for abuse and must be used with caution. Tolerance may develop quickly; *do not* increase the dose of the drug without first consulting your doctor.

Dalmane hypnotic is a safe drug when used alone. When it is combined with other sedative drugs or alcohol, serious adverse reactions may develop.

Darvocet-N analgesic

Manufacturer: Eli Lilly and Company
Generic Name: propoxyphene napsylate, acetaminophen
Equivalent Products: None
Dosage Forms: Darvocet-N 50 tablets: propoxyphene napsylate, 50 mg; acetaminophen, 325 mg. Darvocet-N 100 tablets: propoxyphene napsylate, 100 mg; acetaminophen, 650 mg (both are orange)
Use: Relief of pain
Minor Side Effects: Abdominal pain, constipation, dizziness, headache, light-headedness, nausea, rash, sedation, vomiting, weakness, blurred vision, drowsiness
Major Side Effects: Liver dysfunction
Contraindications: Pregnancy,
Warnings and Precautions: Liver or kidney diseases, history of drug abuse
Interacts With: alcohol and other central nervous system depressants
Comments: Aspirin or acetaminophen should be tried *before* Darvocet-N analgesic. If aspirin or acetaminophen does not relieve pain, Darvocet-N analgesic may be effective. You may want to ask your doctor to prescribe an inexpensive brand of propoxyphene hydrochloride instead of the napsylate.

Darvocet-N analgesic interacts with alcohol and other drugs; avoid the use of other sedative drugs or alcohol while taking this product.

Darvocet-N analgesic has the potential for abuse and must be used with caution. Tolerance may develop quickly; *do not* increase the dose of the drug without first consulting your doctor.

Darvon analgesic

Manufacturer: Eli Lilly and Company

Generic Name: propoxyphene hydrochloride
Equivalent Products: Dolene analgesic (Lederle Laboratories); Pargesic-65 analgesic (Parmed Pharmaceuticals Inc.); Progesic-65 analgesic (Ulmer Pharmacal Company)
Dosage Form: Capsules: 32 mg, 65 mg (both pink)
Use: Relief of mild pain
Minor Side Effects: Abdominal pain, constipation, dizziness, headache, light-headedness, nausea, rash, sedation, vomiting, weakness, blurred vision, drowsiness
Major Side Effects: Liver dysfunction
Contraindications: Pregnancy
Warnings and Precautions: Liver or kidney diseases, history of drug abuse
Interacts With: alcohol and other central nervous system depressants
Comments: An aspirin product should be tried *before* Darvon analgesic. If aspirin does not relieve pain, Darvon analgesic may be effective. You may want to ask your doctor to prescribe an inexpensive brand of propoxyphene.

Darvon analgesic interacts with alcohol and many drugs; avoid the use of other sedative drugs or alcohol while taking this product.

Darvon analgesic has the potential for abuse and must be used with caution. Tolerance may develop quickly; *do not* increase the dose of the drug without first consulting your doctor.

Darvon Compound-65 analgesic

Manufacturer: Eli Lilly and Company
Generic Name: propoxyphene hydrochloride, aspirin, caffeine, phenacetin
Equivalent Products: Dolene Compound-65 analgesic (Lederle Laboratories); Pargesic Compound-65 analgesic (Parmed Pharmaceuticals Inc.); Progesic Compound-65 analgesic (Ulmer Pharmacal Company)
Dosage Form: Capsules: propoxyphene hydrochloride, 65 mg; aspirin, 227 mg; caffeine, 32.4 mg; phenacetin, 162 mg (crimson/gray)
Use: Relief of pain
Minor Side Effects: Abdominal pain, constipation, dizziness, drowsiness, headache, light-headedness, nausea, rash, sedation, vomiting, weakness, blurred vision, ringing in the ears
Major Side Effects: Kidney disease, liver dysfunction
Contraindications: Bleeding ulcers, pregnancy
Warnings and Precautions: Liver or kidney diseases, blood coagulation problems, history of drug abuse, significant allergies
Interacts With: alcohol, ammonium chloride, methotrexate, oral anticoagulants, oral antidiabetics, probenecid, steroids, sulfinpyrazone, vitamin C
Comments: Aspirin should be tried *before* Darvon Compound-65 analgesic. If aspirin does not relieve pain, Darvon Compound-65 analgesic may be effective, and you may want to ask your doctor to prescribe an inexpensive brand of propoxyphene.

Darvon Compound-65 analgesic interacts with alcohol; avoid the use of alcohol while taking this product.

Darvon Compound-65 analgesic may cause allergic reactions and should not be taken by persons with asthma, severe hay fever, or other allergies unless the doctor is aware of these conditions.

If you are taking an anticoagulant ("blood thinner"), remind your doctor.

Darvon Compound-65 analgesic has the potential for abuse and must be used with caution. Tolerance may develop quickly; *do not* increase the dose of the drug without first consulting your doctor.

If your ears feel unusual, or you hear buzzing or ringing, or if your stomach hurts, your dosage may need adjustment. Call your doctor.

Deapril-ST vasodilator (Mead Johnson Pharmaceutical Division), see Hydergine vasodilator.

Delaxin muscle relaxant (Ferndale Laboratories, Inc.), see Robaxin muscle relaxant.

Deltasone steroid hormone (The Upjohn Company), see prednisone steroid hormone.

Demerol analgesic

Manufacturer: Winthrop Laboratories
Generic Name: meperidine hydrochloride
Equivalent Products: meperidine hydrochloride (various manufacturers)
Dosage Forms: Liquid (content per 5 ml): 50 mg; tablets: 50 mg, 100 mg (both white)
Use: Relief of severe pain
Minor Side Effects: Constipation, dry mouth, flushing, light-headedness, nausea, palpitations, rash, sweating, uncoordinated movements, vomiting, drowsiness, urine retention, euphoria
Major Side Effects: Breathing difficulties, faintness, rapid heartbeat, tremors
Contraindications: Pregnancy, history of drug abuse
Warnings and Precautions: Asthma and other respiratory problems, epilepsy, head injuries, liver and kidney diseases
Interacts With: alcohol, monoamine oxidase inhibitors, phenothiazines, antidepressants
Comments: Products containing narcotics (e.g., Demerol analgesic) are usually not used for more than seven to 10 days.

Demerol analgesic interacts with alcohol; avoid the use of other sedative drugs or alcohol while taking Demerol analgesic.

If dizziness or light-headedness occurs when you stand up, place your legs on the floor and "pump" the muscles for a few moments before rising.

Demerol analgesic has the potential for abuse and must be used with caution. Tolerance my develop quickly; *do not* increase the dose of the drug without first consulting your doctor.

Demerol analgesic liquid should be mixed with water before it is swallowed to avoid numbing the inside of the mouth.

Products equivalent to Demerol analgesic are available. Discuss them with your pharmacist.

Demulen oral contraceptive (Searle Laboratories), see oral contraceptives.

Diabinese oral antidiabetic

Manufacturer: Pfizer Laboratories Division
Generic Name: chlorpropamide

Equivalent Products: None
Dosage Form: Tablets: 100 mg, 250 mg (both are blue, "D" shaped)
Use: Treatment of diabetes mellitus
Minor Side Effects: Diarrhea, dizziness, fatigue, headache, loss of appetite, nausea, rash, vomiting, weakness
Major Side Effects: Low blood sugar level, jaundice, sore throat
Contraindications: Acidosis, age (see Comments below), coma, ketosis, severe infections, severe trauma, upcoming surgery, severe liver and kidney diseases, pregnancy
Warnings and Precautions: Liver or kidney diseases
Interacts With: alcohol, anabolic steroids, anticoagulants, aspirin, chloramphenicol, guanethidine, monoamine oxidase inhibitors, phenylbutazone, propranolol, steroids, sulfonamides, tetracycline, thiazide diuretics, thyroid hormones
Comments: Oral antidiabetic drugs are not effective in the treatment of diabetes in children under age 12.

Studies have shown that a good diet and exercise program may be just as effective as oral antidiabetic drugs. However, these drugs allow diabetics more leeway in their lifestyle. Persons taking these drugs should carefully watch their diet and exercise program.

During the first six weeks of Diabinese oral antidiabetic therapy, visit your doctor at least once a week.

While taking Diabinese oral antidiabetic, check your urine for sugar and ketone at least three times a day. A patient taking Diabinese oral antidiabetic will have to be switched to insulin therapy if he develops complications (e.g., ketoacidosis; severe trauma; severe infection, diarrhea, nausea, or vomiting; or the need for major surgery).

Take Diabinese oral antidiabetic at the same time each day.

Ask your doctor how to recognize the first signs of low blood sugar.

Diacin vitamin supplement (Danal Laboratories, Inc.), see nicotinic acid.

Diamox diuretic

Manufacturer: Lederle Laboratories
Generic Name: acetazolamide
Equivalent Products: Rozolamide diuretic (Robinson Laboratory, Inc.)
Dosage Forms: Tablets: 125 mg, 250 mg (white); 500 mg (orange); sustained-release capsules: 500 mg (orange)
Use: Treatment of certain types of glaucoma, fluid retention, epilepsy
Minor Side Effects: Constipation, diarrhea, drowsiness, loss of appetite, nausea, tingling in the fingers and toes, vomiting
Major Side Effects: Blood in the urine, convulsions, darkened skin, jaundice, visual disturbances
Contraindications: Severe diseases of the kidney, liver, and adrenal glands; low blood sodium or potassium; pregnancy
Warnings and Precautions: Emphysema, allergy to sulfa drugs, certain liver and kidney diseases
Interacts With: amphetamine, methenamine, quinidine sulfate
Comments: Diamox diuretic causes frequent urination. Expect this effect; it should not alarm you.

Diamox diuretic may cause drowsiness; to prevent oversedation, avoid the use of other sedative drugs or alcohol.

Diamox diuretic can cause potassium loss. To avoid potassium loss, take Diamox diuretic with a glass of fresh or frozen orange juice. You may also eat a banana each day. The use of Diasal or Co-Salt salt substitutes helps prevent potassium loss.

Persons taking this product and digitalis should watch carefully for symptoms of increased toxicity (e.g., nausea, blurred vision, palpitations).

If you are allergic to a sulfa drug, you may likewise be allergic to Diamox diuretic.

Products equivalent to Diamox diuretic are available and vary widely in cost. Ask your doctor to prescribe a generic preparation; then ask your pharmacist to fill it with the least expensive brand.

Di-Azo analgesic (Kay Pharmacal Company, Inc.), see Pyridium analgesic.

Dibent antispasmodic (W.E. Hauck, Inc.), see Bentyl antispasmodic.

digoxin heart drug

Digoxin is a generic drug.
Equivalent Products: Lanoxin digitalis drug (Burroughs Wellcome Co.)
Dosage Forms: Lanoxin tablets: 0.125 mg (yellow), 0.25 mg (white), 0.5 mg (green)
Use: To strengthen heartbeat and regulate heart rhythm
Minor Side Effects: Nausea, vomiting, diarrhea
Major Side Effects: Perception of "halos" around lights, loss of appetite, palpitations, visual disturbances (such as green-colored vision)
Contraindications: None
Warnings and Precautions: Kidney disease, water retention, pregnancy
Interacts With: aminoglycoside antibiotics, amphotericin B, cholestipol hydrochloride, cholestyramine, diuretics, phenylbutazone, propantheline, propranolol
Comments: The pharmacologic activity of digoxin heart drug preparations varies widely due to how well the tablets dissolve in the stomach and bowels. Because of this variability, do not change brands of the drug without checking with your doctor.

Elderly people will very likely have side effects from digoxin heart drug, and they should have regular checkups.

Using digoxin heart drug for weight loss is very dangerous; the drug should never be used for this purpose.

Take digoxin heart drug at the same time each day.

While taking digoxin heart drug, do not take any nonprescription item for cough, cold, or sinus problems without first checking with your doctor.

Dilantin anticonvulsant

Manufacturer: Parke, Davis & Company
Generic Name: phenytoin sodium or diphenylhydantoin
Equivalent Products: Diphenylan Sodium anticonvulsant (The Lannett Company, Inc.)

Dosage Forms: Capsules: 30 mg, 100 mg (white with pink stripe); flavored tablets: 50 mg (yellow); liquid (content per 5 ml): 30 mg, 125 mg

Use: Control of epilepsy and other convulsive disorders

Minor Side Effects: Constipation, headache, nausea, rash, vomiting, change in color of urine, drowsiness

Major Side Effects: Confusion, dizziness, gum enlargement, nervousness, slurred speech, uncoordinated movements

Contraindications: Severe liver disease, blood disease, pregnancy

Warnings and Precautions: Certain liver or kidney diseases

Interacts With: chloramphenicol, corticosteroids, disulfiram, isoniazid, oral anticoagulants, propranolol, thyroid hormones

Comments: Gums may enlarge to the point of covering the teeth. Gum enlargement can be minimized, at least partially, by good dental care— frequent brushing and massaging the gums with the rubber tip of a good toothbrush.

Do not stop taking Dilantin anticonvulsant suddenly. You may start to convulse.

Dilantin anticonvulsant may cause drowsiness; to prevent oversedation, avoid the use of other sedative drugs or alcohol.

Products equivalent to Dilantin anticonvulsant are available and vary widely in cost. Ask your doctor to prescribe a generic preparation; then ask your pharmacist to fill it with the least expensive brand. But, once you begin therapy, it is important not to switch from brand to brand.

Dimetane antihistamine

Manufacturer: A.H. Robins Company

Generic Name: brompheniramine maleate

Equivalent Products: Bromatane antihistamine (Henry Schein, Inc.), Rolabromophen antihistamine (Robinson Laboratory, Inc.), Spentane antihistamine (Spencer-Mead, Inc.), Veltane antihistamine (Lannett Co., Inc.)

Dosage Forms: Liquid (content per 5 ml): 2 mg; tablets: 4 mg (peach), 8 mg (Persian rose), 12 mg (peach)

Use: Treatment of itching and swelling due to allergy

Minor Side Effects: Blurred vision, confusion, constipation, diarrhea, difficult urination, dizziness, drowsiness, headache, insomnia, nasal congestion, nausea, nervousness, palpitations, rash, restlessness, vomiting, dry mouth, reduced sweating

Major Side Effects: Low blood pressure, rash from exposure to sunlight, severe abdominal cramps, sore throat

Contraindications: Asthma, certain types of glaucoma, certain types of peptic ulcer, enlarged prostate, obstructed bladder, obstructed intestine, pregnancy

Warnings and Precautions: Age (see Comments)

Interacts With: alcohol, other central nervous system depressants

Comments: Although Dimetane antihistamine is frequently prescribed for the prevention and treatment of the common cold, a government panel of experts has concluded that the product may not be effective for this use.

Dimetane antihistamine interacts with alcohol; avoid the use of alcohol while taking this product.

While taking Dimetane antihistamine, do not take any nonprescription item for cough, cold, or sinus problems without first checking with your doctor.

Dimetane antihistamine may cause dryness of the mouth. To reduce this feeling, chew gum or suck on a piece of hard candy.

Dimetane antihistamine reduces sweating; avoid excessive work or exercise in hot weather.

Products equivalent to Dimetane antihistamine are available and vary widely in cost. Ask your doctor to prescribe a generic preparation; then ask your pharmacist to fill it with the least expensive brand.

The elderly are more likely to suffer side effects when taking Dimetane antihistamine than are other people. Children taking this product may become restless and excited.

Dimetane expectorant

Manufacturer: A.H. Robins Company
Generic Name: phenylephrine hydrochloride, phenylpropanolamine hydrochloride, brompheniramine maleate, guaifenesin
Equivalent Products: Puretane expectorant (Purepac Pharmaceutical Co.)
Dosage Form: Liquid (content per 5 ml): phenylephrine hydrochloride, 5 mg; phenylpropanolamine hydrochloride, 5 mg; brompheniramine maleate, 2 mg; guaifenesin, 100 mg
Use: Relief of symptoms of allergy and the common cold
Minor Side Effects: Diarrhea, dizziness, drowsiness, dry mouth, headache, heartburn, difficult urination, loss of appetite, nausea, rash, restlessness, vomiting, weakness, blurred vision, confusion, constipation, insomnia, nasal congestion, palpitations, reduced sweating
Major Side Effects: Low blood pressure, severe abdominal pain, sore throat, high blood pressure, chest pain
Contraindications: Asthma, some glaucomas, certain ulcers, enlarged prostate, obstructed bladder, obstructed intestine, pregnancy, severe heart disease
Warnings and Precautions: Diabetes, high blood pressure, thyroid disease, liver and kidney diseases
Interacts With: guanethidine, monoamine oxidase inhibitors
Comments: If you need an expectorant, you need more moisture in your environment. Drink nine to 10 glasses of water each day. The use of a vaporizer or humidifier may also be beneficial. Consult your doctor.

Dimetane expectorant may cause drowsiness; to prevent oversedation, avoid the use of other sedative drugs or alcohol.

While taking Dimetane expectorant, do not take any nonprescription item for cough, cold, or sinus problems without first checking with your doctor.

Although Dimetane expectorant is frequently prescribed for the prevention and treatment of the common cold, a government panel of experts has concluded that the product may not be effective for this use.

Dimetane expectorant may cause dryness of the mouth. To reduce this feeling, chew gum or suck on a piece of hard candy.

Dimetane expectorant reduces sweating; avoid excessive work or exercise in hot weather.

Products equivalent to Dimetane expectorant are available and vary widely in cost. Ask your doctor to prescribe a generic preparation; then ask your pharmacist to fill it with the least expensive brand.

Dimetane expectorant-DC

Manufacturer: A.H. Robins Company

Generic Name: phenylephrine hydrochloride, phenylpropanolamine hydro-chloride, brompheniramine maleate, guaifenesin, codeine phosphate

Equivalent Products: Puretane DC expectorant (Purepac Pharmaceutical Co.)

Dosage Form: Liquid (content per 5 ml): phenylephrine hydrochloride, 5 mg; phenypropanolamine hydrochloride, 5 mg; brompheniramine maleate, 2 mg; guaifenesin, 100 mg; codeine phosphate, 10 mg

Use: Relief of coughing

Minor Side Effects: Diarrhea, dizziness, drowsiness, dry mouth, headache, heartburn, difficult urination, loss of appetite, nausea, rash, restlessness, vomiting, weakness, blurred vision, confusion, constipation, insomnia, nasal congestion, palpitations, reduced sweating.

Major Side Effects: Low blood pressure, severe abdominal pain, sore throat, high blood pressure, chest pain

Contraindications: Asthma, some glaucomas, certain ulcers, enlarged prostate, obstructed bladder, obstructed intestine, pregnancy, severe heart disease

Warnings and Precautions: Diabetes, high blood pressure, thyroid disease, liver and kidney diseases, potential for abuse

Interacts With: guanethidine, monoamine oxidase inhibitors, antidepressants, phenothiazines

Comments: If you need an expectorant, you need more moisture in your environment. Drink nine to 10 glasses of water each day. The use of a vaporizer or humidifier may also be beneficial. Consult your doctor.

Dimetane expectorant-DC may cause drowsiness; to prevent oversedation, avoid the use of other sedative drugs or alcohol.

While taking Dimetane expectorant-DC, do not take any nonprescription item for cough, cold, or sinus problems without first checking with your doctor.

Products containing narcotics (e.g., codeine) are usually not used for more than seven to 10 days.

Dimetane expectorant-DC has the potential for abuse and must be used with caution. Tolerance may develop quickly; *do not* increase the dose of the drug without first consulting your doctor.

Although Dimetane expectorant-DC is frequently prescribed for the prevention and treatment of the common cold, a government panel of experts has concluded that the product may not be effective for this use.

Dimetane expectorant-DC may cause dryness of the mouth. To reduce this feeling, chew gum or suck on a piece of hard candy.

Dimetane expectorant-DC reduces sweating; avoid excessive work or exercise in hot weather.

Products equivalent to Dimetane expectorant-DC are available and vary widely in cost. Ask your doctor to prescribe a generic preparation; then ask your pharmacist to fill it with the least expensive brand.

Dimetapp cold remedy

Manufacturer: A.H. Robins Company

Generic Name: brompheniramine maleate, phenylephrine hydrochloride, phenylpropanolamine hydrochloride

Equivalent Products: Bromatapp cold remedy (Henry Schein, Inc.); Eldetapp cold remedy (Paul B. Elder Company)

Dosage Forms: Liquid (content per 5 ml): brompheniramine maleate, 4 mg; phenylephrine hydrochloride, 5 mg; phenylpropanolamine hydrochloride, 5 mg. Tablets: brompheniramine maleate, 12 mg; phenylephrine hydrochloride, 15 mg; phenylpropanolamine hydrochloride, 15 mg (blue).

Use: Relief of hay fever symptoms and respiratory congestion

Minor Side Effects: Diarrhea, dizziness, drowsiness, dry mouth, headache, heartburn, difficult urination, loss of appetite, nausea, rash, restlessness, vomiting, weakness, blurred vision, confusion, constipation, insomnia, nasal congestion, palpitations, reduced sweating

Major Side Effects: Low blood pressure, severe abdominal pain, sore throat, high blood pressure, chest pain

Contraindications: Asthma, some glaucomas, certain ulcers, enlarged prostate, obstructed bladder, obstructed intestine, pregnancy, severe heart disease

Warnings and Precautions: Diabetes, high blood pressure, thyroid disease, liver and kidney diseases

Interacts With: guanethidine, monoamine oxidase inhibitors

Comments: Although Dimetapp cold remedy is frequently prescribed for the prevention and treatment of the common cold, a government panel of experts has concluded that the product may not be effective for this use.

While taking Dimetapp cold remedy, do not take any nonprescription item for cough, cold, or sinus problems without first checking with your doctor.

Dimetapp cold remedy may cause dryness of the mouth. To reduce this feeling, chew gum or suck on a piece of hard candy.

Dimetapp cold remedy reduces sweating; avoid excessive work or exercise in hot weather.

Dimetapp cold remedy may cause drowsiness; to prevent oversedation, avoid the use of other sedative drugs or alcohol.

Products equivalent to Dimetapp cold remedy are available. Consult your doctor and pharmacist.

Dimetapp cold remedy tablets must be swallowed whole.

Dimetapp cold remedy has sustained action; never take it more frequently than your doctor prescribes. A serious overdose may result.

Diphenylan Sodium anticonvulsant (The Lannett Company), see Dilantin anticonvulsant.

Disophrol Chronotab tablets allergy and congestion remedy (Schering Corporation), see Drixoral allergy and congestion remedy.

Diupres antihypertensive

Manufacturer: Merck Sharp & Dohme

Generic Name: chlorothiazide, reserpine

Equivalent Products: Ro-Chloro-Serp-500 antihypertensive (Robinson Laboratory, Inc.)

Dosage Forms: Diupres-250 tablet: chlorothiazide, 250 mg; reserpine, 0.125 mg (pink). Diupres-500 tablet: chlorothiazide, 500 mg; reserpine, 0.125 mg (pink)

Use: Treatment of high blood pressure

Minor Side Effects: Cramps, diarrhea, dizziness, headache, itch, loss of appetite, nasal congestion, nausea, palpitations, rash, restlessness, vomiting, tingling in the fingers and toes

Major Side Effects: Chest pain, depression, drowsiness, elevated blood sugar, elevated uric acid, glaucoma, muscle spasm, nightmares, sore throat, weakness, blurred vision

Contraindications: Allergy to sulfa drugs, severe kidney disease, pregnancy

Warnings and Precautions: Bronchial asthma, gallstones, mental depression, peptic ulcer, ulcerative colitis, diabetes, gout, liver and kidney diseases

Interacts With: amphetamine, colestipol hydrochloride, decongestants, digitalis, levodopa, lithium carbonate, monoamine oxidase inhibitors, oral antidiabetics, steroids

Comments: A doctor probably should not prescribe Diupres antihypertensive or other "fixed dose" products as the first choice in the treatment of high blood pressure. The patient should receive each of the individual ingredients singly. If response is adequate to the fixed doses contained in Diupres antihypertensive, this product may then be substituted. The advantage of a combination product such as Diupres antihypertensive is based on increased convenience to the patient.

Take Diupres antihypertensive at the same time each day.

Take Diupres antihypertensive with food or milk.

The effects of Diupres antihypertensive therapy may not be apparent for at least two weeks.

Mild side effects (e.g., nasal congestion) are more noticeable during the first two weeks of therapy and become less bothersome after this period.

While taking Diupres antihypertensive, do not take any nonprescription item for cough, cold, or sinus problems without first checking with your doctor.

Diupres antihypertensive may cause drowsiness; to prevent oversedation, avoid the use of other sedative drugs or alcohol.

Diupres antihypertensive can cause potassium loss. To avoid potassium loss, take Diupres antihypertensive with a glass of fresh or frozen orange juice. You may also eat a banana each day. The use of Diasal or Co-Salt salt substitutes helps prevent potassium loss.

Diupres antihypertensive causes frequent urination. Expect this effect; it should not alarm you.

While taking this product (as with many drugs that lower blood pressure), you should limit your consumption of alcoholic beverages in order to prevent dizziness or light-headedness.

If dizziness or light-headedness occurs when you stand up, place your legs on the floor and "pump" the muscles for a few moments before rising.

Persons taking this product and digitalis should watch carefully for symptoms of increased toxicity (e.g., nausea, blurred vision, palpitations).

If you are allergic to a sulfa drug, you may likewise be allergic to Diupres antihypertensive.

Products equivalent to Diupres antihypertensive are available and vary widely in cost. Ask your doctor to prescribe a generic preparation; then ask your pharmacist to fill it with the least expensive brand.

Reserpine causes cancer in rats. It has not yet been shown to cause cancer in people.

Diuril diuretic

Manufacturer: Merck Sharp & Dohme
Generic Name: chlorothiazide sodium
Equivalent Products: Ro-Chlorozide diuretic (Robinson Laboratory, Inc.)
Dosage Forms: Liquid (content per 5 ml): 250 mg; tablets: 250 mg, 500 mg (white)
Use: Treatment of high blood pressure, removal of fluid from the tissues
Minor Side Effects: Cramps, diarrhea, dizziness, headache, loss of appetite, nausea, rash, restlessness, vomiting, tingling in the fingers and toes
Major Side Effects: Elevated blood sugar, elevated uric acid, muscle spasm, sore throat, weakness, blurred vision
Contraindications: Severe kidney disease, allergy to sulfa drugs.
Warnings and Precautions: Bronchial asthma, diabetes, gout, liver and kidney diseases
Interacts With: colestipol hydrochloride, digitalis, lithium carbonate, oral antidiabetics, steroids
Comments: Diuril diuretic causes frequent urination. Expect this effect; it should not alarm you.

Diuril diuretic can cause potassium loss. To avoid potassium loss, take Diuril diuretic with a glass of fresh or frozen orange juice. You may also eat a banana each day. The use of Diasal or Co-Salt salt substitutes helps prevent potassium loss.

While taking this product (as with many drugs that lower blood pressure), you should limit your consumption of alcoholic beverages in order to prevent dizziness or light-headedness.

If dizziness or light-headedness occurs when you stand up, place your legs on the floor and "pump" the muscles for a few moments before rising.

Persons taking this product and digitalis should watch carefully for symptoms of increased toxicity (e.g., nausea, blurred vision, palpitations).

If you are allergic to a sulfa drug, you may likewise be allergic to Diuril diuretic.

Products equivalent to Diuril diuretic are available and vary widely in cost. Ask your doctor to prescribe a generic preparation; then ask your pharmacist to fill it with the least expensive brand.

If you have high blood pressure, do not take any nonprescription item for cough, cold, or sinus problems without first checking with your doctor.

Dolene analgesic (Lederle Laboratories), see Darvon analgesic.

Dolene Compound-65 analgesic (Lederle Laboratories), see Darvon Compound-65 analgesic.

Donnatal sedative and anticholinergic

Manufacturer: A.H. Robins Company
Generic Name: phenobarbital, hyoscyamine sulfate, atropine sulfate, hyoscine hydrobromide
Equivalent Products: Sedralex sedative and anticholinergic (Kay Pharmacal Co., Inc.); Setamine sedative and anticholinergic (Tutag Pharmaceuticals, Inc.); Spalix sedative and anticholinergic (Reid-Provident Laboratories, Inc.);

Spaz sedative and anticholinergic (Corvit)

Dosage Forms: Liquid, capsules (green/white); sustained-action tablets (green); tablets (white). Content of capsule or tablet or 5 ml liquid: phenobarbital, 16.2 mg; hyoscyamine sulfate, 0.104 mg; atropine sulfate, 0.019 mg; hyoscine hydrobromide, 0.007 mg. Sustained action tablets: phenobarbital, 48.6 mg; hyoscyamine sulfate, 0.3111 mg; atropine sulfate, 0.0582 mg; hyoscine hydrobromide, 0.0195 mg

Use: Treatment of bed-wetting, motion sickness, premenstrual tension, stomach and intestinal disorders, urinary frequency

Minor Side Effects: Blurred vision, constipation, dizziness, drowsiness, dry mouth, flushing, headache, insomnia, loss of the sense of taste, nausea, nervousness, palpitations, reduced sweating, vomiting, difficult urination, increased sensitivity to light

Major Side Effects: Impotence, rash, breathing difficulty, cold and clammy skin

Contraindications: Porphyria, certain types of glaucoma, enlarged prostate, obstructed intestine, asthma, bladder obstruction, certain heart diseases

Warnings and Precautions: Pregnancy, severe heart disease, liver and kidney diseases, potential for drug abuse

Interacts With: amantadine, haloperidol, antacids, phenothiazines, alcohol, griseofulvin, nerve depressants, oral anticoagulants, steroids, sulfonamides, tetracycline, antidepressants, phenytoin

Comments: Donnatal sedative and anticholinergic is best taken one-half to one hour before meals. It does not *cure* ulcers but may help them improve.

Donnatal sedative and anticholinergic interacts with many drugs and alcohol; avoid the use of other sedative drugs and alcohol while taking this product.

While taking Donnatal sedative and anticholinergic, do not take any nonprescription item for cough, cold, or sinus problems without first checking with your doctor.

Even though Donnatal sedative and anticholinergic products contain phenobarbital, they have not been shown to have a high potential for abuse.

Products equivalent to Donnatal sedative and anticholinergic are available, but most are priced about the same as Donnatal sedative and anticholinergic. If your doctor prescribes capsules, ask him to prescribe tablets, which are less expensive, instead.

Remind your doctor if you are taking an anticoagulant (blood thinner).

Doxychel antibiotic (Rachelle Laboratories, Inc.), see Vibramycin antibiotic.

Doxy-II antibiotic (USV [P.R.] Development Corp.), see Vibramycin antibiotic.

Dralzine antihypertensive (Lemmon-Pharmacal Company), see Apresoline antihypertensive.

Drixoral allergy and congestion remedy

Manufacturer: Schering Corporation
Generic Name: dexbrompheniramine maleate, pseudoephedrine sulfate
Equivalent Products: Disophrol Chronotab tablets allergy and congestion remedy (Schering Corporation); Duohist allergy and congestion remedy tablets (Henry Schein, Inc.)

Dosage Form: Sustained-action tablets: dexbrompheniramine maleate, 6 mg; pseudoephedrine sulfate, 120 mg (green)

Use: Relief of hay fever symptoms, respiratory and middle ear congestion

Minor Side Effects: Diarrhea, dizziness, drowsiness, dry mouth, headache, heartburn, difficult urination, loss of appetite, nausea, rash, restlessness, vomiting, weakness, blurred vision, confusion, constipation, insomnia, nasal congestion, palpitations, reduced sweating

Major Side Effects: Low blood pressure, severe abdominal pain, sore throat, high blood pressure, chest pain

Contraindications: Asthma, some glaucomas, certain ulcers, enlarged prostate, obstructed bladder, obstructed intestine, pregnancy, severe heart disease

Warnings and Precautions: Diabetes, high blood pressure, thyroid disease, liver and kidney diseases

Interacts With: guanethidine, monoamine oxidase inhibitors

Comments: While taking Drixoral allergy and congestion remedy, do not take any nonprescription item for cough, cold, or sinus problems without first checking with your doctor.

Drixoral allergy and congestion remedy may cause dryness of the mouth. To reduce this feeling, chew gum or suck on a piece of hard candy.

Drixoral allergy and congestion remedy reduces sweating; avoid excessive work or exercise in hot weather.

Drixoral allergy and congestion remedy may cause drowsiness; to prevent oversedation, avoid the use of other sedative drugs or alcohol.

Products equivalent to Drixoral allergy and congestion remedy are available. Consult your doctor and pharmacist.

Drixoral allergy and congestion remedy must be swallowed whole.

Drixoral allergy and congestion remedy has sustained action; never take it more frequently than your doctor prescribes. A serious overdose may result.

D-S-S Plus laxative (Parke, Davis & Company), see Peri-Colace laxative.

Duohist allergy and congestion remedy (Henry Schein, Inc.), see Drixoral allergy and congestion remedy.

Dyazide diuretic and antihypertensive

Manufacturer: Smith Kline & French Laboratories

Generic Name: triamterine, hydrochlorothiazide

Equivalent Products: None

Dosage Form: Capsules: triamterene, 50 mg; hydrochlorothiazide, 25 mg (maroon/white)

Use: Treatment of high blood pressure, removal of fluid from the tissues

Minor Side Effects: Constipation, diarrhea, drowsiness, dry mouth, fatigue, headache, nausea, rash, restlessness, vomiting, weakness

Major Side Effects: Elevated blood sugar, elevated uric acid, muscle cramps or spasms, sore throat

Contraindications: Severe liver and kidney diseases, hyperkalemia (high blood levels of potassium), pregnancy, allergy to sulfa drugs

Warnings and Precautions: Bronchial asthma, diabetes, gout, liver and kidney diseases

Interacts With: colestipol hydrochloride, digitalis, lithium carbonate, oral antidiabetics, potassium salts, steroids

Comments: Dyazide diuretic and antihypertensive causes frequent urination. Expect this effect; it should not alarm you.

Dyazide diuretic and antihypertensive does not cause potassium loss, and potassium supplements are not necessary. Although the price of Dyazide diuretic and antihypertensive is high compared to the prices of other drugs used to treat high blood pressure, this product is preferable for patients with low potassium levels.

While taking this product (as with many drugs that lower blood pressure), you should limit your consumption of alcoholic beverages in order to prevent dizziness or light-headedness.

If dizziness or light-headedness occurs when you stand up, place your legs on the floor and "pump" the muscles for a few moments before rising.

If you are allergic to a sulfa drug, you may likewise be allergic to Dyazide diuretic and antihypertensive.

If you are taking Dyazide diuretic and antihypertensive for high blood pressure, do not take any nonprescription item for cough, cold, or sinus problems without first checking with your doctor.

A doctor probably should not prescribe Dyazide diuretic and antihypertensive or other "fixed dose" products as the first choice in the treatment of high blood pressure. The patient should receive each of the individual ingredients singly, and if the response if adequate to the fixed doses contained in Dyazide diuretic and antihypertensive, this product can then be substituted. The advantage of a combination product such as Dyazide diuretic and antihypertensive is increased convenience to the patient.

E.E.S. antibiotic (Abbott Laboratories), see Erythromycin antibiotic.

Elavil antidepressant

Manufacturer: Merck Sharp & Dohme
Generic Name: amitriptyline hydrochloride
Equivalent Products: Amitril antidepressant (Parke, Davis & Company); Endep antide-pressant (Roche Products, Inc.)
Dosage Form: Tablets: 10 mg (blue), 25 mg (yellow), 50 mg (beige), 75 mg (orange), 100 mg (mauve), 150 mg (blue, capsule-shaped)
Use: Relief of depression
Minor Side Effects: Diarrhea, dizziness, dry mouth, fatigue, hair loss, headache, loss of appetite, nausea, numbness in fingers or toes, palpitations, rash, uncoordinated movements, vomiting, weakness, difficult urination, drowsiness, reduced sweating, photosensitivity
Major Side Effects: Enlarged or painful breasts (in both sexes), imbalance, heart attack, high or low blood pressure, impotence, jaundice, mouth sores, ringing in the ears, sore throat, stroke, tremors, weight loss or gain (in children), fatigue, nervousness, sleep disorders

Contraindications: Recent heart attack
Warnings and Precautions: Certain types of glaucoma, certain types of heart disease, epilepsy, hyperthyroidism, pregnancy, difficult urination
Interacts With: alcohol, amphetamine, barbiturates, epinephrine, guanethidine, monoamine oxidase inhibitors, oral anticoagulants, phenylephrine, clonidine, depressants
Comments: The effects of Elavil antidepressant therapy may not be apparent for at least two weeks.

While taking Elavil antidepressant, do not take any nonprescription item for cough, cold, or sinus problems without first checking with your doctor. And do not stop or start any other drug.

Elavil antidepressant interacts with alcohol; avoid using alcohol while taking this product.

Elavil antidepressant may cause dryness of the mouth. To reduce this feeling, chew gum or suck on a piece of hard candy.

Elavil antidepressant reduces sweating; avoid excessive work or exercise in hot weather.

Products equivalent to Elavil antidepressant are available and vary widely in cost. Ask your doctor to prescribe a generic preparation; then ask your pharmacist to fill it with the least expensive brand.

Avoid long exposure to the sun while taking Elavil antidepressant.

Eldefed adrenergic and antihistamine tablets (Paul B. Elder Co.), see Actifed adrenergic and antihistamine.

Eldetapp cold remedy (Paul B. Elder Company), see Dimetapp cold remedy.

Eldezine antinauseant (Paul B. Elder Company), see Antivert antinauseant.

Elixophyllin bronchodilator

Manufacturer: Cooper Laboratories, Inc.
Generic Name: theophylline
Equivalent Products: Bronkodyl bronchodilator (Breon Laboratories Inc.); Lanophyllin bronchodilator (The Lannet Company, Inc.);
Dosage Forms: Elixir (content per 15 ml): 80 mg. Capsules: 100 mg (off-white soft gelatin), 200 mg (red soft gelatin)
Use: Relief of bronchial asthma, bronchospasm, emphysema, and other lung diseases
Minor Side Effects: Gastrointestinal disturbances (stomach pain, nausea, vomiting), nervousness
Major Side Effects: Convulsions, palpitations, difficult breathing
Contraindications: Pregnancy
Warnings and Precautions: Peptic ulcer, heart disease, liver and kidney diseases
Interacts With: disulfiram, lithium carbonate, oral antidiabetics, propranolol
Comments: Take Elixophyllin bronchodilator with food or milk.

Elixophyllin bronchodilator elixir is 40 proof alcohol; use caution when taking it with other drugs with which alcohol interacts, or switch to a similiar product which does not contain alcohol.

If gastrointestinal distress occurs while taking Elixophyllin bronchodilator, take an over-the-counter product such as Maalox or Gelusil antacid.

Products equivalent to Elixophyllin bronchodilator are available and vary widely in cost. Ask your doctor to prescribe a generic preparation; then ask your pharmacist to fill it with the least expensive brand. Since the usual dose of Elixophyllin bronchodilator is quite high, many people find they can save money by buying the elixir in quarts or gallons.

Call your doctor if you have severe stomach pain, vomiting, or restlessness.

Be sure to take your dose at exactly the right time each day.

Do not use nonprescription items for asthma unless your doctor has told you to do so.

Avoid drinking tea, cocoa, or other beverages that contain "xanthines" while taking Elixophyllin bronchodilator. Consult your pharmacist.

Empirin Compound with Codeine analgesic

Manufacturer: Burroughs Wellcome Co.
Generic Name: aspirin, phenacetin, caffeine, codeine phosphate
Equivalent Products: None
Dosage Form: Tablets #1, #2, #3, #4: aspirin, 227 mg; phenacetin, 162 mg; caffeine, 32 mg; codeine phosphate (see "Comments")
Use: Relief of moderate to severe pain
Minor Side Effects: Drowsiness, nausea, constipation, dry mouth, flushing, light-headedness, palpitations, rash, ringing in ears, sweating, vomiting, urine retention
Major Side Effects: Jaundice, low blood sugar, tremors, rapid heartbeat, breathing difficulties
Contraindications: Bleeding ulcers, pregnancy
Warnings and Precautions: Asthma and other respiratory problems, coagulation problems, epilepsy, potential for drug abuse, head injury, liver and kidney disease
Interacts With: alcohol, ammonium chloride, vitamin C, methotrexate, oral anticoagulants, oral antidiabetics, probenecid, steroids, sulfinpyrazone
Comments: For this and other preparations containing codeine, the number which follows the drug name always refers to the amount of codeine present. Hence, #1 has 1/8 grain codeine; #2 has 1/4 gr; #3 has 1/2 gr; and #4 contains 1 gr. These numbers are standard for amounts of codeine.

Products containing narcotics (e.g., codeine) are usually not used for more than seven to 10 days.

Empirin Compound with Codeine analgesic interacts with alcohol; avoid the use of alcohol while taking this product.

If you are also taking an anticoagulant ("blood thinner"), remind your doctor.

Empirin Compound with Codeine analgesic has the potential for abuse and must be used with caution. Tolerance may develop quickly; *do not* increase the dose of this drug without first consulting your doctor.

Although no exact equivalent is available, similar products are, and they may save you money. Discuss them with your doctor.

Take Empirin Compound with Codeine analgesic with food or milk.

If your ears feel strange, if you hear buzzing or ringing, or if your stomach hurts, your dosage may need adjustment. Call your doctor.

Empracet with Codeine analgesic (Burroughs Wellcome Co.), see Tylenol with Codeine analgesic.

E-Mycin antibiotic (The Upjohn Co.), see erythromycin antibiotic.

Endep antidepressant (Roche Products, Inc.), see Elavil antidepressant.

Enduron diuretic

Manufacturer: Abbott Laboratories
Generic Name: methyclothiazide
Equivalent Products: Aquatensen diuretic (Mallinckrodt, Inc.)
Dosage Form: Tablets: 2.5 mg (orange), 5 mg (salmon)
Use: Treatment of high blood pressure and removal of fluid from the tissues
Minor Side Effects: Cramps, diarrhea, dizziness, headache, nausea, rash, restlessness, vomiting, tingling in the fingers and toes
Major Side Effects: Elevated blood sugar, elevated uric acid, muscle spasms, sore throat, weakness, blurred vision
Contraindications: Severe kidney diseases, allergy to sulfa drugs, pregnancy
Warnings and Precautions: Bronchial asthma, diabetes, gout, liver and kidney diseases
Interacts With: colestipol hydrochloride, digitalis, lithium carbonate, oral antidiabetics, steroids
Comments: Enduron diuretic causes frequent urination. Expect this effect; it should not alarm you.

Enduron diuretic can cause potassium loss. To avoid potassium loss, take Enduron diuretic with a glass of fresh or frozen orange juice. You may also eat a banana each day. The use of Diasal or Co-Salt salt substitutes helps prevent potassium loss.

While taking this product (as with many drugs that lower blood pressure), you should limit your consumption of alcoholic beverages in order to prevent dizziness or light-headedness.

If dizziness or light-headedness occurs when you stand up, place your legs on the floor and "pump" the muscles for a few moments before rising.

Persons taking this product and digitalis should watch carefully for symptoms of increased toxicity (e.g., nausea, blurred vision, palpitations).

If you are allergic to a sulfa drug, you may likewise be allergic to Enduron diuretic.

Products equivalent to Enduron diuretic are available and vary widely in cost. Ask your doctor to prescribe a generic preparation; then ask your pharmacist to fill it with the least expensive brand.

If you have high blood pressure, do not take any nonprescription item for cough, cold, or sinus problems without first checking with your doctor.

Enovid oral contraceptive (Searle Laboratories), see oral contraceptives.

Equagesic analgesic

Manufacturer: Wyeth Laboratories
Generic Name: meprobamate, ethoheptazine citrate, aspirin
Equivalent Products: Meprogesic analgesic (Spencer-Mead)
Dosage Forms: Tablets: meprobamate, 150 mg; ethoheptazine citrate, 75 mg; aspirin, 250 mg (yellow/white/red layered)
Use: Relief of pain in muscles or joints
Minor Side Effects: Diarrhea, dizziness, drowsiness, fatigue, light-headedness, nausea, rash, vomiting, ringing in the ears
Major Side Effects: Palpitations, fainting, fever, sore throat
Contraindications: Bleeding ulcers, porphyria
Warnings and Precautions: Liver or kidney diseases, history of drug abuse, coagulation problems
Interacts With: central nervous system depressants, ammonium chloride, anticoagulants, methotrexate, oral antidiabetics, probenecid, steroids, sulfinpyrazone, vitamin C
Comments: Take Equagesic analgesic with food or milk.

Equagesic analgesic may cause drowsiness; to prevent oversedation, avoid the use of other sedative drugs or alcohol.

If you are also taking an anticoagulant ("blood thinner"), remind your doctor.

Equagesic analgesic has the potential for abuse and must be used with caution. Tolerance develops quickly; *do not* increase the dose of this drug without first consulting your doctor.

If your ears feel strange; if you hear buzzing or ringing; if your stomach hurts; or if you get a rash, sore throat, or fever, call your doctor. Your dosage may need adjustment, or you may have an allergy to one of the drug's ingredients.

Equanil sedative and hypnotic (Wyeth Laboratories), see meprobamate sedative and hypnotic.

erythromycin antibiotic

Erythromycin is a generic drug.
Equivalent Products: E.E.S. antibiotic (Abbott Laboratories); E-Mycin antibiotic tablets (The Upjohn Co.)
Dosage Forms: Drops (content per ml): 100 mg. Liquid (content per 5 ml): 125 mg; 200 mg; 250 mg; 400 mg. Tablets: E.E.S. tablets: 200 mg (white), 400 mg (salmon); E-Mycin tablets: 250 mg (orange)
Use: Treatment of a wide variety of bacterial infections
Minor Side Effects: Abdominal cramps, diarrhea, fatigue, fever, nausea, vomiting
Major Side Effects: Superinfection, vaginal and rectal itching, cough, severe diarrhea, irritation of the mouth, "black tongue," rash
Contraindications: Pregnancy
Warnings and Precautions: Liver disease (Ilosone brand only), kidney disease
Interacts With: No significant drug interactions
Comments: Take erythromycin antibiotic on an empty stomach (one hour before or two hours after a meal).

Erythromycin antibiotic should be taken for at least 10 full days, even if symptoms have disappeared.

The liquid form of erythromycin antibiotic should be stored in the refrigerator.

Generic brands of erythromycin are available and vary widely in cost. Ask your doctor to prescribe a generic preparation; then ask your pharmacist to fill it with the least expensive brand.

Ilosone antibiotic (Dista Products Co.) is a form of erythromycin antibiotic that has approximately the same pharmacological effect, but it may have adverse effects on people with liver disease.

Esidrix diuretic (CIBA Pharmaceutical Company), see hydrochlorothiazide diuretic.

Eskabarb sedative and hypnotic (Smith Kline & French Laboratories), see phenobarbital sedative and hypnotic.

Eskatrol adrenergic and phenothiazine

Manufacturer: Smith Kline & French Laboratories
Generic Name: dextroamphetamine sulfate, prochlorperazine
Equivalent Products: None
Dosage Form: Capsules: dextroamphetamine sulfate, 15 mg; prochlorperazine, 7.5 mg (white/clear with multicolored pellets)
Use: Short-term treatment of obesity
Minor Side Effects: Blurred vision, change in urine color, constipation, diarrhea, dizziness, drooling, drowsiness, dry mouth, headache, insomnia, jitteriness, menstrual irregularities, nasal congestion, nausea, palpitations, rash, reduced sweating, restlessness, uncoordinated movements, unpleasant taste in the mouth
Major Side Effects: Difficulty in swallowing; enlarged or painful breasts (in both sexes); euphoria; fluid retention; impotence; involuntary movements of the face, mouth, tongue, or jaw; muscle stiffness; rapid heartbeat; sore throat; tremors; rise in blood pressure; jaundice
Contraindications: Coma, diabetes, high blood pressure, heart disease, thyroid disease, glaucoma, blood disease, severe liver disease or kidney disease, Parkinson's disease, pregnancy
Warnings and Precautions: Potential for drug abuse, pneumonia, epilepsy, breast cancer, certain liver and kidney diseases
Interacts With: acetazolamide, anticholinergics, guanethidine, levodopa, monoamine oxidase inhibitors, oral antacids, sodium bicarbonate
Comments: To be effective, Eskatrol adrenergic and phenothiazine therapy must be accompanied by a low-calorie diet.

The effects of Eskatrol adrenergic and phenothiazine on appetite control wear off; do not take this drug for more than three weeks at a time. One way to get full benefit from Eskatrol adrenergic and phenothiazine is to take the drug for three weeks, stop for three weeks, then resume Eskatrol adrenergic and phenothiazine therapy. Consult your doctor about this regimen.

Eskatrol adrenergic and phenothiazine has sustained action; *do not* take it more frequently than your doctor prescribes. A serious overdose may result.

To avoid sleeplessness, do not take Eskatrol adrenergic and phenothiazine later than 3:00 P.M.

While taking Eskatrol adrenergic and phenothiazine, do not take any nonprescription item for cough, cold, or sinus problems without first checking with your doctor.

Eskatrol adrenergic and phenothiazine may mask symptoms of fatigue and pose serious danger; do not take this drug as a stimulant to keep awake.

This drug may cause drowsiness; to prevent oversedation, avoid the use of other sedative drugs or alcohol.

Eskatrol adrenergic and phenothiazine reduces sweating; avoid excessive work or exercise in hot weather.

As with any other drug that has antivomiting activity, symptoms of severe disease or toxicity due to overdose of other drugs may be masked by Eskatrol adrenergic and phenothiazine.

Eskatrol adrenergic and phenothiazine has the potential for abuse and must be used with caution. Tolerance to Eskatrol adrenergic and phenothiazine may quickly develop; *do not* increase the dose of this drug without first consulting your doctor.

Estroate estrogen hormone (Kay Pharmacal Company, Inc.), see Premarin estrogen hormone.

Estrocon estrogen hormone (Mallard Incorporated), see Premarin estrogen hormone.

Estropan estrogen hormone (Panray Division, Ormont Drug & Chemical Co., Inc.), see Premarin estrogen hormone.

Etrafon phenothiazine and antidepressant (Schering Corporation), see Triavil phenothiazine and antidepressant.

Exsel seborrheic (Herbert Laboratories), see Selsun seborrheic.

Fastin anorectic

Manufacturer: Beecham Laboratories
Generic Name: phentermine hydrochloride
Equivalent Products: Adipex-8 anorectic (Lemmon Pharmacal Company); phentermine hydrochloride anorectic (various manufacturers)
Dosage Forms: Capsules: 30 mg (blue/white)
Use: Short-term treatment of obesity
Minor Side Effects: Diarrhea, dizziness, dry mouth, headache, insomnia, nausea, palpitations, restlessness, unpleasant taste in the mouth, vomiting
Major Side Effects: High blood pressure, overstimulation of nerves, chest pain
Contraindications: Certain types of heart disease, diabetes, high blood pressure, thyroid disease, glaucoma, pregnancy
Warnings and Precautions: Potential for drug abuse, liver and kidney diseases
Interacts With: acetazolamide, guanethidine, monoamine oxidase inhibitors, phenothiazines, sodium bicarbonate, antidepressants

Comments: The effects of Fastin anorectic on appetite control wear off; do not take this drug for more than three weeks at a time. One way to get full benefit from Fastin anorectic is to take the drug for three weeks, stop for another three weeks, then resume Fastin anorectic therapy. Consult your doctor about this regimen.

To avoid sleeplessness, do not take Fastin anorectic later than 3:00 P.M.

While taking Fastin anorectic, do not take any nonprescription item for cough, cold, or sinus problems without first checking with your doctor.

Fastin anorectic may mask symptoms of fatigue and pose serious danger; so do not take this drug as a stimulant to keep awake.

Fastin anorectic has the potential for abuse and must be used with caution. Tolerance to Fastin may develop quickly; *do not* increase the dose of this drug without first consulting your doctor.

To be effective Fastin anorectic therapy must be accompanied by a low-calorie diet.

Ionamin anorectic (Pennwalt Pharmaceutical Division) is not a generic equivalent of Fastin anorectic, but in the body they become identical substances.

Femest estrogen hormone (Laser, Inc.), see Premarin estrogen hormone.

Fem-H estrogen hormone (Saron Pharmacal Corp.), see Premarin estrogen hormone.

Fenbutal analgesic and sedative (Tutag Pharmaceutical, Inc.), see Fiorinal analgesic and sedative.

Fenylhist antihistamine (Mallard Incorporated), see Benadryl antihistamine.

Fernisone steroid hormone (Ferndale Laboratories, Inc.), see prednisone steroid hormone.

Fiorinal analgesic and sedative

Manufacturer: Sandoz Pharmaceuticals
Generic Name: butalbital, aspirin, phenacetin, caffeine
Equivalent Products: Fenbutal analgesic and sedative (Tutag Pharmaceuticals, Inc.); Lanorinal analgesic and sedative (The Lannett Company, Inc.)
Dosage Forms: Tablets (white) or capsules (bright green/light green): butalbital, 50 mg; aspirin 200 mg; phenacetin, 130 mg; caffeine, 40 mg
Use: Relief of pain associated with tension
Minor Side Effects: Constipation, dizziness, drowsiness, nausea, rash, vomiting, ringing in ears
Major Side Effects: Breathing difficulty; cold, clammy skin; kidney diseases
Contraindications: Porphyria, history of drug abuse, pregnancy, bleeding ulcers
Warnings and Precautions: Coagulation problems, liver and kidney diseases
Interacts With: alcohol, ammonium chloride, anticoagulants, methotrexate, oral antidiabetics, probenecid, steroids, sulfinpyrazone, vitamin C, central

nervous system depressants, griseofulvin, phenytoin, sulfonamides, tetracyclines, antidepressants

Comments: Many headaches are believed to be caused by nervousness or
tension or by prolonged contraction of the head and neck muscles. Fiorinal
analgesic and sedative is reported to relieve these conditions to help control
headache.

Because of the butalbital (barbiturate) content, Fiorinal analgesic and
sedative may be habit-forming; do not take this medication unless absolutely
necessary. Fiorinal analgesic and sedative has the potential for abuse and
must be used with caution. Tolerance to Fiorinal analgesic and sedative may
develop quickly; *do not* increase the dose of the drug without first consulting
your doctor.

If you are also taking an anticoagulant ("blood thinner"), remind your
doctor.

Fiorinal analgesic and sedative interacts with other sedative drugs and
alcohol; avoid using them while taking this product.

Products equivalent to Fiorinal analgesic and sedative are available and
vary widely in cost. Ask your doctor to prescribe a generic preparation; then
ask your pharmacist to fill it with the least expensive brand.

Take Fiorinal analgesic and sedative with food or milk.

If your ears feel strange, if you hear buzzing or ringing, or if your stomach
hurts, your dosage may need adjustment. Call your doctor.

Fiorinal with Codeine analgesic and sedative

Manufacturer: Sandoz Pharmaceuticals
Generic Name: butalbital, aspirin, phenacetin, caffeine, codeine phosphate
Equivalent Products: None
Dosage Form: Capsules #1 (red/yellow), #2 (gray/yellow), #3 (blue/yellow):
butalbital, 50 mg; aspirin, 200 mg; phenacetin, 130 mg; caffeine, 40 mg; and
codeine phosphate (see "Comments")
Use: Relief of pain associated with tension
Minor Side Effects: Blurred vision, constipation, dizziness, drowsiness,
nausea, rash, itching, light-headedness, sedation, vomiting, ringing in the
ears
Major Side Effects: Bleeding ulcers, jaundice, low blood sugar, tremors, rapid
heartbeat, difficulty in breathing, cold and clammy skin, kidney disease
Contraindications: Porphyria, history of drug abuse
Warnings and Precautions: Potential for drug abuse, heart disease, peptic
ulcer, asthma and other respiratory problems, head injury, coagulation
problems, pregnancy
Interacts With: alcohol, ammonium chloride, anticoagulants, methotrexate,
oral antidiabetics, probenecid, steroids, sulfinpyrazone, vitamin C, central
nervous system depressants, griseofulvin, phenytoin, sulfonamides, tetracyclines, antidepressants
Comments: Products containing narcotics (e.g., codeine) should not usually be
taken for more than seven to 10 days.

For this and other preparations containing codeine, the number that
follows the drug name always refers to the amount of codeine present.
Hence, #1 has 1/8 grain codeine; #2 has 1/4 gr; #3 has 1/2 gr. These
numbers are standard for amounts of codeine.

Many headaches are believed to be caused by nervousness or tension or by prolonged contraction of the head and neck muscles. Fiorinal with Codeine pain reliever is reported to relieve these conditions to help control headache.

If you are also taking an anticoagulant ("blood thinner"), remind your doctor.

Fiorinal with Codeine analgesic and sedative interacts with many other drugs and alcohol; avoid the use of other sedative drugs or alcohol while taking this product.

Fiorinal with Codeine analgesic and sedative has the potential for abuse and must be used with caution. Tolerance to Fiorinal with Codeine analgesic and sedative may develop quickly; do not increase the dose of this drug without first consulting your doctor.

Take Fiorinal with Codeine analgesic and sedative with food or milk.

If your ears feel strange, if you hear ringing or buzzing, or if your stomach hurts, your dosage may need adjustment. Call your doctor.

Flagyl anti-infective

Manufacturer: Searle & Co.
Generic Name: metronidazole
Equivalent Products: None
Dosage Form: Tablets: 250 mg (white)
Use: Treatment of certain genitourinary tract infections and amebiasis
Minor Side Effects: Abdominal cramps, change in urine color, constipation, diarrhea, dizziness, dry mouth, flushing, headache, itching, loss of appetite, metallic taste in mouth, mouth sores, nausea, vomiting
Major Side Effects: No major side effects
Contraindications: Pregnancy, blood disease
Warnings and Precautions: Cancer, liver or kidney diseases
Interacts With: alcohol, warfarin
Comments: Flagyl anti-infective should be taken for seven days. Four to six weeks should elapse before a repeat course of treatment.

Avoid the use of alcohol.

Flagyl anti-infective causes cancer in rodents. It has not yet been shown to cause cancer in people.

If you are also taking an anticoagulant, remind your doctor.

If Flagyl anti-infective is being used to treat a sexually transmitted disease, your sexual partner may also need to be treated.

Formitone-HC steroid hormone and anti-infective (Dermik Laboratories, Inc.), see Vioform-Hydrocortisone steroid hormone and anti-infective.

Gamene pediculocide and scabicide (Barnes-Hind Pharmaceuticals, Inc.), see Kwell pediculocide and scabicide.

Gantanol antibacterial

Manufacturer: Roche Products Inc.
Generic Name: sulfamethoxazole
Equivalent Products: None
Dosage Forms: Liquid (content per 5 ml): 500 mg; tablets: 500 mg (green), 1 g (light orange)

Use: Treatment of a variety of bacterial infections, especially of the urinary tract

Minor Side Effects: Abdominal pain, depression, diarrhea, headache, nausea, vomiting

Major Side Effects: Fluid retention, hallucinations, itching, rash, ringing in the ears, sore throat, jaundice

Contraindications: Pregnancy

Warnings and Precautions: Bronchial asthma, severe hay fever, liver and kidney diseases, significant allergies

Interacts With: barbiturates, methenamine hippurate, methenamine mandelate, methotrexate, oral antidiabetics, oxacillin, para-aminobenzoic acid, phenytoin

Comments: Take Gantanol antibacterial with at least a full glass of water. Drink at least nine to 10 glasses of water each day.

Gantanol antibacterial should be taken for at least 10 full days, even if symptoms have disappeared.

Gantanol antibacterial may cause allergic reactions, and should not be taken by persons with asthma, severe hay fever, or other allergies unless the doctor is aware of these conditions.

Gantrisin antibacterial

Manufacturer: Roche Products Inc.

Generic Name: sulfisoxazole

Equivalent Products: Rosoxol antibacterial (Robinson Laboratory, Inc.); SK-Soxazole antibacterial (Smith Kline & French Laboratories); Sulfalar antibacterial (Parke, Davis & Company)

Dosage Forms: Syrup (content per 5 ml): 500 mg; pediatric suspension (content per 5 ml): 500 mg; tablets: 500 mg (white)

Use: Treatment of a variety of bacterial infections, especially of the urinary tract

Minor Side Effects: Abdominal pain, depression, diarrhea, headache, nausea, vomiting

Major Side Effects: Fluid retention, hallucinations, itching, rash, ringing in the ears, sore throat, jaundice

Contraindications: Pregnancy

Warnings and Precautions: Bronchial asthma, severe hay fever, liver and kidney disease, significant allergies

Interacts With: barbiturates, methenamine hippurate, methenamine mandelate, methotrexate, oral antidiabetics, oxacillin, para-aminobenzoic acid, phenytoin

Comments: Take Gantrisin antibacterial with at least a full glass of water. Drink at least nine to 10 glasses of water each day.

Gantrisin antibacterial should be taken for at least 10 full days, even if symptoms have disappeared.

Gantrisin antibacterial may cause allergic reactions and should not be taken by persons with asthma, severe hay fever, or other allergies, unless the doctor is aware of these conditions.

Products equivalent to Gantrisin antibacterial are available and vary widely in cost. Ask your doctor to prescribe a generic preparation, then ask your pharmacist to fill it with the least expensive brand.

Genisis estrogen hormone (Organon Inc.), see Premarin estrogen hormone.

Haldol antipsychotic agent

Manufacturer: McNeil Laboratories, Inc.
Generic Name: haloperidol
Equivalent Products: None
Dosage Forms: Concentrate; tablets: 0.5 mg (white), 1 mg (yellow), 2 mg (pink), 5 mg (green), 10 mg (aqua)
Use: Treatment of certain psychotic disorders, Gilles de la Tourette's syndrome
Minor Side Effects: Blurred vision, change in urine color, constipation, diarrhea, dizziness, drooling, drowsiness, dry mouth, jitteriness, menstrual irregularities, nasal congestion, nausea, rash, restlessness, uncoordinated movements, vomiting, reduced sweating
Major Side Effects: Difficulty in swallowing; enlarged or painful breasts (in both sexes); fluid retention; impotence; involuntary movements of the face, mouth, tongue, or jaw; muscle stiffness; sore throat; tremors; jaundice; rise in blood pressure
Contraindications: Coma, drug-induced depression, shock, blood disease, Parkinson's disease, liver damage, jaundice, kidney disease, stroke, pregnancy
Warnings and Precautions: Asthma and other respiratory disorders, epilepsy, exposure to extreme heat
Interacts With: alcohol, oral antacids, anticholinergics, depressants
Comments: The effects of Haldol antipsychotic agent therapy may not be apparent for at least two weeks.

Haldol antipsychotic agent has persistent action; never take it more frequently than your doctor prescribes. A serious overdose may result.

While taking Haldol antipsychotic agent, do not take any nonprescription item for cough, cold, or sinus problems without first checking with your doctor.

Haldol antipsychotic agent interacts with alcohol; do not use alcohol while taking this product.

Haldol antipsychotic agent may cause dryness of the mouth. To reduce this feeling, chew gum or suck on a piece of hard candy.

Haldol antipsychotic agent reduces sweating; avoid excessive work or exercise in hot weather.

If dizziness or light-headedness occurs when you stand up, place your legs on the floor and "pump" the muscles for a few moments before rising.

As with any other drug that has antivomiting activity, symptoms of severe disease or toxicity due to overdose of other drugs may be masked by Haldol antipsychotic agent.

Heb-Cort steroid hormone and anti-infective (Barnes-Hind Pharmaceuticals, Inc.), see Vioform–Hydrocortisone steroid hormone and anti-infective.

HRC-Proclan expectorant with Codeine (H.R. Cenci Laboratories, Inc.), see Phenergan expectorant with Codeine.

Hydergine vasodilator

Manufacturer: Sandoz Pharmaceuticals
Generic Name: dihydroergocornine mesylate, dihydroergoscristine mesylate, dihydroergocryptine mesylate

Equivalent Products: Deapril-ST vasodilator (Mead Johnson Pharmaceutical Division); Circanol vasodilator (Riker Laboratories, Inc.)
Dosage Forms: Tablets, sublingual tablets: 0.5 mg, 1 mg (all are white)
Use: To reduce symptoms associated with senility
Minor Side Effects: Irritation under the tongue (sublingual tablets only), nausea, vomiting
Major Side Effects: No major side effects
Contraindications: Pregnancy
Warnings and Precautions: Liver or kidney diseases
Interacts With: No significant drug interactions
Comments: Hydergine vasodilator sublingual tablets must be used by placing them under the tongue until they dissolve. After you are sure they have dissolved, swallow several times. Hydergine vasodilator oral tablets must be swallowed. Be sure you know which product you have. See the chapter on "The Right Way to Take Medications."

Although Hydergine vasodilator may increase flow of blood to the brain, objective improvement of symptoms of senility is difficult to document. If you and your doctor agree that you should take Hydergine vasodilator, ask him to prescribe a generic preparation; then ask your pharmacist to fill it with the least expensive brand.

hydrochlorothiazide diuretic

Hydrochlorothiazide is a generic drug.
Equivalent Products: Esidrix diuretic (CIBA Pharmaceutical Company); Hydro-DIURIL diuretic (Merck Sharp & Dohme); hydrochlorothiazide (various manufacturers)
Dosage Forms: Esidrix tablets: 25 mg (pink), 50 mg (yellow), 100 mg (blue). HydroDIURIL tablets: 25 mg (peach), 50 mg (peach), 100 mg (peach)
Use: Treatment of high blood pressure and removal of fluid from body tissues
Minor Side Effects: Cramps, diarrhea, dizziness, headache, loss of appetite, nausea, rash, restlessness, vomiting, tingling in the fingers and toes
Major Side Effects: Elevated blood sugar, elevated uric acid, muscle spasms, sore throat, weakness, blurred vision
Contraindications: Allergy to sulfa drugs, severe kidney disease, pregnancy
Warnings and Precautions: Bronchial asthma, diabetes, gout, liver and kidney diseases
Interacts With: colestipol hydrochloride, digitalis, lithium carbonate, oral antidiabetics, steroids
Comments: Hydrochlorothiazide causes frequent urination. Expect this effect; it should not alarm you.

Hydrochlorothiazide can cause potassium loss. To avoid potassium loss, take the drug with a glass of fresh or frozen orange juice. You may also eat a banana each day. The use of Diasal or Co-Salt salt substitutes helps prevent potassium loss.

While taking this product (as with many drugs that lower blood pressure), you should limit your consumption of alcoholic beverages in order to prevent dizziness or light-headedness.

If dizziness or light-headedness occurs when you stand up, place your legs on the floor and "pump" the muscles for a few moments before rising.

Persons taking this product and digitalis should watch carefully for symptoms of increased toxicity (e.g., nausea, blurred vision, palpitations).

If you are allergic to a sulfa drug, you may likewise be allergic to hydrochlorothiazide.

Brands of hydrochlorothiazide vary widely in cost. Ask your pharmacist to fill your prescription with the least expensive brand.

If you have high blood pressure, do not take any nonprescription item for cough, cold or sinus problems without checking with your doctor first.

HydroDIURIL diuretic (Merck Sharp & Dohme), see hydrochlorothiazide diuretic.

Hydropres antihypertensive and diuretic

Manufacturer: Merck Sharp & Dohme
Generic Name: hydrochlorothiazide, reserpine
Equivalent Products: Hydroserpine tablets (various manufacturers); Hydrotensin antihypertensive and diuretic (Mayrand, Inc.)
Dosage Forms: Hydropres-25 tablets: hydrochlorothiazide, 25 mg; reserpine, 0.125 mg. Hydropres-50 tablets: hydrochlorothiazide, 50 mg; reserpine, 0.125 mg (both are green)
Use: Treatment of high blood pressure
Minor Side Effects: Cramping, diarrhea, dizziness, headache, itch, loss of appetite, nasal congestion, nausea, palpitations, rash, restlessness, vomiting, tingling in the fingers and toes
Major Side Effects: Chest pain, depression, drowsiness, elevated blood sugar, elevated uric acid, muscle spasms, nightmares, sore throat, weakness, blurred vision
Contraindications: Allergy to sulfa drugs, severe kidney disease, pregnancy
Warnings and Precautions: Bronchial asthma, depression, gallstones, peptic ulcer, ulcerative colitis, diabetes, gout, liver and kidney diseases
Interacts With: amphetamine, colestipol hydrochloride, decongestants, digitalis, levodopa, lithium carbonate, monoamine oxidase inhibitors, oral antidiabetics, steroids
Comments: A doctor probably should not prescribe Hydropres antihypertensive and diuretic or other "fixed-dose" products as the first choice in the treatment of high blood pressure. The patient should receive each of the individual ingredients singly, and if response is adequate to the fixed components contained in Hydropres antihypertensive and diuretic this product can then be substituted. The advantage of a combination product such as Hydropres antihypertensive and diuretic is based on increased convenience to the patient.

Take Hydropres antihypertensive and diuretic with food or milk and at the same time each day.

While taking Hydropres antihypertensive and diuretic, do not take any nonprescription item for cough, cold, or sinus problems without first checking with your doctor.

The effects of Hydropres antihypertensive and diuretic therapy may not be apparent for at least two weeks.

Hydropres antihypertensive and diuretic causes frequent urination. Expect this effect; it should not alarm you.

Mild side effects (e.g., nasal congestion) are most noticeable during the first two weeks of therapy and become less bothersome after this period.

Hydropres antihypertensive and diuretic may cause drowsiness; to prevent oversedation, avoid the use of other sedative drugs or alcohol.

Hydropres antihypertensive and diuretic can cause potassium loss. To avoid potassium loss, take the drug with a glass of fresh or frozen orange juice. You may also eat a banana each day. The use of Diasal or Co-Salt salt substitutes helps prevent potassium loss.

While taking this product (as with many drugs that lower blood pressure), you should limit your consumption of alcoholic beverages in order to prevent dizziness or light-headedness.

If dizziness or light-headedness occurs when you stand up, place your legs on the floor and "pump" the muscles for a few moments before rising.

Persons taking this product and digitalis should watch carefully for symptoms of increased toxicity (e.g., nausea, blurred vision, palpitations).

If you are allergic to a sulfa drug, you may likewise be allergic to Hydropres antihypertensive and diuretic.

Products equivalent to Hydropres antihypertensive and diuretic are available and vary widely in cost. Ask your doctor to prescribe a generic preparation; then ask your pharmacist to fill it with the least expensive brand.

Reserpine causes cancer in rats. So far it has not been shown to cause cancer in people.

Hydrotensin antihypertensive and diuretic (Mayrand, Inc.), see Hydropres antihypertensive and diuretic.

Hydrotensin-Plus antihypertensive and diuretic (Mayrand, Inc.), see Ser-Ap-Es antihypertensive and diuretic.

Hygroton diuretic

Manufacturer: USV (P.R.) Development Corp.
Generic Name: chlorthalidone
Equivalent Products: None
Dosage Forms: Tablets: 25 mg (peach), 50 mg (aqua), 100 mg (white)
Use: Treatment of high blood pressure and removal of fluid from body tissues
Minor Side Effects: Constipation, cramping, diarrhea, headache, itch, loss of appetite, nausea, numbness or tingling in fingers and toes, rash
Major Side Effects: Dizziness, elevated blood sugar, impotence, muscle spasms, restlessness, sore throat, weakness
Contraindications: Severe kidney disease, allergy to sulfa drugs, pregnancy
Warnings and Precautions: Bronchial asthma, diabetes, gout, pregnancy, liver and kidney diseases
Interacts With: colestipol hydrochloride, digitalis, lithium carbonate, oral antidiabetics, steroids
Comments: Hygroton diuretic causes frequent urination. Expect this effect; it should not alarm you.

Hygroton diuretic can cause potassium loss. To avoid potassium loss, take the drug with a glass of fresh or frozen orange juice. You may also eat a banana each day. The use of Diasal or Co-Salt salt substitutes helps prevent potassium loss.

While taking this product (as with many drugs that lower blood pressure), you should limit your consumption of alcoholic beverages in order to prevent dizziness or light-headedness.

If dizziness or light-headedness occurs when you stand up, place your legs on the floor and "pump" the muscles for a few moments before rising.

Persons taking this product and digitalis should watch carefully for symptoms of increased toxicity (e.g., nausea, blurred vision, palpitations).

If you are allergic to a sulfa drug, you may likewise be allergic to Hygroton diuretic.

If you have high blood pressure, do not take any nonprescription item for cough, cold, or sinus problems without first checking with your doctor.

Ilosone antibiotic (Dista Products Co.), see erythromycin antibiotic.

Imavate antidepressant (A.H. Robins Company), see Tofranil antidepressant.

Inderal antiarrhythmic

Manufacturer: Ayerst Laboratories
Generic Name: propranolol hydrochloride
Equivalent Products: None
Dosage Form: Tablets: 10 mg (peach), 20 mg (blue), 40 mg (green), 80 mg (yellow)
Use: Angina pectoris, certain heart arrhythmias, high blood pressure, prevention of migraine headaches
Minor Side Effects: Abdominal cramps, constipation, diarrhea, insomnia, nausea, vomiting
Major Side Effects: Dizziness, low blood pressure, rash, shortness of breath, sore throat, tingling in fingers or toes, visual disturbances
Contraindications: Bronchial asthma, certain types of heart disease, severe hay fever, pregnancy
Warnings and Precautions: Certain respiratory problems, diabetes, certain heart problems, liver and kidney diseases
Interacts With: aminophylline, digitalis, epinephrine, isoproterenol, oral antidiabetics, phenytoin
Comments: Inderal antiarrhythmic is a potent medication, and it should not be stopped abruptly. Deaths from heart attacks have occured when the medication was stopped suddenly.

Talk to your doctor about the need for a daily pulse check.

While taking Inderal antiarrhythmic, do not take any nonprescription item for cough, cold, or sinus problems without first checking with your doctor.

Indocin anti-inflammatory

Manufacturer: Merck Sharp & Dohme
Generic Name: indomethacin
Equivalent Products: None
Dosage Form: Capsules: 25 mg, 50 mg (blue/white)
Use: Reduction of pain, redness, and swelling due to arthritis
Minor Side Effects: Diarrhea, nausea, rash, vomiting, drowsiness, constipation, headache, dizziness, ringing in ears
Major Side Effects: Blood in stools, urine, or mouth; blurred vision; fatigue; fluid retention; itching; jaundice; paleness; severe abdominal pain; weight gain; high blood pressure; sore throat

Contraindications: Allergy to aspirin, pregnancy
Warnings and Precautions: Epilepsy, infection, Parkinson's disease, ulcers, psychiatric illness, liver and kidney diseases
Interacts With: aspirin, oral anticoagulants, probenecid, steroids
Comments: Indocin anti-inflammatory is a potent pain-killing drug and is not intended for general aches and pains.

Regular checkups by the doctor, including blood tests, are required by persons taking Indocin anti-inflammatory.

Indocin anti-inflammatory must be taken with food or milk. Never take Indocin anti-inflammatory on an empty stomach or with aspirin.

If you are taking an anticoagulant ("blood thinner"), remind your doctor.

Indocin anti-inflammatory may cause discoloration of the urine or feces. If you notice a change in color, call your doctor.

insulin antidiabetic

Insulin is a generic drug.
Equivalent Products: Insulin is usually prescribed by strength rather than by trade name.
Dosage Forms: Insulin is available only as an injectable. Various types of insulin provide different times of onset and duration of action. The types of insulin and their times of onset and duration are as follows:

	Onset (hr.)	Duration (hr.)
regular insulin	1/2	6
insulin zinc suspension, prompt	1/2	14
isophane (NPH)	1	24
insulin zinc suspension	1	24
globin zinc insulin	2	24
Protamine Zinc Insulin (PZI)	6	36
insulin zinc suspension, extended	6	36

Use: Treatment of diabetes mellitus
Minor Side Effects: Low blood sugar level
Major Side Effects: No major side effects when used as directed.
Contraindications: None
Warnings and Precautions: Use only under the direction of a doctor, and be sure to follow your prescribed diet.
Interacts With: guanethidine, monoamine oxidase inhibitors, propranolol, steroids, tetracycline, thyroid hormone
Comments: Insulin is stored in the refrigerator in the pharmacy, but once the bottle has been opened, most forms (except U-500 strength) may be kept at room temperature for the normal life of the vial.

Insulin comes in various strengths, currently U-40, U-80, U-100, U-500. Eventually, U-40 and U-80 will be taken off the market, and insulin strength will be less confusing. But until then, be *sure* to buy the right strength of the drug and the right syringes. Purchase disposable syringes, and remember to dispose of them properly.

Special injection kits are available for blind diabetics. Ask your doctor for help in obtaining them.

Doses of insulin may be prepared in advance. Ask your pharmacist for advice.

Thoroughly blend insulin before withdrawing a dose into the syringe. While taking insulin, do not take any nonprescription item for cough, cold, or sinus problems without first checking with your doctor.

Iodocort steroid hormone and anti-infective (Ulmer Pharmacal Company), see Vioform-Hydrocortisone steroid hormone and anti-infective.

Ionamin anorectic (Pennwalt Pharmaceutical Division), see Fastin anorectic.

Iosel 250 seborrheic (Owen Drug Company), see Selsun seborrheic.

Isolait vasodilator (Paul B. Elder Company), see Vasodilan vasodilator.

Isopto Carpine ophthalmic solution

Manufacturer: Alcon Labs, Inc.
Generic Name: pilocarpine hydrochloride
Equivalent Products: pilocarpine hydrochloride ophthalmic solution (various manufacturers); Almocarpine ophthalmic solution (Ayerst Laboratories); Mi-Pilo ophthalmic solution (Barnes Hind Pharmaceuticals, Inc.); Adsorbocarpine ophthalmic solution (Burton, Parsons & Company, Inc.); Mistura P ophthalmic solution (Lederle Laboratories); Pilocar ophthalmic solution, Pilomiotin ophthalmic solution (Smith, Miller & Patch); P.V. Carpine Liquifilm ophthalmic solution (Allergan Pharmaceuticals)
Dosage Forms: Drops; ocular therapeutic system*
Use: Treatment of glaucoma
Minor Side Effects: Brow-ache, loss of night vision, blurred vision
Major Side Effects: No major side effects
Contraindications: Certain eye conditions
Warnings and Precautions: Liver or kidney disease
Interacts With: No significant drug interactions
Comments: Be careful about the contamination of solutions used for the eyes. See the chapter on "The Right Way to Take Medications."
   *The ocular therapeutic system mentioned above is an oval ring of plastic that contains pilocarpine. This ring is placed in the eye, and the drug is released gradually over a period of seven days. Use of these rings has made possible the control of glaucoma for some patients. If you are having trouble controlling glaucoma, ask your doctor about the possibility of using one of these devices.

Isordil antianginal

Manufacturer: Ives Laboratories, Inc.
Generic Name: isosorbide dinitrate
Equivalent Products: Sorbitrate antianginal (Stuart Pharmaceuticals); Isotrate Timecelles antianginal (W.E. Hauck, Inc.); Sorbide antianginal (Mayrand, Inc.); Vasotrate antianginal (Reid Provident Laboratories, Inc.)
Dosage Forms: Sublingual tablets: 2.5 mg (yellow), 5 mg (pink); tablets: 5 mg (pink), 10 mg (white); chewable tablets: 10 mg (yellow); sustained-action tablets: 40 mg (green); sustained-action capsules: 40 mg (blue/clear with beads)

Use: Prevention (tablets and capsules) and relief (chewable and sublingual tablets) of chest pain due to heart disease

Minor Side Effects: Dizziness, flushing, headache, nausea, vomiting

Major Side Effects: Palpitations, rash, weakness, low blood pressure

Contraindications: Pregnancy

Warnings and Precautions: Head injuries, liver and kidney diseases

Interacts With: alcohol, nitroglycerin

Comments: Although sublingual tablets are effective, there is some question about the effectiveness of regular tablets. Carefully discuss the merits of the drug with your doctor. If you agree to take it, ask for one of the less expensive equivalent products.

  Before using a sublingual tablet to relieve chest pain, be certain pain arises from the heart and is not due to a muscle spasm or to indigestion.

  After continued use (two to three weeks) of Isordil antianginal, many side effects disappear. Alcoholic beverages may enhance the severity of side effects, and they should be avoided or used with caution.

  If your chest pain is not relieved by use of sublingual tablets, if pain arises from a different location or differs in severity, consult your doctor immediately.

  See the chapter on "The Right Way to Take Medications."

Isotrate Timecelles antianginal (W.E. Hauck, Inc.), see Isordil antianginal.

Janimine antidepressant (Abbott Laboratories), see Tofranil antidepressant.

J-Gan-V.C. expectorant plain (J. Pharmacal Co.), see Phenergan VC expectorant plain.

Kaochlor potassium replacement (Warren-Teed Pharmaceuticals Inc.), see potassium chloride.

Kaon-Cl potassium replacement (Warren-Teed Pharmaceuticals Inc.), see potassium chloride.

Kay Ciel potassium replacement (Cooper Laboratories Inc.), see potassium chloride.

Keflex antibiotic

Manufacturer: Eli Lilly and Company

Generic Name: cephalexin

Equivalent Products: None

Dosage Forms: Drops (content per ml): 100 mg; liquid (content per 5 ml): 125 mg, 250 mg; capsules: 250 mg (white/green), 500 mg (light green/dark green); tablets (capsule-shaped): 500 mg (green)

Use: Treatment of bacterial infections

Minor Side Effects: Abdominal pain, diarrhea, dizziness, fatigue, headache, itching, nausea, vomiting

Major Side Effects: Superinfection, vaginal and rectal itching, cough, severe diarrhea, irritation of the mouth, "black tongue", rash

Contraindications: Pregnancy
Warnings and Precautions: Allergy to penicillin, liver and kidney diseases
Interacts With: colestipol hydrochloride, furosemide, gentamicin
Comments: Persons who are allergic to penicillin should observe extreme caution when using Keflex antibiotic or any other cephalosporin antibiotic. Although the medical and pharmaceutical literature contains many different opinions, general consensus is that about 10% of all persons who are allergic to penicillin will also be allergic to a cephalosporin like Keflex antibiotic.

Keflex antibiotic is frequently prescribed for many infections for which penicillin is adequate. For example, penicillin is the usual drug of choice for treatment of a strep throat, even though Keflex antibiotic may be prescribed. Ask your doctor if you really need Keflex antibiotic, or if you could take penicillin, which is less expensive.

Keflex antibiotic should be taken for at least 10 full days, even if symptoms have disappeared.

Diabetics using Clinitest urine-testing product may get a false high sugar reading. Change to Clinistix urine-testing product or Tes-Tape urine-testing product to avoid this problem.

Take Keflex antibiotic on an empty stomach (one hour before or two hours after a meal).

The liquid form of Keflex antibiotic should be stored in the refrigerator.

Kenacort steroid hormone (E.R. Squibb & Sons), see Aristocort steroid hormone.

Kenalog steroid hormone

Manufacturer: E.R. Squibb & Sons
Generic Name: triamcinolone acetonide
Equivalent Products: SK-Triamcinolone steroid hormone (Smith Kline & French Laboratories)
Dosage Forms: Cream; lotion; ointment; spray
Use: Relief of skin inflammation associated with conditions such as eczema or poison ivy
Minor Side Effects: Burning sensation, dryness, irritation of affected area, itching, rash
Major Side Effects: Secondary infection
Contraindications: No absolute contraindications
Warnings and Precautions: Bacterial or viral skin infections, diseases that severely impair blood circulation
Interacts With: No significant drug interactions
Comments: The spray form of Kenalog steroid hormone produces a cooling sensation, which may be uncomfortable for some persons. When the spray is used about the face, cover the eyes and do not inhale the spray.

If the affected area is extremely dry or is scaling, the skin may be moistened before applying the product by soaking in water or by applying water with a clean cloth. The ointment form is probably the better product for dry skin.

Do not use Kenalog steroid hormone with an occlusive wrap of transparent plastic film unless directed to do so by your doctor.

Aristogel gel and Aristoderm lotion (manufactured by Lederle Laboratories) are, for all practical purposes, the same as Kenalog steroid hormone. See the chapter "The Right Way to Take Medications."

Kestrin estrogen hormone (Hyprex Pharmaceuticals), see Premarin estrogen hormone.

K-LOR potassium replacement (Abbott Laboratories), see potassium chloride.

Klorvess potassium replacement (Dorsey Laboratories), see potassium chloride.

K-Lyte potassium replacement

Manufacturer: Mead Johnson Pharmaceutical Division
Generic Name: potassium bicarbonate, potassium citrate
Equivalent Products: None
Dosage Form: Effervescent tablets (lime or orange flavored)
Use: Prevention or treatment of potassium deficiency
Minor Side Effects: Diarrhea, nausea, vomiting
Major Side Effects: Confusion, numbness or tingling in the arms or legs
Contraindications: Severe kidney disease
Warnings and Precautions: Liver or kidney disease, pregnancy
Interacts With: spironolactone, triamterene
Comments: Potassium supplements usually have a low rate of patient compliance. If a potassium product is prescribed, be sure to take the medication as directed and do not stop taking it without first consulting your doctor.

K-Lyte potassium replacement may be taken with meals.

Take K-Lyte potassium replacement with at least a full glass of water. K-Lyte potassium replacement tablets must be completely dissolved in water before swallowing.

Consult your doctor about using salt substitutes instead of K-Lyte potassium replacement; they are similar, less expensive, and more convenient.

K-Lyte/Cl potassium replacement (Mead Johnson Pharmaceuticals Division), see potassium chloride replacement.

Korostatin antifungal vaginal tablets (Holland-Rantos Company), see Mycostatin antifungal agent.

K-Phen expectorant with Codeine (Kay Pharmacal Company, Inc.), see Phenergan expectorant with Codeine.

Kwell pediculocide and scabicide

Manufacturer: Reed & Carnrick
Generic Name: gamma benzene hexachloride (lindane)
Equivalent Products: Gamene pediculocide and scabicide (Barnes-Hind Pharmaceuticals, Inc.)

Dosage Forms: Lotion; shampoo; cream
Use: Treatment of head lice, crab lice and their nits; scabies
Minor Side Effects: Rash, skin irritation if improperly used
Major Side Effects: See "Comments"
Contraindications: Children under age two, pregnancy
Warnings and Precautions: Use only as directed
Interacts With: No significant drug interactions
Comments: Complete directions for the use of Kwell pediculocide and scabicide are supplied by the manufacturer. Ask your pharmacist for these directions if he does not supply them.

Side effects to Kwell pediculocide and scabicide products are rare if the directions for using the drug are followed. However, serious toxicity (convulsions and even death) can result if Kwell pediculocide and scabicide is swallowed; call your doctor or pharmacist immediately.

Lice are easily transmitted from one person to another. All family members should be carefully examined. Personal items (clothing, towels) need only be machine-washed on the "hot" temperature cycle and dried. No unusual cleaning measures are required. Combs, brushes, and other such washable items may be cleaned with Kwell pediculocide and scabicide shampoo.

Lanophyllin bronchodilator (The Lannett Company, Inc.), see Elixophyllin bronchodilator.

Lanorinal analgesic and sedative (The Lannett Company, Inc.), see Fiorinal analgesic and sedative.

Lanoxin heart drug (Burroughs Wellcome Co.), see digoxin heart drug.

Larotid antibiotic (Roche Products Inc.), see amoxicillin antibiotic.

Lasix diuretic

Manufacturer: Hoechst-Roussel Pharmaceuticals, Inc.
Generic Name: furosemide
Equivalent Products: None
Dosage Forms: Liquid (content per 1 ml): 10 mg; tablets: 20 mg, 40 mg (both are white)
Use: Treatment of high blood pressure and removal of fluid from body tissues
Minor Side Effects: Blurred vision, diarrhea, loss of appetite, nausea, rash, vomiting, cramping, constipation, tingling in the fingers and toes, dizziness
Major Side Effects: Jaundice, anorexia, pancreatitis, blurred vision, ringing in the ears, anemia
Contraindications: Severe kidney disease, pregnancy
Warnings and Precautions: Liver or kidney disease, allergy to sulfa drugs
Interacts With: cephalosporins, clofibrate, digitalis, lithium carbonate, steroids
Comments: Lasix diuretic causes more frequent urination. Expect this effect; it should not alarm you.

Lasix diuretic has potent activity. If another drug to decrease blood pressure is also prescribed, your doctor may decide to decrease the dose of one of the drugs to avoid an excessive drop in blood pressure.

Lasix diuretic can cause potassium loss. To avoid potassium loss, take the drug with a glass of fresh or frozen orange juice. You may also eat a banana each day. The use of Diasal or Co-Salt salt substitutes helps prevent potassium loss.

While taking this product (as with many drugs that lower blood pressure), you should limit your consumption of alcoholic beverages in order to prevent dizziness or light-headedness.

If dizziness or light-headedness occurs when you stand up, place your legs on the floor and "pump" the muscles for a few moments before rising.

Persons taking this product and digitalis should watch carefully for symptoms of increased toxicity (e.g., nausea, blurred vision, palpitations).

If you are allergic to a sulfa drug, you may likewise be allergic to Lasix diuretic.

A generic furosemide product is available, but it is not equivalent to Lasix diuretic.

If you have high blood pressure, do not take any nonprescription item for cough, cold, or sinus problems without first checking with your doctor.

Letter thyroid hormone (Armour Pharmaceutical Company), see thyroid hormone.

Levoid thyroid hormone (Nutrition Control Products), see thyroid hormone.

Librax anticholinergic and sedative

Manufacturer: Roche Products Inc.
Generic Name: chlordiazepoxide hydrochloride, clidinium bromide
Equivalent Products: Lidinium anticholinergic and sedative (Spencer-Mead Inc.)
Dosage Form: Capsules: chlordiazepoxide hydrochloride, 5 mg; clidinium bromide, 2.5 mg (green)
Use: Treatment of peptic ulcer or irritable bowel syndrome
Minor Side Effects: Confusion, rash, uncoordinated movements, depression, fatigue, headache, slurred speech, blurred vision, constipation, dizziness, drowsiness, dry mouth, insomnia, loss of the sense of taste, nausea, nervousness, palpitations, photosensitivity, reduced sweating, vomiting, difficult urination
Major Side Effects: Tremors, double vision, jaundice, low blood pressure, impotence
Contraindications: Certain types of glaucoma, enlarged prostate, obstructed intestine, asthma, bladder obstruction, certain heart diseases, porphyria
Warnings and Precautions: Suicidal tendencies, pregnancy, severe heart disease, liver and kidney diseases
Interacts With: amantadine hydrochloride, haloperidol, other central nervous system depressants, antacids, phenothiazines
Comments: Librax anticholinergic and sedative is best taken one-half to one hour before meals. The drug does not *cure* ulcers but may help them improve.

Librax anticholinergic and sedative may cause drowsiness; to prevent oversedation, avoid the use of other sedatives or alcohol.

Librax anticholinergic and sedative has a slight potential for abuse, but taken as directed, there is little danger. *Do not* increase the dose of this drug without first consulting your doctor.

Librax anticholinergic and sedative always produces certain side effects. These include dry mouth, blurred vision, reduced sweating, difficult urination, constipation, and palpitations. To reduce dryness of the mouth, chew gum or suck on a piece of hard candy. Avoid excessive work in hot weather.

Call your doctor if you notice a rash, flushing, or pain in the eye.

Products equivalent to Librax anticholinergic and sedative are available and vary widely in cost. Ask your doctor to prescribe a generic preparation and then ask your pharmacist to fill it with the least expensive brand.

Librium sedative and hypnotic

Manufacturer: Roche Products Inc.
Generic Name: chlordiazepoxide hydrochloride
Equivalent Products: chlordiazepoxide hydrochloride (various manufacturers); Chlordiazachel sedative and hypnotic (Rachelle Laboratories, Inc.); SK-Lygen sedative and hypnotic (Smith Kline & French Laboratories); Sereen sedative and hypnotic (Foy Laboratories, Inc.); Tenax sedative and hypnotic (Reid-Provident Laboratories, Inc.)
Dosage Forms: Capsules: 5 mg (green/yellow), 10 mg (green/black), 25 mg (green/white); tablets: 5 mg, 10 mg, 25 mg (green)
Use: Relief of anxiety, nervousness, tension; relief of muscle spasms; withdrawal from alcohol addiction
Minor Side Effects: Confusion, constipation, depression, difficult urination, dizziness, drowsiness, dry mouth, fatigue, headache, nausea, rash, slurred speech, uncoordinated movements
Major Side Effects: Blurred vision, decreased sexual drive, double vision, jaundice, low blood pressure, stimulation, tremors
Contraindications: Certain types of glaucoma
Warnings and Precautions: Pregnancy, suicidal tendencies, liver and kidney diseases, potential for abuse
Interacts With: central nervous system depressants
Comments: Librium sedative and hypnotic currently is used by many people to relieve nervousness. It is effective for this purpose, but it is important to try to eliminate the cause of the anxiety as well. Phenobarbital is equally effective for most people and costs much less. Consult your doctor.

Librium sedative and hypnotic has the potential for abuse and must be used with caution. Tolerance may develop quickly; *do not* increase the dose of this drug without first consulting your doctor.

Taken alone, Librium sedative and hypnotic is a safe drug; when it is combined with other sedative drugs or with alcohol, serious adverse reactions may develop.

Librium sedative and hypnotic may cause drowsiness. Try to avoid driving and operating machinery while taking it.

Products equivalent to Librium sedative and hypnotic are available and vary widely in cost. Ask your doctor to prescribe a generic preparation, and then ask your pharmacist to fill it with the least expensive brand.

Lidex steroid hormone

Manufacturer: Syntex Laboratories, Inc.
Generic Name: fluocinonide

Equivalent Products: None
Dosage Forms: Cream; ointment
Use: Relief of skin inflammation associated with conditions such as eczema or poison ivy
Minor Side Effects: Burning sensation, dryness, irritation of affected area, itching, rash
Major Side Effects: Secondary infection
Contraindications: No absolute contraindications
Warnings and Precautions: Diseases in which blood circulation is severely impaired, viral and bacterial skin infections
Interacts With: No significant drug interactions
Comments: Topsin steroid hormone is another product manufactured by Syntex Laboratories, Inc. Topsin steroid hormone contains fluocinonide, but in a gel. For all practical purposes, Topsin steriod hormone is the same as Lidex cream steroid hormone, and they are similar in price.

If the affected area is extremely dry or is scaling, the skin may be moistened before applying the product by soaking in water or by applying water with a clean cloth. The ointment form is probably the better product for dry skin.

Do not use Lidex steroid hormone with an occlusive wrap of transparent plastic film unless directed to do so by your doctor. See the chapter "The Right Way To Take Medications."

Lidinium anticholinergic and sedative (Spencer-Mead Inc.), see Librax anticholinergic and sedative.

Lisacort steroid hormone (Fellows Medical Division), see prednisone steroid hormone.

Loestrin oral contraceptive (Parke, Davis & Company), see oral contraceptives.

Lomotil anticholinergic and antispasmodic

Manufacturer: Searle & Co.
Generic Name: diphenoxylate hydrochloride, atropine sulfate
Equivalent Products: Lonox anticholinergic and antispasmodic (Geneva Generics, Inc.); Colonil anticholinergic and antispasmodic (Mallinckrodt, Inc.)
Dosage Forms: Liquid (content per 5 ml): diphenoxylate hydrochloride, 2.5 mg; atropine sulfate, 0.025 mg; tablets: diphenoxylate hydrochloride, 2.5 mg; atropine sulfate, 0.025 mg (white)
Use: Treatment of diarrhea
Minor Side Effects: Abdominal pain, difficult urination, dizziness, drowsiness, flushing, headache, itching, nausea, rash, sedation, swollen gums, vomiting, blurred vision, constipation, nervousness, sweating, dry mouth, insomnia, loss of sense of taste
Major Side Effects: Breathing difficulties, coma, euphoria, numbness in fingers or toes, impotence, palpitations
Contraindications: Age (children under age two), jaundice, glaucoma, enlarged prostate, obstructed intestine, bladder obstruction, certain heart diseases, porphyria

Warnings and Precautions: Age (all children), potential for drug abuse, pregnancy, severe heart disease, liver and kidney diseases
Interacts With: amantadine, haloperidol, antacids, phenothiazines, monoamine oxidase inhibitors, alcohol
Comments: While taking Lomotil anticholinergic and narcotic, drink at least eight to nine glasses of water each day to replace the fluid that is being lost.

Lomotil anticholinergic and antispasmodic ordinarily should not be used for more than three to five days. Unless your doctor prescribes otherwise, do not take Lomotil anticholinergic and antispasmodic for over five days.

People commonly take Lomotil anticholinergic and antispasmodic with them when traveling to foreign countries. If your doctor prescribes Lomotil anticholinergic and antispasmodic to take with you, do not use the medication unless you absolutely have to. Make sure that diarrhea is not just a temporary occurrence (two to three hours).

Lomotil anticholinergic and antispasmodic has abuse potential and must be used with caution. Tolerance to Lomotil anticholinergic and antispasmodic may develop quickly; *do not* increase the dose of this drug without first consulting your doctor.

Products equivalent to Lomotil anticholinergic and antispasmodic are available and vary widely in cost. Ask your doctor to prescribe a generic preparation; then ask your pharmacist to fill it with the least expensive brand.

Call your doctor if you notice a rash or pain in the eye.

Lonox anticholinergic and antispasmodic (Geneva Generics, Inc.), see Lomotil anticholinergic and antispasmodic.

Lo/Ovral oral contraceptive (Wyeth Laboratories), see oral contraceptives.

Lotrimin antifungal agent

Manufacturer: Delbay Pharmaceuticals, Inc.
Generic Name: clotrimazole
Equivalent Products: None
Dosage Forms: Cream; solution
Use: Treatment of fungal infections of the skin
Minor Side Effects: Redness, stinging sensation
Major Side Effects: Blistering, irritation, peeling of the skin
Contraindications: Pregnancy
Warnings and Precautions: Liver and kidney diseases
Interacts With: No significant drug interactions
Comments: Lotrimin antifungal agent should be rubbed well into the affected area and the surrounding skin.

Improvement may not be seen for one week. If the condition for which you are takin Lotrimin antifungal agent has not improved after four weeks, consult your doctor.

See the chapter "The Right Way To Take Medications."

Luminal Ovoids sedative and hypnotic (Winthrop Laboratories), see phenobartibal sedative and hypnotic.

Macrodantin antibacterial

Manufacturer: Eaton Laboratories
Generic Name: nitrofurantoin (macrocrystals)
Equivalent Products: None
Dosage Form: Capsules: 25 mg (white), 50 mg (yellow/white), 100 mg (yellow)
Use: Treatment of bacterial urinary tract infections such as pyelonephritis, pyelitis, or cystitis
Minor Side Effects: Abdominal cramps, loss of appetite, nausea, vomiting, change in urine color
Major Side Effects: Rash, superinfection, fever, chills, cough, chest pain, vaginal and rectal itching, irritation of the mouth, "black tongue"
Contraindications: Pregnancy, severe kidney disease
Warnings and Precautions: Liver or kidney disease
Interacts With: No significant drug interactions
Comments: Macrodantin antibacterial is similar to the generic product nitrofurantoin. However, Macrodantin antibacterial is much better tolerated (causes less nausea and stomach distress) than other nitrofurantoin products.

If you have a urinary tract infection, you should drink at least nine to 10 glasses of water each day.

To reduce nausea and vomiting, take Macrodantin antibacterial with a meal or glass of milk.

Mallergan expectorant with Codeine (Mallard Incorporated), see Phenergan expectorant with Codeine.

Mallergan VC expectorant with Codeine, (Mallard Incorporated), see Phenergan VC expectorant with Codeine.

Marax adrenergic, sedative, and smooth muscle relaxant

Manufacturer: Roerig
Generic Name: theophylline, ephedrine sulfate, hydroxyzine hydrochloride
Equivalent Products: Theophozine adrenergic, sedative, and smooth muscle relaxant (Spencer-Mead Inc.); Theozine adrenergic, sedative, and smooth muscle relaxant (Henry Schein, Inc.)
Dosage Forms: Tablets (blue or white) or syrup (content per 15 ml): theophylline, 130 mg; ephedrine sulfate, 25 mg; hydroxyzine hydrochloride, 10 mg
Use: Control of asthmatic bronchospasm
Minor Side Effects: Difficult urination, insomnia, stimulation, nausea, vomiting, drowsiness, stomach pain, restlessness
Major Side Effects: High blood pressure, chest pain, convulsions, difficult breathing, palpitations, cold and clammy skin
Contraindications: Severe heart disease, porphyria
Warnings and Precautions: Certain types of glaucoma, certain kinds of heart disease, enlarged prostate, hyperthyroidism, pregnancy, high blood pressure, diabetes, history of drug abuse
Interacts With: central nervous system depressants, guanethidine, lithium carbonate, monoamine oxidase inhibitors, propranolol

Comments: Take Marax adrenergic, sedative, and smooth muscle relaxant with food or milk.

Marax adrenergic, sedative, and smooth muscle relaxant may cause drowsiness; to prevent oversedation, avoid the use of other sedative drugs or alcohol.

While taking Marax adrenergic, sedative, and smooth muscle relaxant, do not take any nonprescription item for cough, cold, or sinus problems without first checking with your doctor.

Never take Marax adrenergic, sedative, and smooth muscle relaxant more frequently than your doctor prescribes. A serious overdose may result.

Products equivalent to Marax adrenergic, sedative, and smooth muscle relaxant are available and vary widely in cost. Ask your pharmacist for the least expensive brand.

Call your doctor if you develop severe stomach pain or nausea, or insomnia and restlessness. This product may aggravate an ulcer.

Medrol steroid hormone

Manufacturer: The Upjohn Company
Generic Name: methylprednisolone
Equivalent Products: methylprednisolone (various manufacturers)
Dosage Form: Tablets: 2 mg (oval pink); 4 mg (oval white); 8 mg (oval peach); 16 mg (oval white); 24 mg (oval yellow); 32 mg (oval peach)
Use: Relief of inflammations (e.g., arthritis, dermatitis, poison ivy); endocrine and rheumatic disorders; asthma; blood diseases; certain cancers; and gastrointestinal disturbances (e.g., ulcerative colitis)
Minor Side Effects: Dizziness, headache, increased sweating, menstrual irregularities
Major Side Effects: Abdominal distention, fluid retention, glaucoma, growth impairment in children, hemorrhage, high blood pressure, impaired wound healing, peptic ulcer, potassium loss, weakness, cataracts
Contraindications: Usually systemic fungal infections
Warnings and Precautions: Peptic ulcer, pregnancy, tuberculosis, diabetes
Interacts With: antidiabetics, aspirin, barbiturates, diuretics, estrogens, indomethacin, oral anticoagulants, phenytoin
Comments: When Medrol steroid hormone is used for short periods of time, such as in the treatment of allergy or poison ivy, it is often taken on a decreasing dosage schedule (i.e., one tablet four times daily for several days, then one tablet three times daily, then one tablet twice daily; then one tablet daily).

When Medrol steroid hormone is used for long periods of time, as in the treatment of arthritis, an every-other-day dosage schedule is preferred. In other words, instead of taking one tablet daily, you can take two tablets every other day and still receive the same pharmacologic effect. This treatment consideration is the reason for the large variety of tablet strengths.

If your doctor tells you to take the entire daily dose of the medication at one time, take it as close to 8:00 A.M. as possible to receive optimal response.

Medrol steroid hormone can cause potassium loss. To avoid potassium loss, take Medrol steroid hormone with a glass of fresh or frozen orange juice. You may also eat a banana each day. The use of Diasal or Co-Salt salt substitutes helps prevent potassium loss.

Blood pressure and body weight should be monitored at regular intervals. Stomach x-rays are desirable for persons with suspected or known peptic ulcers.

Products equivalent to Medrol steroid hormone are available and vary widely in cost. Ask your doctor to prescribe a generic preparation, and have your pharmacist fill your prescription with the least expensive brand.

Do not stop taking Medrol steroid hormone without your doctor's knowledge.

If you are taking Medrol steroid hormone daily for a long period, you should carry with you a notice that you are taking a steroid.

Mellaril phenothiazine

Manufacturer: Sandoz Pharmaceuticals
Generic Name: thioridazine hydrochloride
Equivalent Products: None
Dosage Forms: Tablets: 10 mg (buff), 15 mg (pink), 25 mg (orange), 50 mg (white), 100 mg (buff), 150 mg (yellow), 200 mg (pink)
Use: Control of agitation, aggressiveness, hyperactivity in children; relief of depression, certain types of psychoses; withdrawal from alcohol addiction
Minor Side Effects: Blurred vision, change in urine color, constipation, diarrhea, dizziness, drooling, drowsiness, dry mouth, jitteriness, menstrual irregularities, nasal congestion, nausea, rash, restlessness, uncoordinated movements, vomiting, reduced sweating
Major Side Effects: Difficulty in swallowing; enlarged or painful breasts (in both sexes); fluid retention; impotence; involuntary movements of the face, mouth, tongue, or jaw; muscle stiffness; sore throat; tremors; jaundice; rise in blood pressure
Contraindications: Coma, drug-induced depression, shock, blood disease, Parkinson's disease, liver damage, jaundice, kidney disease, stroke, pregnancy
Warnings and Precautions: Asthma and other respiratory disorders, epilepsy, exposure to extreme heat
Interacts With: alcohol, antacids, anticholinergics, central nervous system depressants
Comments: The effects of Mellaril phenothiazine therapy may not be apparent for at least two weeks.

Mellaril phenothiazine has persistent action; so never take it more frequently than your doctor prescribes. A serious overdose may result.

While taking Mellaril phenothiazine, do not take any nonprescription item for cough, cold, or sinus problems without first checking with your doctor.

Mellaril phenothiazine interacts with alcohol; avoid using alcohol while taking this product.

Mellaril phenothiazine may cause dryness of the mouth. To reduce this feeling, chew gum or suck on a piece of hard candy.

Mellaril phenothiazine reduces sweating; avoid excessive work or exercise in hot weather.

If dizziness or light-headedness occurs when you stand up, place the legs on the floor and "pump" the muscles for a few moments before rising.

As with any other drug that has antivomiting activity, symptoms of severe disease or toxicity due to overdose of other drugs may be masked by Mellaril phenothiazine.

Menogen estrogen hormone (General Pharmaceutical Products, Inc.), see Premarin estrogen hormone.

Menotab estrogen hormone (Fleming & Company), see Premarin estrogen hormone.

meprobamate sedative and hypnotic

Meprobamate is a generic drug.
Equivalent Products: Equanil sedative and hypnotic (Wyeth Laboratories); Miltown sedative and hypnotic (Wallace Laboratories)
Dosage Form: Equanil tablets: 200 mg, 400 mg (white); Equanil Wyseals: 400 mg (yellow); Equanil capsules: 400 mg (red/clear with pellets); Miltown tablets: 200 mg, 400 mg (both white), 600 mg (white, capsule-shaped)
Use: Relief of anxiety or tension, sleeping aid
Minor Side Effects: Diarrhea, dizziness, headache, nausea, palpitations, sedation, vomiting, rash, sore throat, fever
Major Side Effects: Fainting
Contraindications: Porphyria, pregnancy
Warnings and Precautions: Epilepsy, potential for drug abuse, liver and kidney diseases
Interacts With: central nervous system depressants
Comments: Meprobamate sedative and hypnotic may cause drowsiness; to prevent oversedation, avoid the use of other sedative drugs or alcohol.
Meprobamate sedative and hypnotic has the potential for abuse and must be used with caution. Tolerance may develop quickly; *do not* increase the dose of this drug without first consulting your doctor.
Brands of meprobamate sedative and hypnotic vary widely in cost. Ask your pharmacist to fill your prescription with the least expensive brand.
Call your doctor if you get a rash, sore throat, or fever.
If you have been taking meprobamate sedative and hypnotic for two to three months, do not stop taking it abruptly. Talk to your doctor about tapering off slowly.

Meprogesic analgesic (Spencer-Mead Inc.), see Equagesic analgesic.

Meticorten steroid hormone (Shering Corporation), see prednisone steroid hormone.

Midahist DH expectorant (Vangard Laboratories), see Novahistine DH expectorant.

Midahist expectorant (Vangard Laboratories), see Novahistine expectorant.

Miltown sedative and hypnotic (Wallace Laboratories), see meprobamate sedative and hypnotic.

Minipress antihypertensive

Manufacturer: Pfizer Laboratories Division

Generic Name: prazosin hydrochloride
Equivalent Products: None
Dosage Form: Capsules: 1 mg (white); 2 mg (pink and white); 5 mg (blue and white)
Use: Treatment of high blood pressure
Minor Side Effects: Dizziness, headache, drowsiness, tiredness, weakness, palpitations, nausea, vomiting, diarrhea, constipation, abdominal pain, tingling in fingers and toes, rash, itching, impotence, dry mouth, nasal congestion, ringing in the ears
Major Side Effects: Depression, blurred vision, nosebleed, low blood pressure, fainting
Contraindications: Pregnancy
Warnings and Precautions: No major warning or precautions
Interacts With: No known drug interactions
Comments: The effects of Minipress antihypertensive may not be apparent for at least two weeks.

Mild side effects (e.g., nasal congestion) are most noticeable during the first two weeks of therapy and become less bothersome after this period.

Initial dosages of Minipress antihypertensive may be given under supervision in order to adjust dosages to control side effects.

While taking Minipress antihypertensive, do not take any nonprescription item for cough, cold or sinus problems without first checking with your doctor.

While taking this product (as with many drugs that lower blood pressure), you should limit your consumption of alcoholic beverages in order to prevent dizziness or light-headedness.

If dizziness or light-headedness occurs when you stand up, place your legs on the floor and "pump" the muscles for a few moments before rising.

There are no known drug interactions with Minipress antihypertensive. However, if you are taking Minipress antihypertensive and begin therapy with another antihypertensive drug, your doctor will probably reduce the dosage of the Minipress antihypertensive to 1 or 2 mg three times a day, then recalculate your correct dose over the next couple of weeks.

Minocin antibiotic

Manufacturer: Lederle Laboratories
Generic Name: minocycline hydrochloride
Equivalent Products: Vectrin antibiotic (Parke, Davis & Company)
Dosage Form: Capsules: 50 mg (orange), 100 mg (blue and orange)
Use: Treatment of a wide variety of bacterial infections
Minor Side Effects: Diarrhea, loss of appetite, nausea, vomiting, photosensitivity
Major Side Effects: Anemia, itching, sore throat, superinfection, rash, vaginal and rectal itching, irritation of the mouth, "black tongue"
Contraindications: Allergy to tetracycline, pregnancy
Warnings and Precautions: Age (children under age nine), liver and kidney diseases
Interacts With: barbiturates, carbamazepine, dairy products, diuretics, iron-containing products, antacids, phenytoin
Comments: Take Minocin antibiotic on an empty stomach (one hour before or two hours after a meal).

Minocin antibiotic should be taken for at least 10 full days, even if symptoms have disappeared.

Minocin antibiotic is taken once or twice a day. Never increase the dosage unless your doctor tells you to do so.

While taking Minocin antibiotic, avoid prolonged exposure to sunlight.

Do not take Minocin antibiotic at the same time as milk or other dairy products or iron preparations. Separate taking the drugs by at least one hour.

Products equivalent to Minocin antibiotic are available and vary widely in cost. Ask your doctor to prescribe a generic preparation; then ask your pharmacist to fill it with the least expensive brand.

Mi-Pilo ophthalmic solution (Barnes-Hind Pharmaceuticals, Inc.), see Isopto Carpine ophthalmic solution.

Mistura P ophthalmic solution (Lederle Laboratories), see Isopto Carpine ophthalmic solution.

Modicon oral contraceptive (Ortho Pharmaceutical Corporation), see oral contraceptives.

Monistat 7 antifungal agent

Manufacturer: Ortho Pharmaceutical Corporation
Generic Name: miconazole nitrate
Equivalent Products: None
Dosage Form: Cream
Use: Treatment of fungal infections of the vagina
Minor Side Effects: Burning sensation, irritation, itching
Major Side Effects: Headache, pelvic cramps
Contraindications: No major contraindications
Warnings and Precautions: Liver or kidney diseases, pregnancy (see "Comments")
Interacts With: No significant drug interactions
Comments: Usually, one seven-day course of Monistat 7 antifungal agent therapy is sufficient, but it may be repeated for another seven days.

Monistat 7 antifungal agent is effective in the treatment of fungal infections in pregnant and nonpregnant women, as well as in women taking oral contraceptives. However, because small amounts of the drug may be absorbed through the vagina wall, Monistat 7 antifungal agent should not be used during the first three months of pregnancy.

See the chapter "The Right Way To Take Medications."

Use until the prescribed amount of medication is gone.

Call your doctor if you develop burning or itching.

Avoid sexual intercourse, or ask your partner to use a condom until treatment is complete to avoid reinfection.

Motrin anti-inflammatory

Manufacturer: The Upjohn Company
Generic Name: ibuprofen

Equivalent Products: None
Dosage Form: Tablets: 300 mg (white), 400 mg (orange)
Use: Reduction of pain and swelling due to arthritis; relief of mild pain
Minor Side Effects: Bloating, cramps, diarrhea, drowsiness, flatulence, headache, heartburn, nausea, ringing in the ears, vomiting
Major Side Effects: Blood in stools, depression, fluid retention, hearing loss, jaundice, palpitations, tremors, visual disturbances
Contraindications: Allergy to aspirin
Warnings and Precautions: Anemia, pregnancy, ulcers, heart disease, liver and kidney diseases
Interacts With: anticoagulants, aspirin, oral antidiabetics, phenytoin, sulfonamides
Comments: In numerous tests Motrin anti-inflammatory has been shown to be as effective as aspirin in the treatment of arthritis, but aspirin is still the drug of choice for the disease. Because of the high cost of Motrin anti-inflammatory, consult your doctor about prescribing proper doses of aspirin instead.

If you are allergic to aspirin, you may not be able to use Motrin anti-inflammatory.

Do not take aspirin while taking Motrin anti-inflammatory without first consulting your doctor.

You should note improvement in your condition soon after you start using Motrin anti-inflammatory; however, full benefit may not be obtained for as long as a month. It is important not to stop taking Motrin anti-inflammatory even though symptoms have diminished or disappeared.

Motrin anti-inflammatory is not a substitute for rest, physical therapy, or other measures recommended by your doctor to treat your condition.

Mycolog anti-infective and steroid hormone

Manufacturer: E.R. Squibb & Sons
Generic Name: gramicidin, neomycin sulfate, nystatin, triamcinolone acetonide
Equivalent Products: None
Dosage Forms: Cream; ointment
Use: Relief of skin inflammation associated with conditions such as dermatitis, eczema, or poison ivy
Minor Side Effects: Burning sensation, dryness, irritation, itching, rash
Major Side Effects: No major side effects
Contraindications: No absolute contraindications
Warnings and Precautions: Bacterial and viral infections of the skin, diseases that severely impair blood circulation, tuberculosis
Interacts With: No significant drug interactions
Comments: If the affected area is extremely dry or is scaling, the skin may be moistened before applying the medication by soaking in water or by applying water with a clean cloth. The ointment form is probably better for dry skin.

Do not use Mycolog anti-infective and steroid hormone with an occlusive wrap of transparent plastic film unless instructed to do so by your doctor. See the chapter "The Right Way To Take Medication."

Mycostatin antifungal agent

Manufacturer: E.R. Squibb & Sons
Generic Name: nystatin
Equivalent Products: Candex antifungal agent cream or lotion (Dome Laboratories); Korostatin antifungal agent vaginal tablets (Holland-Rantos Company, Inc.); Nilstat antifungal agent cream or lotion, vaginal tablets, oral tablets, oral suspension (Lederle Laboratories); nystatin (various manufacturers)
Dosage Forms: Cream; ointment; powder; oral suspension; oral tablets: 500,000 units (brown); vaginal tablets (yellow)
Use: Treatment of fungus infections
Minor Side Effects: Diarrhea, itching, nausea, rash, vomiting
Major Side Effects: No major side effects
Contraindications: Pregnancy
Warning and Precautions: Liver or kidney diseases
Interacts With: No significant drug interactions
Comments: If using Mycostatin antifungal agent powder for a foot infection, sprinkle the powder liberally into the shoes and socks.

Moist lesions or sores are best treated with dusting powder.

To treat an infection in the mouth, your doctor may prescribe Mycostatin antifungal agent oral suspension. If so, rinse the drug around in your mouth as long as possible before swallowing.

Mycostatin antifungal agent vaginal tablets should be inserted high into the vagina by means of the enclosed applicator. Do not douche while using Mycostatin antifungal agent. Use until your doctor tells you to stop.

See the chapter "The Right Way To Take Medications."

Use continuously, including during a menstrual period.

If you are using Mycostatin antifungal agent to treat a vaginal infection, avoid sexual intercourse or ask your partner to wear a condom until treatment is completed to avoid reinfection.

Naldecon adrenergic and antihistamine

Manufacturer: Bristol Laboratories
Generic Name: phenylpropanolamine hydrochloride, phenylephrine hydrochloride, phenyltoloxamine citrate, chlorpheniramine maleate
Equivalent Products: Col-Decon adrenergic and antihistamine (Columbia Medical Co.), Quadra-hist adrenergic and antihistamine (Henry Schein, Inc.)
Dosage Forms: Syrup (content per 5 ml): phenylpropanolamine hydrochloride, 20 mg; phenylephrine hydrochloride, 5 mg; phenyltoloxamine citrate, 7.5 mg; chlorpheniramine maleate, 2.5 mg. Tablets: phenylpropanolamine hydrochloride, 40 mg; phenylephrine hydrochloride, 10 mg; phenyltoloxamine citrate, 15 mg; chlorpheniramine maleate, 5 mg. Pediatric syrup (content per 5 ml), pediatric drops (content per 1 ml): phenylpropanolamine hydrochloride, 5 mg; phenylephrine hydrochloride, 1.25 mg; phenyltoloxamine citrate, 2 mg; chlorpheniramine maleate, 0.5 mg.
Use: Relief of upper respiratory tract infections, symptoms of hay fever or other allergies, sinusitis
Minor Side Effects: Diarrhea, dizziness, drowsiness, dry mouth, headache, heartburn, difficult urination, loss of appetite, nausea, rash, restlessness, vomiting, weakness, blurred vision, confusion, constipation, insomnia,

nasal congestion, palpitations, reduced sweating

Major Side Effects: Low blood pressure, severe abdominal pain, sore throat, high blood pressure, chest pain

Contraindications: Asthma, some glaucomas, certain ulcers, enlarged prostate, obstructed bladder, obstructed intestine, pregnancy, severe heart disease

Warnings and Precautions: Diabetes, high blood pressure, thyroid disease, liver and kidney diseases

Interacts With: guanethidine, monoamine oxidase inhibitors

Comments: Although Naldecon adrenergic and antihistamine is frequently prescribed for the prevention and treatment of the common cold, a government panel of experts has concluded that the product may not be effective for this use.

While taking Naldecon adrenergic and antihistamine, do not take any nonprescription item for cough, cold, or sinus problems without first checking with your doctor.

Naldecon adrenergic and antihistamine may cause dryness of the mouth. To reduce this feeling, chew gum or suck on a piece of hard candy.

Naldecon adrenergic and antihistamine reduces sweating; avoid excessive work or exercise in hot weather.

Naldecon adrenergic and antihistamine may cause drowsiness; to prevent oversedation, avoid the use of other sedative drugs or alcohol.

Products equivalent to Naldecon adrenergic and antihistamine are available. Consult your doctor and pharmacist.

Naldecon adrenergic and antihistamine tablets must be swallowed whole.

Naldecon adrenergic and antihistamine has sustained action; never take it more frequently than your doctor prescribes. A serious overdose may result.

Nalfon anti-inflammatory

Manufacturer: Dista Products Company

Generic Name: fenoprofen calcium

Equivalent Products: None

Dosage Forms: Capsules: 300 mg (yellow/ocher opaque pulvules); tablets: 600 mg (yellow)

Use: Relief of pain and swelling due to arthritis

Minor Side Effects: Bloating, cramps, diarrhea, flatulence, headache, heartburn, nausea, ringing in the ears, vomiting, drowsiness

Major Side Effects: Blood in stools, depression, fluid retention, hearing loss, jaundice, palpitations, tremors, visual disturbances

Contraindications: Allergy to aspirin

Warnings and Precautions: Anemia, pregnancy, ulcers, heart disease, liver and kidney diseases

Interacts With: anticoagulants, aspirin, oral antidiabetics, phenytoin, sulfonamides

Comments: In numerous tests, Nalfon anti-inflammatory has been shown to be as effective as aspirin in the treatment of arthritis, but aspirin is still the drug of choice for the disease. Because of the high cost of Nalfon anti-inflammatory, consult your doctor about prescribing proper doses of aspirin instead.

If you are allergic to aspirin, you may not be able to use Nalfon anti-inflammatory. Do not take aspirin while taking Nalfon anti-inflammatory without first consulting your doctor.

You should note improvement in your condition soon after you start using Nalfon anti-inflammatory; however, full benefit may not be obtained for as long as a month. It is important not to stop taking Nalfon anti-inflammatory even though symptoms have diminished or disappeared.

Nalfon anti-inflammatory is not a substitute for rest, physical therapy, or other measures recommended by your doctor to treat your condition.

Naprosyn anti-inflammatory

Manufacturer: Syntex Puerto Rico, Inc.
Generic Name: naproxen
Equivalent Products: None
Dosage Form: Tablets: 250 mg (yellow)
Use: Relief of pain and swelling due to arthritis
Minor Side Effects: Bloating, cramps, diarrhea, flatulence, headache, heartburn, nausea, ringing in the ears, vomiting, drowsiness
Major Side Effects: Blood in stools, depression, fluid retention, hearing loss, jaundice, palpitations, tremors, visual disturbances
Contraindications: Allergy to aspirin
Warnings and Precautions: Anemia, pregnancy, ulcers, heart disease, liver and kidney diseases
Interacts With: anticoagulants, aspirin, oral antidiabetics, phenytoin, sulfonamides
Comments: In numerous tests, Naprosyn anti-inflammatory has been shown to be as effective as aspirin in the treatment of arthritis, but aspirin is still the drug of choice for the disease. Because of the high cost of Naprosyn anti-inflammatory, consult your doctor about prescribing proper doses of aspirin instead.

If you are allergic to aspirin, you may not be able to use Naprosyn anti-inflammatory without first consulting your doctor.

You should note improvement in your condition soon after you start using Naprosyn anti-inflammatory; however, full benefit may not be obtained for as long as a month. It is important not to stop taking Naprosyn anti-inflammatory even though symptoms have diminished or disappeared.

Naprosyn anti-inflammatory is not a substitute for rest, physical therapy, or other measures recommended by your doctor to treat your condition.

Nebralin sedative and hypnotic (Dorsey Laboratories), see Nembutal sedative and hypnotic.

Nembutal sedative and hypnotic

Manufacturer: Abbott Laboratories
Generic Name: pentobarbital

Equivalent Products: Nebralin sedative and hypnotic (Dorsey Laboratories); pentobarbital sedative and hypnotic (various manufacturers)
Dosage Form: Capsules: 30 mg (yellow), 50 mg (white/orange), 100 mg (yellow)
Use: Relief of anxiety or tension, sleeping aid
Minor Side Effects: Drowsiness, nausea, vomiting
Major Side Effects: Difficult breathing, cold and clammy skin, rash, or other allergic reactions
Contraindications: Porphyria, history of drug abuse, pregnancy
Warnings and Precautions: Liver and kidney diseases
Interacts With: alcohol, central nervous system depressants, griseofulvin, oral anticoagulants, phenytoin, steroids, sulfonamides, tetracyclines, tricyclic antidepressants
Comments: Drugs used for sleep should be taken one-half to one hour before bedtime.

While taking Nembutal sedative and hypnotic, avoid the use of other sedative drugs or alcohol.

Nembutal sedative and hypnotic has abuse potential and must be used with caution. Tolerance may develop quickly; *do not* increase the dose of this drug without first consulting your doctor.

If you are also taking an anticoagulant ("blood thinner"), remind your doctor.

Products equivalent to Nembutal sedative and hypnotic are available and vary widely in cost. Ask your doctor to prescribe a generic preparation; then ask your pharmacist to fill it with the least expensive brand.

Butisol Sodium sedative and hypnotic (sodium butabarbital), manufactured by McNeil Laboratories, and Seconal Sodium sedative and hypnotic (secobarbital sodium), manufactured by Eli Lilly and Company, have identical uses, side effects, contraindications, warning and precautions, and comments as Nembutal sedative and hypnotic.

Neofed adrenergic (The Vale Chemical Co., Inc.), see Sudafed adrenergic.

Neosporin antibiotic ophthalmic solution

Manufacturer: Burroughs Wellcome Co.
Generic Name: gramicidin, neomycin sulfate, polymyxin B sulfate
Equivalent Products: None
Dosage Form: Drops
Use: Short-term treatment of bacterial infections of the eye
Minor Side Effects: Burning, stinging, blurred vision
Major Side Effects: Worsening of the condition
Contraindications: Known sensitivity to any of the drug components
Warnings and Precautions: No major warnings or precautions
Interacts With: No significant drug interactions
Comments: Like other eyedrops, Neosporin antibiotic ophthalmic solution may cause some clouding or blurring of vision. This side effect will go away quickly.

Be careful about the contamination of solutions used for the eyes. See the chapter "The Right Way To Take Medications."

Niac vitamin supplement (O'Neal, Jones & Feldman), see nicotinic acid.

Niacalex vitamin supplement (Merrell-National Laboratories), see nicotinic acid.

NICL vitamin supplement (Saron Pharmaceutical Corp.), see nicotinic acid.

Nicobid vitamin supplement (Armour Pharmaceutical Company), see nicotinic acid.

Nicocap vitamin supplement (ICN Pharmaceuticals, Inc.), see nicotinic acid.

Nico-400 Plateau Caps vitamin supplement (Marion Laboratories, Inc.), see nicotinic acid.

Nico-Span vitamin supplement (Key Pharmaceuticals, Inc.), see nicotinic acid.

nicotinic acid vitamin supplement

Nicotinic acid is a generic drug.

Equivalent Products: nicotinic acid (niacin) (various manufacturers); Diacin vitamin supplement (Danal Laboratories, Inc.); Niac vitamin supplement (O'Neal, Jones & Feldman); SK-Niacin vitamin supplement (Smith Kline & French Laboratories); Nicalex vitamin supplement (Merrell-National Laboratories); NICL vitamin supplement (Saron Pharmacal Corp.); Nicobid vitamin supplement (Armour Pharmaceutical Company); Nicocap vitamin supplement (ICN Pharmaceuticals, Inc.); Nico-400 Plateau Caps vitamin supplement (Marion Laboratories, Inc.); nico-Span vitamin supplement (Key Pharmaceuticals, Inc.); Tega-Span vitamin supplement (Ortega Pharmaceutical Co.); Wampocap vitamin supplement (Wallace Laboratories)

Dosage Forms: Nicotinic acid tablets: 25 mg, 50 mg, 100 mg; time-release capsules: 125 mg, 200 mg, 250 mg, 300 mg, 400 mg, 500 mg; capsules: 500 mg (various colors); liquid (content per 5 ml): 50 mg

Use: To correct niacin deficiency, lower blood cholesterol levels, promote blood flow to the brain and extremities

Minor Side Effects: Dizziness, dryness of skin, flushing and warmth, headache, itching, nausea, palpitations, tingling in fingers or toes, vomiting

Major Side Effects: Activation of peptic ulcers

Contraindications: Hemorrhage, peptic ulcer, low blood pressure, severe liver disease

Warnings and Precautions: Diabetes, gall bladder disease, glaucoma, gout, liver and kidney diseases, pregnancy

Interacts With: No significant drug interactions

Comments: Nicotinic acid is also known as vitamin B_3 or niacin.

The flushing, warmth, and dizziness experienced usually go away after several days of continuous therapy.

If dizziness or light-headedness occurs when you stand up, place your legs on the floor and "pump" the muscles for a few moments before rising.

Nicotinic acid products vary widely in cost. Ask your pharmacist to fill your prescription with the least expensive brand.

Nilstat antifungal agent (Lederle Laboratories), see Mycostatin antifungal agent

Nitro-Bid Plateau Caps antianginal

Manufacturer: Marion Laboratories, Inc.
Generic Name: nitroglycerin
Equivalent Products: Cardabid antianginal (Saron Pharmacal Corp.); Nitrobon antianginal (Forest Laboratories, Inc.); Nitrodyl antianginal (Bock Pharmacal Company); Nitrospan antianginal, (USV [P.R.] Development Corp.)
Dosage Form: Time-release capsules: 2.5 mg (violet/white with white beads), 6.5 mg (black/orange with white beads)
Use: Prevention of chest pain (angina) due to heart disease; possibly effective for management of attacks of angina
Minor Side Effects: Dizziness, headache, flushing of face
Major Side Effects: Palpitations
Contraindications: Low blood pressure, recent heart attack, severe anemia, glaucoma
Warnings and Precautions: Pregnancy
Interacts With: alcohol, other vasodilators
Comments: Nitro-Bid Plateau Caps antianginal capsules *must* be swallowed.
Nitro-Bid Plateau Caps antianginal probably will not continue to relieve chest pain after it has been used for one to three months because tolerance to nitroglycerin develops quickly. Discuss the merits of the drug with your doctor before accepting a prescription.
Side effects generally disappear after two to three weeks of continued therapy.
Products equivalent to Nitro-Bid Plateau Caps antianginal are available and vary widely in cost. Ask your doctor to prescribe a generic preparation; then ask your pharmacist to fill it with the least expensive brand.

Nitrobon antianginal (Forest Laboratories, Inc.), see Nitro-Bid Plateau Caps antianginal.

Nitrodyl antianginal (Bock Pharmacal Company), see Nitro-Bid Plateau Caps antianginal.

Nitrospan antianginal (USV [P.R.] Development Corp.) see Nitro-Bid Plateau Caps antianginal.

Nitrostat antianginal

Manufacturer: Parke, Davis & Company
Generic Name: nitroglycerin
Equivalent Products: nitroglycerin (various manufacturers)
Dosage Form: Sublingual tablets: 0.15 mg, 0.3 mg, 0.4 mg, 0.6 mg (all are white)
Use: Relief of chest pain (angina) due to heart disease
Minor Side Effects: Dizziness, flushing of face, headache
Major Side Effects: Palpitations, fainting
Contraindications: Head injuries, recent heart attack, stroke
Warnings and Precautions: Liver or kidney disease, pregnancy

Interacts With: alcohol, other vasodilators

Comments: Frequently, chest pain will be relieved in two to five minutes simply by sitting down. When you have chest pain, sit down for a few minutes.

When you take nitroglycerin, sit down, lower your head, and breathe deeply.

Do not swallow Nitrostat antianginal tablets; they must be placed under the tongue. Do not drink water or swallow for five minutes after taking Nitrostat antianginal.

If you require more nitroglycerin tablets than usual to relieve chest pain, contact your doctor. You may have developed a tolerance to the drug, or the nitroglycerin may not be working effectively because of interference with other medication to prevent chest pain.

If your chest pain is not relieved by nitroglycerin, if pain arises from a different location or differs in severity, call your doctor immediately.

Nitroglycerin tablets must be stored in a tightly capped, glass container. Never store or carry the tablets in a metal box or plastic vial or in the refrigerator. If you do not use 100 tablets within three months, ask your pharmacist for the smaller bottle which contains 25 tablets.

Side effects of nitroglycerin therapy usually disappear within about two weeks.

Before using a sublingual tablet to relieve chest pain, be certain pain arises from the heart and is not due to a muscle spasm or indigestion.

Norgesic analgesic

Manufacturer: Riker Laboratories, Inc.

Generic Name: aspirin, phenacetin, caffeine, orphenadrine citrate

Equivalent Products: None

Dosage Forms: Tablets: aspirin, 225 mg; caffeine, 30 mg; orphenadrine citrate, 25 mg; phenacetin, 160 mg (tri-layered green, white, yellow). Norgesic Forte analgesic tablets: aspirin, 450 mg; caffeine, 60 mg; orphenadrine citrate, 50 mg; phenacetin, 320 mg (tri-layered, elongated green, white, and yellow)

Use: Relief of pain in muscles or joints

Minor Side Effects: Blurred vision, diarrhea, dilation of pupils, drowsiness, dry mouth, headache, nausea, rash, vomiting, weakness, ringing in the ears

Major Side Effects: Palpitations, rapid heartbeat, urinary retention

Contraindications: Enlarged prostate, glaucoma, obstructed bladder or bowel, pregnancy, myasthenia gravis, bleeding ulcers, severe kidney disease

Warnings and Precautions: Liver, kidney, or heart diseases, blood coagulation problems

Interacts With: alcohol, ammonium chloride, anticoagulants, central nervous system depressants, methotrexate, oral antidiabetics, probenecid, steroids, sulfinpyrazone, vitamin C

Comments: Norgesic analgesic is not a substitute for rest, physical therapy, or other measures recommended by your doctor to treat your condition.

Take Norgesic analgesic with food or milk.

Norgesic analgesic interacts with sedative drugs and alcohol. Do not use them while taking this product.

If you are also taking an anticoagulant ("blood thinner"), remind your doctor.

If you hear buzzing or ringing, if your ears feel strange, or if your stomach hurts, your dosage may need adjustment. Call your doctor.

Norinyl oral contraceptive (Syntex Laboratories, Inc.), see oral contraceptives.

Norlestrin oral contraceptive (Parke, Davis & Company), see oral contraceptives.

Norpace antiarrhythmic

Manufacturer: Searle Laboratories
Generic Name: disopyramide phosphate
Equivalent Products: None
Dosage Form: Capsules: 100 mg (white/orange); 150 mg (brown/orange)
Use: Treatment of some heart arrhythmias
Minor Side Effects: Difficult urination; dry mouth; blurred vision; dry nose, eyes, throat; nausea; pain; bleeding; gas; dizziness; muscle weakness; headache; loss of appetite; diarrhea; vomiting; rash; nervousness
Major Side Effects: Low blood pressure, edema and weight gain, shortness of breath, fainting, chest pain, low blood sugar, psychosis
Contraindications: Cardiogenic shock, some types of heart disease
Warnings and Precautions: Certain kinds of heart disease, glaucoma, urinary retention, liver and kidney disease, hypokalemia (low blood potassium), pregnancy
Interacts With: No known drug interactions
Comments: Norpace antiarrhythmic is similar in action to procainamide and to quinidine sulfate.
   While taking Norpace antiarrhythmic, do not take any nonprescription item for cough, cold, or sinus problems without first checking with your doctor.

Novahistine DH expectorant

Manufacturer: Dow Pharmaceuticals
Generic Name: codeine phosphate, phenylpropanolamine hydrochloride, chlorpheniramine maleate
Equivalent Products: Midahist DH expectorant (Vangard Laboratories)
Dosage Form: Liquid (content per 15 ml): codeine phosphate, 10 mg; phenylpropanolamine hydrochloride, 18.75 mg; chlorpheniramine maleate, 2 mg
Use: Relief of symptoms of common cold or allergy
Minor Side Effects: Diarrhea, dizziness, drowsiness, dry mouth, headache, heartburn, difficult urination, loss of appetite, nausea, rash, restlessness, vomiting, weakness, blurred vision, confusion, constipation, insomnia, nasal congestion, palpitations, reduced sweating
Major Side Effects: Low blood pressure, severe abdominal pain, sore throat, high blood pressure, chest pain
Contraindications: Asthma, some glaucomas, certain ulcers, enlarged prostate, obstructed bladder, obstructed intestine, pregnancy, severe heart disease
Warnings and Precautions: Diabetes, high blood pressure, thyroid disease, liver and kidney diseases
Interacts With: guanethidine, monoamine oxidase inhibitors, phenothiazines
Comments: Products containing narcotics (e.g., codeine) are usually not used

for more than seven to 10 days.

While taking Novahistine DH expectorant, do not take any nonprescription item for cough, cold, or sinus problems without first checking with your doctor.

Novahistine DH expectorant may cause drowsiness; to prevent oversedation, avoid the use of other sedative drugs or alcohol.

Novahistine DH expectorant has the potential for abuse and must be used with caution. Tolerance may develop quickly; *do not* increase the dose of this drug without first consulting your doctor.

Although Novahistine DH expectorant is frequently prescribed for the prevention and treatment of the common cold, a government panel of experts has concluded that the product may not be effective for this use.

Novahistine DH expectorant may cause dryness of the mouth. To reduce this feeling, chew gum or suck on a piece of hard candy.

Novahistine DH expectorant reduces sweating; avoid excessive work or exercise in hot weather.

Products equivalent to Novahistine DH expectorant are available and vary widely in cost. Ask your doctor to prescribe a generic preparation, and have your pharmacist fill your prescription with the least expensive brand.

Novahistine elixir adrenergic and antihistamine

Manufacturer: Dow Pharmaceuticals
Generic Name: chlorpheniramine maleate, phenylpropanolamine hydrochloride
Equivalent Products: Ornade 2 Liquid for Children adrenergic and antihistamine (Smith Kline & French Laboratories); Spen-Histine elixir adrenergic and antihistamine (Spencer-Mead Inc.)
Dosage Form: Liquid (content per 5 ml): chlorpheniramine maleate, 2 mg; phenylpropanolamine hydrochloride, 18.75 mg
Use: Relief of hay fever symptoms, respiratory or middle ear congestion
Minor Side Effects: Diarrhea, dizziness, drowsiness, dry mouth, headache, heartburn, difficult urination, loss of appetite, nausea, rash, restlessness, vomiting, weakness, blurred vision, confusion, constipation, insomnia, nasal congestion, palpitations, reduced sweating
Major Side Effects: Low blood pressure, severe abdominal pain, sore throat, high blood pressure, chest pain
Contraindications: Asthma, some glaucomas, certain ulcers, enlarged prostate, obstructed bladder, obstructed intestine, pregnancy, severe heart disease
Warnings and Precautions: Diabetes, high blood pressure, thyroid disease, liver and kidney diseases
Interacts With: guanethidine, monoamine oxidase inhibitors
Comments: Although Novahistine elixir adrenergic and antihistamine is frequently prescribed for the prevention and treatment of the common cold, a government panel of experts has concluded that the product may not be effective for this use.

While taking Novahistine elixir adrenergic and antihistamine do not take any nonprescription item for cough, cold, or sinus problems without first checking with your doctor.

Novahistine elixir adrenergic and antihistamine may cause dryness of the mouth. To reduce this feeling, chew gum or suck on a piece of hard candy.

Novahistine elixir adrenergic and antihistamine reduces sweating; avoid excessive work or exercise in hot weather.

Novahistine elixir adrenergic and antihistamine may cause drowsiness; to prevent oversedation, avoid the use of other sedative drugs or alcohol.

Products equivalent to Novahistine elixir adrenergic and antihistamine are available and vary widely in cost. Ask your doctor to prescribe a generic preparation and have your pharmacist fill your prescription with the least expensive brand.

Novahistine elixir adrenergic and antihistamine and products equivalent to it may be purchased without a prescription.

Novahistine expectorant

Manufacturer: Dow Pharmaceuticals

Generic Name: codeine phosphate, guaifenesin, phenylpropanolamine hydrochloride

Equivalent Products: Midahist expectorant (Vangard Laboratories)

Dosage Form: Liquid (content per 5 ml): codeine phosphate, 10 mg; guaifenesin, 100 mg; phenylpropanolamine hydrochloride, 18.75 mg

Use: Relief of symptoms of allergy and the common cold

Minor Side Effects: Diarrhea, dizziness, drowsiness, dry mouth, headache, heartburn, difficult urination, loss of appetite, nausea, rash, restlessness, vomiting, weakness, blurred vision, confusion, constipation, insomnia, nasal congestion, palpitations, reduced sweating

Major Side Effects: Low blood pressure, severe abdominal pain, sore throat, high blood pressure, chest pain

Contraindications: Asthma, some glaucomas, certain ulcers, enlarged prostate, obstructed bladder, obstructed intestine, pregnancy, severe heart disease

Warnings and Precautions: Diabetes, high blood pressure, thyroid disease, liver and kidney diseases, potential for abuse

Interacts With: guanethidine, monoamine oxidase inhibitors, phenothiazines

Comments: Novahistine expectorant and products equivalent to it may be purchased without a prescription.

If you need an expectorant, you need more moisture in your environment. Drink nine to 10 glasses of water each day. The use of a vaporizer or humidifier may also be beneficial. Consult your doctor.

Products containing narcotics (e.g., codeine) are usually not used for more than seven to 10 days.

Novahistine expectorant may cause drowsiness; to prevent oversedation, avoid the use of other sedative drugs or alcohol.

While taking Novahistine expectorant, do not take any nonprescription item for cough, cold, or sinus problems without first checking with your doctor.

Novahistine expectorant has the potential for abuse and must be used with caution. Tolerance may develop quickly; *do not* increase the dose of this drug without first consulting your doctor.

Although Novahistine expectorant is frequently prescribed for the prevention and treatment of the common cold, a government panel of experts has concluded that the product may not be effective for this use.

Novahistine expectorant may cause dryness of the mouth. To reduce this feeling, chew gum or suck on a piece of hard candy.

Novahistine expectorant reduces sweating; avoid excessive work or exercise in hot weather.

Products equivalent to Novahistine expectorant are available and vary widely in cost. Ask your doctor to prescribe a generic preparation, and have your pharmacist fill your prescription with the least expensive brand.

o.b.c.t. adrenergic (Pharmics, Inc.), see Tenuate adrenergic

Omnipen antibiotic (Wyeth Laboratories), see ampicillin antibiotic.

Oral Contraceptives

Oral contraceptives is a descriptive term.

Examples: Brevicon oral contraceptive, Norinyl oral contraceptive (Syntex Laboratories, Inc.); Demulen oral contraceptive, Enovid oral contraceptive, Ovulen oral contraceptive (Searle Laboratories); Loestrin oral contraceptive, Norlestrin oral contraceptive (Parke, Davis & Company); Lo/Ovral oral contraceptive, Ovral oral contraceptive (Wyeth Laboratories); Modicon oral contraceptive, Ortho-Novum oral contraceptive (Ortho Pharmaceutical Corporation); Ovcon oral contraceptive (Mead Johnson Pharmaceutical Division); Zorane oral contraceptive (Lederle Laboratories)

Dosage Forms: Tablets in packages. Some contain 20 or 21 tablets; others 28. When 28 are present, 7 are blank or contain iron (see "Comments").

Use: Birth control

Minor Side Effects: Abdominal cramps, diarrhea, dizziness, nausea, nervousness, vomiting

Major Side Effects: Blood clots, breakthrough bleeding (spotting), cancer, changes in menstrual flow, depression, elevated blood sugar, enlarged or tender breasts, eye damage, fluid retention, gall bladder disease, high blood pressure, reduced ability to conceive after the drug is stopped, increase or decrease in hair growth, jaundice, migraine, painful menstruation, rash, stroke, weight changes, skin color changes

Contraindications: Cancer (known or suspected), certain types of heart disease, history of blood disease or clots, pregnancy, previous stroke, vaginal bleeding, liver disease

Warnings and Precautions: Age (women over age 40), any eye ailment, bleeding abnormalities, depression, diabetes, gall bladder disease, high blood pressure, migraine

Interacts With: oral anticoagulants, steroids, rifampin

Comments: Oral contraceptives currently are considered the most effective available method of birth control. The table below shows various methods of birth control and their effectiveness.

Birth Control Method	Effectiveness*
Oral contraceptive	less than 1
Intrauterine device (IUD)	up to 6
Diaphragm	up to 20
Aerosol foam	up to 29
Condom	up to 36
Gel or cream	up to 36
Rhythm	up to 47

*Pregnancies per each 100 women.

Take an oral contraceptive at the same time every day to get into the habit of taking the pills. If you skip one day, take a tablet for the day you missed as soon as you think of it and another tablet at the regular time.

Missing a day increases your chances of pregnancy; use other methods of contraception for the rest of the cycle and continue taking the tablets.

If you do not start to menstruate on schedule at the end of the pill cycle, begin the next cycle of pills at the prescribed time, anyway. Many women taking oral contraceptives have irregular menstruation. Do not be alarmed, but consult your doctor.

Stop taking oral contraceptive tablets at least three months before you wish to become pregnant. Use another type of contraceptive during this three-month period.

Some oral contraceptive packets contain 28 tablets rather than the usual 20 or 21 tablets. The 28-tablet packets contain seven placebos (sugar pills) or iron tablets. The placebos help you remember to take a tablet each day even while you are menstruating, and the iron tablets help replace the iron that is lost in menstruation.

Nausea is common, especially during the first two or three months, but may be prevented by taking the tablets at bedtime. If nausea persists for more than three months, consult your doctor.

Although many brands of oral contraceptives are available, most differ in only minor ways, and you may have to try several brands before you find the product that is ideal for you.

Your pharmacist will give you a booklet explaining birth control pills with every prescription. Read this booklet carefully. It contains exact directions on how to use the medication correctly.

If you use oral contraceptives, you should not smoke cigarettes; taking oral contraceptives and smoking may cause heart disease.

You should visit your doctor for a checkup at least twice a year while you are taking oral contraceptives.

Warning: If you have a family history of cancer, you should inform your doctor of it before taking oral contraceptives.

Orasone steroid hormone (Rowell Laboratories, Inc.), see prednisone steroid hormone.

Orinase oral antidiabetic

Manufacturer: The Upjohn Company
Generic Name: tolbutamide
Equivalent Products: tolbutamide (various manufacturers)
Dosage Form: Tablets: 500 mg (white)
Use: Treatment of diabetes mellitus
Minor Side Effects: Dizziness, fatigue, headache, nausea, rash, vomiting, weakness, diarrhea, loss of appetite
Major Side Effects: Low blood sugar, jaundice, sore throat
Contraindications: Acidosis, age (see "Comments"), coma, ketosis, severe infection, severe trauma, upcoming surgery, severe liver and kidney diseases, pregnancy
Warnings and Precautions: Liver or kidney diseases
Interacts With: alcohol, anabolic steroids, anticoagulants, aspirin, chloramphe-

nicol, guanethidine, propranolol, monoamine oxidase inhibitors, phenylbutazone, steroids, sulfonamides, tetracycline, thiazide diuretics, thyroid hormones

Comments: Oral antidiabetic drugs are not effective in treating diabetes in
children under age 12.

Studies have shown that a good diet and exercise program may be just as
effective as oral antidiabetic drugs. However, these drugs allow diabetics
more leeway in their lifestyle. Persons taking these drugs should carefully
watch their diet and exercise program.

Take Orinase oral antidiabetic at the same time each day.

Ask your doctor how to recognize the first signs of low blood sugar.

Products equivalent to Orinase oral antidiabetic are available and vary
widely in cost. Ask your doctor to prescribe a generic preparation; then ask
your pharmacist to fill it with the least expensive brand.

During the first six weeks of Orinase oral antidiabetic therapy, visit your
doctor at least once a week.

Check your urine for sugar and ketone at least three times a day.

A patient taking Orinase oral antidiabetic will have to be switched to insulin
therapy if complications develop (e.g., ketoacidosis; severe trauma; severe
infection; diarrhea; nausea or vomiting; or the need for major surgery).

Ornade antihistamine, anticholinergic, and adrenergic

Manufacturer: Smith Kline & French Laboratories
Generic Name: chlorpheniramine maleate, isopropamide iodide, phenylpropanolamine hydrochloride
Equivalent Products: Allernade cold remedy (Rugby Laboratories), Capade cold
remedy (Spencer-Mead Inc.)
Dosage Form: Capsules: chlorpheniramine maleate, 8 mg; isopropamide
iodide, 2.5 mg; phenylpropanolamine hydrochloride, 50 mg (blue/clear with
red and white beads)
Use: Relief of upper respiratory tract congestion
Minor Side Effects: Diarrhea, dizziness, drowsiness, dry mouth, headache,
heartburn, difficult urination, loss of appetite, nausea, rash, restlessness,
vomiting, weakness, blurred vision, confusion, constipation, insomnia,
nasal congestion, palpitations, reduced sweating
Major Side Effects: Low blood pressure, severe abdominal pain, sore throat,
high blood pressure, chest pain
Contraindications: Asthma, some glaucomas, certain ulcers, enlarged prostate, obstructed bladder, obstructed intestine, pregnancy, heart disease
Warnings and Precautions: Diabetes, high blood pressure, thyroid disease,
liver and kidney diseases
Interacts With: monoamine oxidase inhibitors, guanethidine
Comments: Although Ornade antihistamine, anticholinergic, and adrenergic is
frequently prescribed for the prevention and treatment of the common cold, a
government panel of experts has concluded that the product may not be
effective for this use.

Ornade antihistamine, anticholinergic, and adrenergic has sustained
action; never take it more frequently than your doctor prescribes. A
serious overdose may result.

Ornade antihistamine, anticholinergic, and adrenergic may cause drowsiness; to prevent oversedation, avoid the use of other sedative drugs or alcohol.

Ornade antihistamine, anticholinergic, and adrenergic may cause dryness of the mouth. To reduce this feeling, chew gum or suck on a piece of hard candy.

Ornade antihistamine, anticholinergic, and adrenergic reduces sweating; avoid excessive work or exercise in hot weather.

While taking Ornade antihistamine, anticholinergic, and adrenergic, do not take any nonprescription item for cough, cold, or sinus problems without first checking with your doctor.

If you are having a test for thyroid function, tell your doctor you are taking Ornade antihistamine, anticholinergic, and adrenergic because the drug may influence the results of the test.

Ornade 2 Liquid for Children adrenergic and antihistamine (Smith Kline & French Laboratories), see Novahistine Elixir adrenergic and antihistamine.

Ortho-Novum oral contraceptive (Ortho Pharmaceutical Corporation), see oral contraceptives.

Otobione otic suspension (Schering Corporation), see Cortisporin otic sterile solution.

Ovcon oral contraceptive (Mead Johnson Pharmaceutical Division), see oral contraceptives.

Ovest estrogen hormone (Trimen Laboratories), see Premarin estrogen hormone.

Ovral oral contraceptive (Wyeth Laboratories), see oral contraceptives.

Ovulen oral contraceptive (Searle Laboratories), see oral contraceptives.

Oxalid anti-inflammatory (USV [P.R.] Development Corp.), see Butazolidin anti-inflammatory.

Oxlopar antibiotic (Parke, Davis & Company), see Terramycin antibiotic.

Oxybiotic antibiotic (Star Pharmaceuticals, Inc.), see Terramycin antibiotic.

Oxy-Tetrachel antibiotic (Rachelle Laboratories, Inc.), see Terramycin antibiotic.

Palopause estrogen hormone (Palmedico, Inc.), see Premarin estrogen hormone.

Panmycin antibiotic (The Upjohn Company), see tetracycline hydrochloride antibiotic.

Panwarfin anticoagulant (Abbott Laboratories), see Coumadin anticoagulant.

Paracort steroid hormone (Parke, Davis & Company), see prednisone steroid hormone.

Parafon Forte analgesic

Manufacturer: McNeil Laboratories
Generic Name: chlorzoxazone, acetaminophen
Equivalent Products: None
Dosage Form: Tablets: chlorzoxazone, 250 mg; acetaminophen, 300 mg (green)
Use: Relief of pain from strained muscles
Minor Side Effects: Change in urine color, diarrhea, dizziness, drowsiness, fatigue, light-headedness, nausea, overstimulation, rash
Major Side Effects: Jaundice
Contraindications: Pregnancy
Warnings and Precautions: Liver or kidney diseases
Interacts With: No significant drug interactions
Comments: Parafon Forte analgesic is not a substitute for rest, physical therapy, or other measures recommended by your doctor to treat your condition.
  Parafon Forte analgesic may cause drowsiness; to prevent oversedation, avoid the use of other sedative drugs or alcohol.

Parest sedative and hypnotic (Parke, Davis & Company), see Quaalude sedative and hypnotic.

Pargesic Compound-65 analgesic (Ulmer Pharmacal Company), see Darvon Compound-65 analgesic.

Pargesic-65 analgesic (Parmed Pharmaceuticals Inc.), see Darvon analgesic.

Pavabid Plateau Caps smooth muscle relaxant

Manufacturer: Marion Laboratories, Inc.
Generic Name: papaverine hydrochloride
Equivalent Products: Cerebid smooth muscle relaxant (Saron Pharmacal Corp.); Cerespan smooth muscle relaxant (USV [P.R.] Development Corp.); Pavased smooth muscle relaxant (Mallard Incorporated); Dylate smooth muscle relaxant (Paul B. Elder Company); papaverine hydrochloride (various manufacturers)
Dosage Forms: Pavabid Plateau Caps (time-release capsules): 150 mg (black/white); capsulets: 300 mg (orange)
Use: To promote blood flow to the heart muscle and brain
Minor Side Effects: Abdominal distress, constipation, diarrhea, dizziness, drowsiness, fatigue, headache, loss of appetite, nausea, rash, sweating
Major Side Effects: No major side effects

Contraindications: Pregnancy
Warnings and Precautions: Glaucoma, liver and kidney diseases
Interacts With: No significant drug interactions
Comments: Pavabid Plateau Caps smooth muscle relaxant increases the flow of blood to the heart muscle and brain, but this activity has not been shown to alleviate the aftereffects of a stroke or chest pain. Discuss the merits of Pavabid Plateau Caps smooth muscle relaxant with your doctor before accepting a prescription. Ask him to prescribe a generic preparation; then ask your pharmacist to fill it with the least expensive brand.

Pavabid Plateau Caps smooth muscle relaxant may cause drowsiness; to prevent oversedation, avoid the use of other sedative drugs or alcohol.

While taking Pavabid Plateau Caps smooth muscle relaxant, do not take any nonprescription item for cough, cold, or sinus problems without first checking with your doctor.

Pavased smooth muscle relaxant (Mallard Incorporated), see Pavabid Plateau Caps smooth muscle relaxant.

PBR/12 sedative and hypnotic (Scott-Alison Pharmaceuticals, Inc.), see phenobarbital sedative and hypnotic.

penicillin G antibiotic

Penicillin G is a generic drug.
Equivalent Products: Pentids antibiotic (E.R. Squibb & Sons); penicillin G (various manufacturers)
Dosage Forms: Liquid (content per 5 ml): 125 mg, 250 mg; Pentids tablets: 125 mg, 250 mg (off-white), 500 mg (yellow)
Use: Treatment of a wide variety of bacterial infections
Minor Side Effects: Diarrhea, nausea, vomiting
Major Side Effects: Superinfection, vaginal and rectal itching, cough, severe diarrhea, irritation of the mouth, "black tongue," rash
Contraindications: Known allergy to penicillin G or to ampicillin
Warnings and Precautions: Asthma, pregnancy, liver and kidney diseases
Interacts With: chloramphenicol, erythromycin, tetracycline
Comments: A prescription for penicillin G antibiotic may indicate drug strength in units: 200,000 unit tablets, for example. 200,000 units are equal to 125 mg; 400,000 units are equal to 250 mg; and 800,000 units are equal to 500 mg

The pharmacology and toxicology of the antibiotics penicillin and ampicillin are almost identical. Severe allergy (shown by a drop in blood pressure or breathing difficulties) has been reported, but it does *not* usually occur in patients taking the oral forms of the drug (tablets or liquids).

Penicillin G antibiotic, for all practical purposes, has the same antibacterial activity as penicillin potassium phenoxymethyl antibiotic. However, unlike the latter, penicillin G antibiotic is readily destroyed by acids in the stomach; do not drink orange juice or other beverages with high acidic content when you take this medication.

Take penicillin G antibiotic on an empty stomach (one hour before or two hours after a meal).

Penicillin G antibiotic should be taken for at least 10 full days, even if symptoms have disappeared.

Penicillin G antibiotic may cause allergic reactions and should not be taken by persons with asthma, severe hay fever, or other allergies unless the doctor is aware of these conditions.

The liquid form of penicillin G antibiotic should be stored in the refrigerator.

Brands of penicillin G antibiotic vary widely in cost. Ask your pharmacist to fill your prescription with the least expensive brand.

Diabetics using Clinitest urine test may get a false high reading of sugar. Change to Clinistix or Tes-Tape urine tests to avoid this problem.

penicillin potassium phenoxymethyl antibiotic

Penicillin potassium phenoxymethyl is a generic drug.

Equivalent Products: penicillin potassium phenoxymethyl (various manufacturers); Pen-Vee K antibiotic (Wyeth Laboratories)

Dosage Forms: Liquid (content per 5 ml): 125 mg, 250 mg; Pen-Vee K tablets: 125 mg, 250 mg, 500 mg (white)

Use: Treatment of a wide variety of bacterial infections

Minor Side Effects: Diarrhea, nausea, vomiting

Major Side Effects: Superinfection, vaginal and rectal itching, cough, severe diarrhea, irritation of the mouth, "black tongue," rash

Contraindications: Known allergy to penicillin or ampicillin

Warnings and Precautions: Asthma, pregnancy, liver and kidney diseases, significant allergies

Interacts With: chloramphenicol, erythromycin, tetracycline

Comments: Penicillin potassium phenoxymethyl antibiotic may be written as penicillin V—an older name for phenoxymethyl penicillin.

A prescription for penicillin potassium phenoxymethyl antibiotic may indicate drug strength in units: 200,000 unit tablets, for example, 200,000 units are equal to 125 mg; 400,000 units are equal to 250 mg; 800,000 units are equal to 500 mg.

The pharmacology and toxicology of the antibiotics penicillin and ampicillin are almost identical. Severe allergy (shown by a drop in blood pressure or breathing difficulties) has been reported, but it does *not* usually occur in patients taking the oral forms (tablets or liquids).

Penicillin potassium phenoxymethyl antibiotic has approximately the same antibacterial activity as the less expensive product penicillin G antibiotic (e.g., Pentids tablets). However, penicillin potassium phenoxymethyl antibiotic is more stable in the stomach and is worth the extra cost.

Take penicillin potassium phenoxymethyl antibiotic on an empty stomach (one hour before or two hours after a meal).

Penicillin potassium phenoxymethyl antibiotic should be taken for at least 10 full days, even if symptoms have disappeared.

Penicillin potassium phenoxymethyl antibiotic may cause allergic reaction and should not be taken by persons with asthma, severe hay fever, or other allergies unless the doctor is aware of these conditions.

Diabetics using Clinitest urine test may get a false high reading of sugar. Change to Clinistix or Tes-Tape urine tests to avoid this problem.

The liquid form of penicillin potassium phenoxymethyl antibiotic should be stored in the refrigerator.

Brands of penicillin potassium phenoxymethyl antibiotic vary in cost. Ask your pharmacist to fill your prescription with the least expensive brand.

Pentazine expectorant with Codeine (Century Pharmaceuticals, Inc.), see Phenergan expectorant with Codeine.

Pentids antibiotic (E.R. Squibb & Sons), see penicillin G antibiotic.

Pen-Vee K antibiotic (Wyeth Laboratories), see penicillin potassium phenoxymethyl antibiotic.

Percodan analgesic

Manufacturer: Endo Laboratories, Inc.
Generic Name: aspirin, caffeine, oxycodone hydrochloride, oxycodone terephthalate, phenacetin
Equivalent Products: None
Dosage Forms: Tablets: aspirin, 224 mg; caffeine, 32 mg; oxycodone hydrochloride, 4.5 mg; oxycodone terephthalate, 0.38 mg; phenacetin, 160 mg (yellow)
Use: Relief of pain
Minor Side Effects: Constipation, dizziness, itching, light-headedness, nausea, sedation, vomiting, dry mouth, flushing, palpitations, rash, ringing ears, sweating, odd movements
Major Side Effects: Jaundice, low blood sugar, tremors, rapid heartbeat, kidney disease
Contraindications: Bleeding ulcers, pregnancy
Warnings and Precautions: Breathing or respiratory difficulties (e.g., asthma), epilepsy, head injury, blood coagulation problems, potential for drug abuse
Interacts With: alcohol, ammonium chloride, methotrexate, oral anticoagulants, oral antidiabetics, probenecid, steroids, sulfinpyrazone
Comments: Products containing narcotics (e.g., oxycodone) are usually not used for more than seven to 10 days.

Percodan analgesic interacts with alcohol; avoid alcohol while taking this product.

If you are also taking an anticoagulant ("blood thinner"), remind your doctor.

Percodan analgesic has the potential for abuse and must be used with caution. Tolerance may develop quickly; *do not* increase the dose of this drug without first consulting your doctor.

Although no product exactly equivalent to Percodan analgesic is available, similar products are available, and they may save you money. Consult your doctor.

Take Percodan analgesic with food or milk.

If your ears feel strange, if you hear buzzing or ringing, or if your stomach hurts, your dosage may need adjustment. Call your doctor.

Periactin antihistamine

Manufacturer: Merck Sharp & Dohme
Generic Name: cyproheptadine hydrochloride

184

Equivalent Products: None
Dosage Forms: Syrup (content per 5 ml): 2 mg; tablets: 4 mg (white)
Use: Relief of hay fever symptoms, itching, and rash
Minor Side Effects: Diarrhea, dizziness, drowsiness, dry mouth, headache, heartburn, difficult urination, loss of appetite, nausea, nervousness, rash, reduced sweating, restlessness, vomiting, weakness, blurred vision, confusion, insomnia, nasal congestion, palpitations
Major Side Effects: Low blood pressure, rash from exposure to sunlight, severe abdominal pain, sore throat
Contraindications: Asthma attacks, certain types of glaucoma, certain types of peptic ulcer, enlarged prostate, obstructed bladder, obstructed intestine, pregnancy
Warnings and Precautions: Age (see "Comments")
Interacts With: Alcohol and other central nervous system depressants
Comments: Although Periactin antihistamine is frequently prescribed for the prevention and treatment of the common cold, a government panel of experts has concluded that the product may not be effective for this use.

Periactin antihistamine may cause drowsiness; to prevent oversedation, avoid the use of other sedative drugs or alcohol.

Periactin antihistamine may cause dryness of the mouth. To reduce this feeling, chew gum or suck on a piece of hard candy.

Periactin antihistamine reduces sweating; avoid excessive work or exercise in hot weather.

While taking Periactin antihistamine, do not take any nonprescription item for cough, cold, or sinus problems without first checking with your doctor.

The elderly are more likely to suffer side effects from this drug than are other people. Children under 12 who take Periactin antihistamine may become excited or restless.

Peri-Colace laxative

Manufacturer: Mead Johnson Pharmaceutical Division
Generic Name: casanthranol, dioctyl sodium sulfosuccinate
Equivalent Products: Bu-Lax Plus laxative (Ulmer Pharmacal Company); Comfolax Plus laxative (Searle Laboratories); D-S-S Plus laxative (Parke, Davis & Company)
Dosage Form: Capsules: casanthranol, 30 mg; dioctyl sodium sulfosuccinate, 100 mg (white/red)
Use: Relief of constipation
Minor Side Effects: Cramps, nausea, vomiting, diarrhea
Major Side Effects: No major side effects
Contraindications: Abdominal pain, nausea, vomiting, pregnancy
Warnings and Precautions: Liver or kidney diseases
Interacts With: No significant drug interactions
Comments: Take Peri-Colace laxative with at least a glassful of water. Drink at least nine to 10 glasses of water each day.

The full effect of Peri-Colace laxative may not be apparent for several days.

Peri-Colace laxative and products equivalent to it may be purchased without a prescription.

Products equivalent to Peri-Colace laxative are available and vary widely in cost. Ask your doctor to prescribe a generic preparation; then ask your pharmacist to fill it with the least expensive brand.

Persantine antianginal

Manufacturer: Boehringer Ingelheim Ltd.
Generic Name: dipyridamole
Equivalent Products: None
Dosage Form: Tablets: 25 mg (orange)
Use: Prevention of chest pain (angina) due to heart disease
Minor Side Effects: Dizziness, fainting, flushing, headache, nausea, rash, weakness
Major Side Effects: Worsening of chest pain
Contraindications: Pregnancy
Warnings and Precautions: Low blood pressure, liver and kidney diseases
Interacts With: anticoagulants
Comments: The effectiveness of Persantine antianginal for prevention of angina is controversial. Persantine antianginal is more frequently prescribed to prevent blood clot formation, although use of Persantine antianginal for this purpose is not approved by the FDA.

Take Persantine antianginal on an empty stomach (one hour before or two hours after a meal) and take only the prescribed amount.

The effects of Persantine antianginal therapy may not be apparent for at least two months.

Pfiklor potassium replacement (Pfizer Laboratories Division), see potassium chloride replacement.

Phenaphen with Codeine analgesic   (A.H. Robins Company),   see Tylenol with Codeine analgesic.

Phenergan expectorant plain

Manufacturer: Wyeth Laboratories
Generic Name: promethazine hydrochloride, potassium guaiacolsulfonate, sodium citrate, citric acid
Equivalent Products: Proclan expectorant (H.R. Cenci Laboratories, Inc.); Promethazine Hydrochloride expectorant plain (Lederle Laboratories); Promex expectorant (Lemmon Pharmacal Company)
Dosage Form: Liquid (content per 5 ml): promethazine hydrochloride, 5 mg; potassium guaiacolsulfonate, 44 mg; sodium citrate, 197 mg; citric acid, 60 mg
Use: Relief of coughing
Minor Side Effects: Blurred vision, change in urine color, confusion, constipation, diarrhea, difficult urination, dizziness, drowsiness, headache, insomnia, nasal congestion, nausea, nervousness, palpitations, rash, restlessness, vomiting, dry mouth, loss of appetite, weakness, trembling, reduced sweating
Major Side Effects: Low blood pressure, rash from exposure to sunlight, severe abdominal pain, sore throat, jaundice
Contraindications: Asthma attacks, certain types of glaucoma, certain types of peptic ulcers, enlarged prostate, obstructed bladder, obstructed intestine, pregnancy, depression
Warnings and Precautions: Liver and kidney diseases, heart diseases

Interacts With: amphetamine, anticholinergics, levopoda, antacids, trihexyphenidyl

Comments: If you need an expectorant, you need more moisture in your environment. Drink nine to 10 glasses of water each day. The use of a humidifier or vaporizer may also be beneficial. Consult your doctor.

Phenergan expectorant plain may cause drowsiness; to prevent oversedation, avoid the use of other sedative drugs or alcohol.

Phenergan expectorant plain may cause dryness of the mouth. To reduce this feeling, chew gum or suck on a piece of hard candy.

Phenergan expectorant plain reduces sweating; avoid excessive work or exercise in hot weather.

While taking Phenergan expectorant plain, do not take any nonprescription item for cough, cold, or sinus problems without first checking with your doctor.

Products equivalent to Phenergan expectorant plain are available and vary widely in cost. Ask your doctor to prescribe a generic preparation; then ask your pharmacist to fill it with the least expensive brand.

Phenergan expectorant with Codeine

Manufacturer: Wyeth Laboratories

Generic Name: promethazine hydrochloride, codeine phosphate, potassium guaiacolsulfonate, sodium citrate, citric acid

Equivalent Products: HRC-Proclan expectorant with Codeine (H.R. Cenci Laboratories, Inc.); K-Phen expectorant with Codeine (Kay Pharmacal Company, Inc.); Mallergan expectorant with Codeine (Mallard Incorporated); Pentazine expectorant with Codeine (Century Pharmaceuticals, Inc.); Promethazine Hydrochloride expectorant with Codeine (Lederle Laboratories)

Dosage Form: Liquid (content per 5 ml): promethazine hydrochloride, 5 mg; codeine phosphate, 10 mg; potassium guaiacolsulfonate, 44 mg; sodium citrate, 197 mg; citric acid, 60 mg

Use: Cough suppressant

Minor Side Effects: Blurred vision, change in urine color, confusion, constipation, diarrhea, difficult urination, dizziness, drowsiness, headache, insomnia, nasal congestion, nausea, nervousness, palpitations, rash, restlessness, vomiting, dry mouth, loss of appetite, weakness, trembling, reduced sweating

Major Side Effects: Low blood pressure, rash from exposure to sunlight, severe abdominal pain, sore throat, jaundice

Contraindications: Asthma attacks, certain types of glaucoma, certain types of peptic ulcer, enlarged prostate, obstructed bladder, obstructed intestine, pregnancy, depression

Warnings and Precautions: Liver and kidney disease, heart diseases, potential for abuse

Interacts With: amphetamine, anticholinergics, levopoda, antacids, trihexyphenidyl

Comments: If you need an expectorant, you need more moisture in your environment. Drink nine to 10 glasses of water each day. The use of a vaporizer or humidifier may also be beneficial. Consult your doctor.

Products containing narcotics (e.g., codeine) are usually not used for more than seven to 10 days.

Phenergan expectorant with Codeine has the potential for abuse and must be used with caution. Tolerance may develop quickly; *do not* increase the dose of this drug without first consulting your doctor.

Phenergan expectorant with Codeine may cause drowsiness; to prevent oversedation, avoid the use of other sedative drugs or alcohol.

Phenergan expectorant with Codeine may cause dryness of the mouth. To reduce this feeling, chew gum or suck on a piece of hard candy.

Phenergan expectorant with Codeine reduces sweating; therefore, avoid excessive work or exercise in hot weather.

While taking Phenergan expectorant with Codeine, do not take any nonprescription item for cough, cold, or sinus problems without first checking with your doctor.

Products equivalent to Phenergan expectorant with Codeine are available and vary widely in cost. Ask your doctor to prescribe a generic preparation; then ask your pharmacist to fill it with the least expensive brand.

Phenergan VC expectorant plain

Manufacturer: Wyeth Laboratories

Generic Name: citric acid, phenylephrine hydrochloride, potassium guaiacolsulfonate, promethazine hydrochloride, sodium citrate

Equivalent Products: Proclan VC expectorant plain (H.R. Cenci Laboratories, Inc.); J-Gan-VC expectorant plain (J. Pharmacal Co.)

Dosage Form: Liquid (content per 5 ml): citric acid, 60 mg; phenylephrine hydrochloride, 5 mg; potassium guaiacolsulfonate, 44 mg; promethazine hydrochloride, 5 mg; sodium citrate, 197 mg

Use: Decongestant, relief of coughing

Minor Side Effects: Diarrhea, dizziness, drowsiness, dry mouth, headache, heartburn, difficult urination, change in urine color, loss of appetite, nausea, rash, restlessness, vomiting, weakness, blurred vision, confusion, constipation, insomnia, nasal congestion, palpitations, trembling, reduced sweating

Major Side Effects: Low blood pressure, severe abdominal pain, sore throat, high blood pressure, chest pain, jaundice

Contraindications: Asthma, depression, some glaucomas, certain ulcers, enlarged prostate, obstructed bladder, obstructed intestine, pregnancy, severe heart disease

Warnings and Precautions: Diabetes, high blood pressure, thyroid disease, liver and kidney diseases

Interacts With: amphetamine, anticholinergics, trihexyphenidyl, guanethidine, levopoda, monoamine oxidase inhibitors, antacids, antidepressants

Comments: If you need an expectorant, you need more moisture in your environment. Drink nine to 10 glasses of water each day. The use of a vaporizer or humidifier may also be beneficial.

Phenergan VC expectorant plain may cause drowsiness; to prevent oversedation, avoid the use of other sedative drugs or alcohol.

Phenergan VC expectorant plain may cause dryness of the mouth. To reduce this feeling, chew gum or suck on a piece of hard candy.

Phenergan VC expectorant plain reduces sweating; therefore, avoid excessive work or exercise in hot weather.

While taking Phenergan VC expectorant plain, do not take any nonprescription item for cough, cold, or sinus problems without first checking with your doctor.

Products equivalent to Phenergan VC expectorant plain are available and vary widely in cost. Ask your doctor to prescribe a generic preparation; then ask your pharmacist to fill it with the least expensive brand.

Phenergan VC expectorant with Codeine

Manufacturer: Wyeth Laboratories

Generic Name: citric acid, codeine phosphate, phenylephrine hydrochloride, potassium guaiacolsulfonate, promethazine hydrochloride, sodium citrate

Equivalent Products: Mallergan VC expectorant with Codeine (Mallard Incorporated); Promethazine Hydrochloride VC expectorant with Codeine (Lederle Laboratories)

Dosage Form: Liquid (content per 5 ml): citric acid, 60 mg; codeine phosphate, 10 mg; phenylephrine hydrochloride, 5 mg; potassium guaiacolsulfonate, 44 mg; promethazine hydrochloride, 5 mg; sodium citrate, 197 mg

Use: Relief of symptoms of the common cold

Minor Side Effects: Diarrhea, dizziness, drowsiness, dry mouth, headache, heartburn, difficult urination, change in urine color, loss of appetite, nausea, rash, restlessness, vomiting, weakness, blurred vision, confusion, constipation, insomnia, nasal congestion, palpitations, trembling, reduced sweating

Major Side Effects: Low blood pressure, severe abdominal pain, sore throat, high blood pressure, chest pain, jaundice

Contraindications: Asthma, depression, some glaucomas, certain ulcers, enlarged prostate, obstructed bladder, obstructed intestine, pregnancy, severe heart disease

Warnings and Precautions: Diabetes, high blood pressure, thyroid disease, liver and kidney diseases, potential for abuse

Interacts With: amphetamine, anticholinergics, trihexyphenidyl, guanethidine, levodopa, monoamine oxidase inhibitors, antacids

Comments: If you need an expectorant, you need more moisture in your environment. Drink nine to 10 glasses of water each day. The use of a vaporizer or humidifier may also be beneficial. Consult your doctor.

Phenergan VC expectorant with Codeine may cause drowsiness; to prevent oversedation, avoid the use of other sedative drugs or alcohol.

Phenergan VC expectorant with Codeine may cause dryness of the mouth. To reduce this feeling, chew gum or suck on a piece of hard candy.

Phenergan VC expectorant with Codeine reduces sweating; therefore, avoid excessive work or exercise in hot weather.

While taking Phenergan VC expectorant with Codeine, do not take any nonprescription item for cough, cold, or sinus problems without first checking with your doctor.

Products equivalent to Phenergan VC expectorant with Codeine are available and vary widely in cost. Ask your doctor to prescribe a generic preparation, then ask your pharmacist to fill it with the least expensive brand.

Products containing narcotics (e.g., codeine) are not usually taken for more than seven to 10 days.

Phenergan VC expectorant with Codeine has the potential for abuse and must be used with caution. Tolerance may develop quickly; *do not* increase the dose of this drug without first consulting your doctor.

phenobarbital sedative and hypnotic

Phenobarbital is a generic drug.

Equivalent Products: phenobarbital (various manufacturers); SK-Phenobarbital sedative and hypnotic, Eskabarb sedative and hypnotic (Smith Kline & French Laboratories); Luminal Ovoids sedative and hypnotic (Winthrop Laboratories); Pheno-Squar sedative and hypnotic (Mallard Incorporated); Solfoton sedative and hypnotic (Wm. P. Poythress & Co. Inc.); PBR/12 sedative and hypnotic (Scott-Alison Pharmaceuticals, Inc.)

Dosage Forms: Liquid (content per 5 ml): 20 mg; tablets: 15 mg, 30 mg, 65 mg, 100 mg, (most commonly white); time-release capsules: 100 mg (various colors)

Use: Control of convulsions, relief of anxiety or tension, sleeping aid

Minor Side Effects: Drowsiness, nausea, vomiting

Major Side Effects: Breathing difficulty, cold and clammy skin, other allergic reactions

Contraindications: Porphyria

Warnings and Precautions: Potential for drug abuse, pregnancy, liver and kidney diseases

Interacts With: alcohol, central nervous system depressants, griseofulvin, oral anticoagulants, phenytoin, steroids, sulfonamides, tetracycline, antidepressants

Comments: Phenobarbital sedative and hypnotic interacts with other sedative drugs or alcohol; avoid them while using this drug.

Phenobarbital sedative and hypnotic has the potential for abuse and must be used with caution. Tolerance may develop quickly; *do not* increase the dose of this drug without first consulting your doctor.

If you are also taking an anticoagulant ("blood thinner"), remind your doctor.

Phenobarbital sedative and hypnotic is manufactured in a wide variety of tablets, and they vary in cost. Ask your pharmacist to fill your prescription with the least expensive brand.

Pheno-Squar sedative and hypnotic (Mallard Incorporated), see phenobarbital sedative and hypnotic.

Phenyl-Idium analgesic (Columbia Medical Co.), see Pyridium analgesic.

Pilocar ophthalmic solution (Smith, Miller & Patch), see Isopto Carpine ophthalmic solution.

Pilomiotin ophthalmic solution (Smith, Miller & Patch), see Isopto Carpine ophthalmic solution.

Polaramine antihistamine

Manufacturer: Schering Corporation
Generic Name: dexchlorpheniramine maleate
Equivalent Products: None
Dosage Forms: Liquid (content per 5 ml): 2 mg; sustained-action tablets: 4 mg, 6 mg (both are red); tablets: 2 mg (red)
Use: Relief of allergic symptoms

Minor Side Effects: Diarrhea, dizziness, drowsiness, dry mouth, headache, heartburn, difficult urination, loss of appetite, nausea, nervousness, rash, restlessness, vomiting, weakness, blurred vision, confusion, insomnia, nasal congestion, palpitations

Major Side Effects: Low blood pressure, rash from exposure to sunlight, severe abdominal pain, sore throat

Contraindications: Asthma, certain types of glaucoma, certain types of peptic ulcers, enlarged prostate, obstructed intestine, pregnancy

Warnings and Precautions: Liver and kidney diseases

Interacts With: Alcohol and other central nervous system depressants

Comments: Although Polaramine antihistamine is frequently prescribed for the prevention and treatment of the common cold, a government panel of experts has concluded that the product may not be effectcive for this use.

The 4-mg and 6-mg sustained-action tablets must be swallowed whole. Never take Polaramine antihistamine sustained action tablets more frequently than your doctor prescribes. A serious overdose may result. Whereas sedation is the usual response to overdosage in adults, children may experience symptoms of excitation leading to convulsions or death.

Polaramine antihistamine interacts with sedative drugs and alcohol. Avoid them while using this product.

Polaramine antihistamine may cause dryness of the mouth. To reduce this feeling, chew gum or suck on a piece of hard candy.

While taking Polaramine antihistamine, do not take any nonprescription item for cough, cold, or sinus problems without first checking with your doctor.

Polycillin antibiotic (Bristol Laboratories), see ampicillin antibiotic.

Polymox antibiotic (Bristol Laboratories), see amoxicillin antibiotic.

Poly-Vi-Flor vitamin and fluoride supplement

Manufacturer: Mead Johnson Nutritional Division

Generic Name: vitamins A, D, E, C, B_1, B_2, niacin, B_6, B_{12}; folic acid; sodium fluoride

Equivalent Products: None

Dosage Forms: Chewable tablets: vitamin A, 2500 I.U.; D, 400 I.U.; E, 15 I.U.; C, 60 mg; B_1, 1.05 I.U.; B_2, 1.2 I.U.; niacin, 13 mg; B_6, 1.05 mg; B_{12}, 4.5 mcg; folic acid, 0.3 mg; sodium fluoride, 1.0 mg (green and orange); drops

Use: Protection against tooth decay and vitamin deficiencies in children

Minor Side Effects: Rash (rare)

Major Side Effects: No major side effects

Contraindications: Areas where the drinking water contains a fluoride concentration greater than 0.7 parts per million

Warnings and Precautions: No major warnings or precautions

Interacts With: No significant drug interactions

Comments: Poly-Vi-Flor vitamin and fluoride supplement should never be referred to as candy or "candy-flavored vitamins." Your child may take you literally and swallow too many.

If you are unsure of the fluoride content of your drinking water, ask your doctor, or call your County Health Department.

Mead Johnson Nutritional Division also manufactures a similar product,

Tri-Vi-Flor vitamin and fluoride supplement, which contains only vitamins A, C and D and sodium fluoride.

potassium chloride replacement

Potassium chloride is a generic drug.

Equivalent Products: potassium chloride (various manufacturers); Kaochlor potassium replacement (Warren-Teed Pharmaceuticals Inc.); Kay Ciel potassium replacement (Cooper Laboratories Inc.); K-LOR potassium replacement (Abbott Laboratories); Klorvess potassium replacement (Dorsey Laboratories); Pfiklor potassium replacement (Pfizer Laboratories Division); Kaon-Cl potassium replacement (Warren-Teed Pharmaceuticals Inc.); K-Lyte/ Cl potassium replacement (Mead Johnson Pharmaceutical Division); Slow-K potassium replacement (CIBA Pharmaceutical Company)

Dosage Forms: Effervescent tablets; liquid, powders; sustained-action tablets (various strengths, manufacturers, and colors)

Use: Prevention or treatment of potassium deficiency, especially that caused by diuretics

Minor Side Effects: Diarrhea, nausea, vomiting

Major Side Effects: Confusion, numbness or tingling in arms or legs

Contraindications: Severe kidney disease

Warnings and Precautions: Peptic ulcers, certain types of heart disease, liver and kidney diseases, pregnancy

Interacts With: spironolactone, triamterene

Comments: Potassium products may be taken with food. Liquid and powder products may be added to one-half to one glassful of cold water, then swallowed.

Potassium supplements usually have a low rate of patient compliance. If a potassium product is prescribed, take the medication as directed and do not stop taking it without first consulting your doctor.

Ask your doctor about using a salt substitute instead of potassium chloride; salt substitutes are similar, less expensive and more convenient.

Potassium chloride products vary widely in cost. Ask your pharmacist to fill your prescription with the least expensive brand.

Do not crush or chew Slow-K potassium replacement tablets.

Take K-Lyte/Cl with at least a full glass of water. K-Lyte/Cl tablets must be completely dissolved in water before they are swallowed.

If your kidneys are normal, it is difficult to produce toxicity by taking an overdose.

Prednicen-M steroid hormone (The Central Pharmacal Company), see prednisone steroid hormone.

prednisone steroid hormone

Prednisone steroid hormone is a generic drug.

Equivalent Products: prednisone steroid hormone (various manufacturers); Meticorten steroid hormone, (Schering Corporation); Orasone steroid hormone (Rowell Laboratories, Inc.); Deltasone steroid hormone (The Upjohn Company); Fernisone steroid hormone (Ferndale Laboratories, Inc.); Lisacort steroid hormone (Fellows Medical Division); Paracort steroid hormone (Parke, Davis & Company); Prednicen-M steroid hormone (The Central Pharmacal Company); Ropred steroid hormone (Robinson Laboratory, Inc.);

Servisone steroid hormone (Lederle Laboratories); SK-Prednisone steroid hormone (Smith Kline & French Laboratories)

Dosage Form: Tablets: 1 mg, 2.5 mg, 5 mg, 10 mg, 20 mg, 50 mg (various colors)

Use: Treatment of inflammations such as arthritis, dermatitis, poison ivy, endocrine and rheumatoid disorders; asthma; blood disease; certain cancers and gastrointestinal disorders such as ulcerative colitis

Minor Side Effects: Dizziness, headache, increased sweating, menstrual irregularities

Major Side Effects: Abdominal distention, cataracts, fluid retention, glaucoma, growth impairment in children, hemorrhage, high blood pressure, impaired wound healing, peptic ulcer, potassium loss, weakness

Contraindications: Usually systemic fungal infections

Warnings and Precautions: Peptic ulcer, pregnancy, tuberculosis, diabetes

Interacts With: antidiabetics, aspirin, barbiturates, diuretics, estrogens, indomethacin, oral anticoagulants, phenytoin

Comments: When prednisone steroid hormone is used for short periods of time, such as in the treatment of allergy or poison ivy, it is often taken on a decreasing-dosage schedule (i.e., one tablet four times daily for several days; then one tablet three times daily; then one tablet twice daily; then one tablet daily).

When prednisone steroid hormone is used for long periods of time, such as in the treatment of arthritis, an every-other-day dosage schedule is preferred. In other words, instead of taking 5 mg daily, you can take 10 mg every other day and still receive the same pharmacologic effect.

If your doctor tells you to take the entire daily dose of the medication at one time, take it as close to 8:00 A.M. as possible to receive optimal response.

Prednisone steroid hormone can cause potassium loss. To avoid potassium loss, take prednisone steroid hormone with a glass of fresh or frozen orange juice. You may also eat a banana each day. The use of Diasal or Co-Salt salt substitutes helps prevent potassium loss.

Blood pressure and body weight should be monitored at regular intervals. Stomach X-rays are desirable for persons with suspected or known peptic ulcers.

Brands of prednisone steroid hormone vary widely in cost. Ask your pharmacist to fill your prescription with the least expensive brand.

Do not stop taking this drug without your doctor's knowledge.

If you are taking prednisone steroid hormone chronically, you should carry with you a notice that you are taking a steroid.

Premarin estrogen hormone

Manufacturer: Ayerst Laboratories

Generic Name: conjugated estrogens

Equivalent Products: Menotab estrogen hormone (Fleming & Company); Ovest estrogen hormone (Trimen Laboratories, Inc.); Co-Estro estrogen hormone (Robinson Laboratory, Inc.); Estropan estrogen hormone (Panray Division, Ormont Drug & Chemical Co., Inc.); Femest estrogen hormone (Laser, Inc.); Fem-H estrogen hormone (Saron Pharmacal Corp.); Genisis estrogen hormone (Organon Inc.); Menogen estrogen hormone (General Pharmaceutical Products, Inc.); Palopause estrogen hormone (Palmedico, Inc.); Kestrin estrogen hormone (Hyrex Pharmaceuticals); Sodestrin estrogen hormone (Tutag Pharmaceuticals, Inc.); Conest estrogen hormone (Century Pharmaceuticals); Estroate estrogen hormone (Kay Pharmacal Company, Inc.); Estrocon estrogen hormone (Mallard Incorporated)

Dosage Form: Tablets: 0.3 mg (green), 0.625 mg (dark red), 1.25 mg (yellow), 2.5 mg (dark blue)

Use: Estrogen replacement therapy, treatment of symptoms due to menopause, enlarged breasts after childbirth, prostatic cancer in men, uterine bleeding, some cases of breast cancer

Minor Side Effects: Bleeding, bloating, cramps, loss of appetite, nausea, tender breasts, vomiting

Major Side Effects: Allergic rash, severe headache, weight gain (more than two pounds a week), gall bladder disease, high blood pressure, vision changes, skin color changes

Contraindications: Pregnancy; also most patients with breast cancer, blood clotting disorders, endometrial cancer, vaginal bleeding

Warnings and Precautions: Asthma, epilepsy, heart disease, kidney disease, migraine. Studies have shown that estrogens increase the risk of cancer. In three independent studies, the rate of endometrial cancer development was 4.5 to 13.9 times greater in estrogen users than in nonusers.

Interacts With: oral anticoagulants, steroids

Comments: The name "Premarin" comes from the natural source of the drug: *pre-pre*gnant; *mar-mar*e's; *in-ur*ine. Thus, Premarin estrogen hormone is obtained by collecting samples of urine from pregnant mares.

Your pharmacist has a brochure which describes the benefits and risks involved with estrogen therapy. He is required by law to give you a copy each time he fills a prescription. Read this material carefully.

Products equivalent to Premarin estrogen hormone are available and vary widely in cost. Ask your doctor to prescribe a generic preparation; then ask your pharmacist to fill it with the least expensive brand.

Presamine antidepressant (USV [P.R.] Development Corp.), see Tofranil antidepressant.

Principen antibiotic (E.R. Squibb & Sons), see ampicillin antibiotic.

Pro-Banthine anticholinergic

Manufacturer: Searle & Co.

Generic Name: propantheline bromide

Equivalent Products: propantheline bromide (various manufacturers)

Dosage Forms: Sustained-action tablets: 30 mg (peach); tablets: 7.5 mg (white), 15 mg (peach)

Use: Treatment of peptic ulcer and irritable bowel syndrome

Minor Side Effects: Blurred vision, constipation, dizziness, drowsiness, dry mouth, headache, insomnia, loss of the sense of taste, nausea, nervousness, vomiting, difficult urination, reduced sweating, photosensitivity, palpitations

Major Side Effects: Impotence, rash

Contraindications: Certain types of glaucoma, enlarged prostate, obstructed intestine, asthma, bladder obstruction, certain heart diseases, porphyria

Warnings and Precautions: Pregnancy, severe heart disease, certain liver and kidney diseases

Interacts With: amantadine, haloperidol, antacids, phenothiazines

Comments: Pro-Banthine anticholinergic is best taken one-half to one hour before meals.

This drug does not *cure* ulcers but may help them improve.

Pro-Banthine anticholinergic always produces certain side effects. These include dry mouth, blurred vision, reduced sweating, difficult urination, constipation, and palpitations. To reduce dryness of the mouth, chew gum or suck on a piece of hard candy. Avoid excessive work in hot weather.

Some forms of Pro-Banthine anticholinergic have sustained action; never take these forms more frequently than your doctor prescribes. A serious overdose may result.

Pro-Banthine anticholinergic is also available in tablets with phenobarbital for persons who are especially nervous or anxious. Although phenobarbital is present, Pro-Banthine anticholinergic with phenobarbital has not been shown to have high potential for abuse.

Products equivalent to Pro-Banthine anticholinergic are available and vary widely in cost. Ask your doctor to prescribe a generic preparation; then ask your pharmacist to fill it with the least expensive brand.

Call your doctor if you notice a rash or pain in the eye.

Procamide antiarrhythmic (Amfre-Grant Inc.), see Pronestyl antiarrhythmic.

Proclan expectorant (H.R. Cenci Laboratories, Inc.), see Phenergan expectorant plain.

Proclan VC expectorant plain (H.R. Cenci Laboratories, Inc.), see Phenergan VC expectorant plain.

Progesic Compound-65 analgesic (Ulmer Pharmcal Company), see Darvon Compound-65 analgesic.

Progesic-65 analgesic (Ulmer Pharmaceutical Company), see Darvon analgesic.

Proloid thyroid hormone

Manufacturer: Warner/Chilcott

Generic Name: thyroglobulin

Equivalent Products: thyroglobulin (various manufacturers)

Dosage Form: Tablets: ¼ grain, ½ gr, 1 gr, 1½ gr, 2 gr, 3 gr, 5 gr (all grey)

Use: Thyroid replacement therapy

Minor Side Effects: No minor side effects when used as directed

Major Side Effects: Chest pain, diarrhea, headache, heat intolerance, insomnia, palpitations, sweating, weight loss

Contraindications: No major contraindications

Warnings and Precautions: Heart disease, high blood pressure, diabetes

Interacts With: oral antidiabetics, cholestyramine, digitalis, oral anticoagulants, phenytoin

Comments: If you are undergoing thyroid replacement therapy, do not take any nonprescription item for cough, cold, or sinus problems without first checking with your doctor.

Persons taking this product and digitalis should watch carefully for symptoms of increased toxicity (e.g., nausea, blurred vision, palpitations).

Thyroid tablets may work as well as Proloid thyroid hormone and are often less expensive. Check with your doctor.

Products equivalent to Proloid thyroid hormone are available and vary widely in cost. Ask your doctor to prescribe a generic preparation; then ask your pharmacist to fill it with the least expensive brand.

Be sure to follow your doctor's directions exactly.

Most side effects from this drug can be controlled by dosage adjustment. Check with your doctor.

Promapar phenothiazine (Parke, Davis & Company), see Thorazine phenothiazine.

Promethazine Hydrochloride expectorant plain (Lederle Laboratories), see Phenergan expectorant plain.

Promethazine Hydrochloride expectorant with Codeine (Lederle Laboratories), see Phenergan expectorant with Codeine.

Promethazine Hydrochloride VC expectorant with Codeine (Lederle Laboratories), see Phenergan VC expectorant with Codeine.

Promex expectorant (Lemmon Pharmacal Company), see Phenergan expectorant plain.

Pronestyl antiarrhythmic

Manufacturer: E.R. Squibb & Sons
Generic Name: procainamide hydrochloride
Equivalent Products: Sub-Quin antiarrhythmic (Scrip-Physician Supply Co.); procainamide hydrochloride (various manufacturers); Procamide antiarrhythmic (Amfre-Grant Inc.)
Dosage Forms: Capsules: 250 mg (yellow), 375 mg (red/white), 500 mg (yellow/orange); tablets: 250 mg (orange), 375 mg (deep orange), 500 mg (red)
Use: Treatment of some heart arrhythmias
Minor Side Effects: Bitter taste in the mouth, diarrhea, itching, loss of appetite, nausea, rash, vomiting
Major Side Effects: Chills, depression, fever, giddiness, weakness, pain in the joints
Contraindications: Certain types of heart disease, myasthenia gravis, allergy to procaine, pregnancy
Warnings and Precautions: Liver or kidney diseases
Interacts With: No significant drug interactions
Comments: Pronestyl antiarrhythmic capsules or tablets must be swallowed whole.

While taking Pronestyl antiarrhythmic do not take any nonprescription item for cough, cold, or sinus problems without first checking with your doctor.

Products equivalent to Pronestyl antiarrhythmic are available and vary widely in cost. Ask your doctor to prescribe a generic preparation; then ask your pharmacist to fill it with the least expensive brand.

Pronestyl antiarrhythmic must be taken exactly as directed in order for it to work properly. It is especially important that it be taken on time.

Provera progesterone hormone

Manufacturer: The Upjohn Company
Generic Name: medroxyprogesterone acetate
Equivalent Products: Amen progesterone hormone (Carnrick Laboratories)
Dosage Form: Tablets: 2.5 mg (pink), 10 mg (white)
Use: Treatment of abnormal menstrual bleeding, difficult menstruation, or lack of menstruation.
Minor Side Effects: Acne
Major Side Effects: Cessation of menstrual flow, itching, migraine, tender breasts, rash, spotting or breakthrough or unusual vaginal bleeding, visual disturbances, weight gain or loss
Contraindications: Cancer of the breast or genitals, clotting disorders, pregnancy, vaginal bleeding of unknown cause
Warnings and Precautions: Liver or kidney diseases
Interacts With: oral anticoagulants, steroids
Comments: Call your doctor at once if any unusual vaginal bleeding, vision changes, or severe headaches occur. People taking Provera progesterone hormone occasionally develop clotting disorders.

Puretane expectorant (Purepac Pharmaceutical Co.), see Dimetane expectorant.

Puretane expectorant-DC (Purepac Pharmaceutical Co.), see Dimetane expectorant-DC.

P.V. Carpine Liquifilm ophthalmic solution (Allergan Pharmaceuticals), see Isopto Carpine ophthalmic solution.

Pyridium analgesic

Manufacturer: Warner/Chilcott
Generic Name: phenazopyridine hydrochloride
Equivalent Products: Azo-Standard analgesic (Webcon Pharmaceuticals); Di-Azo analgesic (Kay Pharmacal Company, Inc.); Phenyl-Idium analgesic (Columbia Medical Co.); Urodine analgesic (Robinson Laboratory, Inc.); Azo-Stat analgesic (O'Neal, Jones & Feldman); phenazopyridine hydrochloride (various manufacturers)
Dosage Form: Tablets: 100 mg, 200 mg (maroon)
Use: Treatment of the burning and pain of urinary tract disorders
Minor Side Effects: Nausea, vomiting, change in urine color
Major Side Effects: Jaundice, anemia
Contraindications: Severe kidney disease, pregnancy
Warnings and Precautions: Liver or kidney disease

Interacts With: No significant drug interactions
Comments: Take Pyridium analgesic with at least a glassful of water. Drink at least nine to 10 glasses of water each day.

Products equivalent to Pyridium analgesic are available and vary widely in cost. Ask your doctor to prescribe a generic preparation; then ask your pharmacist to fill it with the least expensive brand.

Quaalude sedative and hypnotic

Manufacturer: William H. Rorer, Inc.
Generic Name: methaqualone
Equivalent Products: Sopor sedative and hypnotic (Arnar-Stone Laboratories, Inc.); Parest sedative and hypnotic (Parke, Davis & Company)
Dosage Form: Tablets: 150 mg, 300 mg (both white)
Use: Sleeping aid
Minor Side Effects: Anxiety, reduced sweating, diarrhea, dizziness, dry mouth, fatigue, hangover, headache, loss of appetite, nausea, numbness of the fingers or toes, rash, vomiting
Major Side Effects: Sore throat
Contraindications: History of drug abuse, pregnancy
Warnings and Precautions: Liver and kidney disease
Interacts With: central nervous system depressants.
Comments: Quaalude sedative and hypnotic and other brands of methaqualone are known on the "street" as "sopors" and "ludes."

Since Quaalude sedative and hypnotic and other brands of methaqualone may produce drowsiness within 10 to 20 minutes, they should be taken only at bedtime.

Avoid the use of other sedative drugs or alcohol while taking Quaalude sedative and hypnotic.

Quaalude sedative and hypnotic has the potential for abuse and must be used with caution. Tolerance may develop quickly; *do not* increase the dose of this drug without first consulting your doctor.

Products equivalent to Quaalude sedative and hypnotic are available and vary widely in cost. Ask your doctor to prescribe a generic preparation; then ask your pharmacist to fill it with the least expensive brand.

Quadra-hist adrenergic and antihistamine (Henry Schein, Inc.), see Naldecon adrenergic and antihistamine.

Quibron expectorant and smooth muscle relaxant

Manufacturer: Mead Johnson Pharmaceutical Division
Generic Name: guaifenesin, theophylline
Equivalent Products: Slo-Phyllin expectorant and smooth muscle relaxant (Dooner Laboratories, Inc.); Cerylin expectorant and smooth muscle relaxant (Spencer-Mead Inc.)
Dosage Forms: Liquid (content per 15 ml): guaifenesin, 90 mg; theophylline, 150 mg. Capsules: guaifenesin, 180 mg; theophylline, 300 mg (yellow)
Use: Prevention and treatment of asthmatic attacks or related conditions
Minor Side Effects: Mild stimulation, nausea, vomiting

Major Side Effects: Convulsions, palpitations, difficult breathing
Contraindications: Pregnancy
Warnings and Precautions: Peptic ulcer, heart disease, certain liver and kidney diseases
Interacts With: lithium carbonate, propranolol
Comments: Quibron expectorant and smooth muscle relaxant should not be taken more frequently than once every six hours or within 12 hours of any similar product given rectally.

Take Quibron expectorant and smooth muscle relaxant with food or milk.

Products equivalent to Quibron expectorant and smooth muscle relaxant are available and vary widely in cost. Ask your doctor to prescribe a generic preparation; then ask your pharmacist to fill it with the least expensive brand.

Call your doctor if you develop stomach pain, vomiting, or restlessness because this product may aggravate an ulcer.

Be sure to take your dosage at exactly the right time.

Drink at least eight to 10 glasses of water each day.

Do not use nonprescription items for asthma unless your doctor has told you to do so.

Avoid drinking tea, cocoa, or other beverages which contain xanthines while taking Quibron expectorant and smooth muscle relaxant. Consult your pharmacist.

Quinidex antiarrhythmic (A.H. Robins Company), see quinidine sulfate antiarrhythmic.

quinidine sulfate antiarrhythmic

Quinidine sulfate is a generic drug.
Equivalent Products: Cin-Quin antiarrhythmic (Rowell Laboratories, Inc.); Quinidex antiarrhythmic (A.H. Robins Company); Quinora antiarrhythmic (Key Pharmaceuticals, Inc.); quinidine sulfate (various manufacturers)
Dosage Forms: Capsules: 100 mg, 200 mg, 300 mg; tablets: 100 mg, 200 mg, 300 mg (various colors)
Use: Treatment of certain types of heart arrhythmias
Minor Side Effects: Abdominal pain, diarrhea, headache, nausea, vomiting
Major Side Effects: Anemia, blurred vision, dizziness, ringing in the ears
Contraindications: Pregnancy
Warnings and Precautions: Certain types of heart disease, liver and kidney diseases
Interacts With: acetazolamide, cholinergics, antacids, oral anticoagulants, sodium bicarbonate
Comments: If you are being treated for a heart arrhythmia, do not take any nonprescription item for cough, cold, or sinus problems without first checking with your doctor.

Brands of quinidine sulfate antiarrhythmic vary widely in cost. Ask your pharmacist to fill your prescription with the least expensive brand.

Quinora antiarrhythmic (Key Pharmaceuticals, Inc.), see quinidine sulfate antiarrhythmic.

Raurine antihypertensive (O'Neal, Jones & Feldman), see reserpine antihypertensive.

Rau-Sed antihypertensive (E.R. Squibb & Sons), see reserpine antihypertensive.

Rauzide antihypertensive and diuretic

Manufacturer: E.R. Squibb & Sons
Generic Name: rauwolfia serpentina, bendroflumethiazide
Equivalent Products: None
Dosage Form: Tablets: rauwolfia serpentina, 50 mg; bendroflumethiazide, 4 mg (green)
Use: Treatment of high blood pressure
Minor Side Effects: Cramps, diarrhea, dizziness, headache, itching, loss of appetite, nasal congestion, nausea, palpitations, rash, restlessness, vomiting, tingling of the fingers and toes
Major Side Effects: Chest pain, depression, drowsiness, elevated blood sugar, elevated uric acid, glaucoma, muscle spasms, nightmares, sore throat
Contraindications: Allergy to sulfa drugs, depression, peptic ulcer, ulcerative colitis, severe kidney disease, pregnancy
Warnings and Precautions: Bronchial asthma, diabetes, gallstones, liver and kidney diseases
Interacts With: amphetamine, antidiabetics, colestipol hydrochloride, decongestants, digitalis, levodopa, lithium carbonate, monoamine oxidase inhibitors, steroids
Comments: A doctor should probably not prescribe Rauzide antihypertensive and diuretic or other "fixed dose" products as the first choice in the treatment of high blood pressure. The patient should receive each of the individual ingredients singly, and if response is adequate to the fixed doses contained in Rauzide antihypertensive and diuretic, this product can then be substituted. The advantage of a combination product such as Rauzide antihypertensive and diuretic is based on increased convenience to the patient.

Take Rauzide antihypertensive and diuretic with food or milk.

Rauzide antihypertensive and diuretic causes frequent urination. Expect this effect; it should not alarm you.

The effects of Rauzide antihypertensive and diuretic therapy may not be apparent for at least two weeks.

Mild side effects (e.g., nasal congestion) are most noticeable during the first two weeks of therapy and become less bothersome after this period.

Rauzide antihypertensive and diuretic can cause potassium loss. To avoid potassium loss, take Rauzide antihypertensive and diuretic with a glass of fresh or frozen orange juice. You may also eat a banana each day. The use of Diasal or Co-Salt salt substitutes helps prevent potassium loss.

Rauzide may cause drowsiness or depression; to prevent oversedation, avoid the use of other sedative drugs. If you feel continually tired or depressed, consult your doctor.

While taking this product (as with many drugs that lower blood pressure), you should limit your consumption of alcoholic beverages in order to prevent dizziness or light-headedness.

If dizziness or light-headedness occurs when you stand up, place your legs on the floor and "pump" the muscles for a few moments before rising.

Persons taking this product and digitalis should watch carefully for symptoms of increased toxicity, (e.g., nausea, blurred vision, palpitations).

While taking Rauzide antihypertensive and diuretic, do not take any nonprescription item for cough, cold, or sinus problems without first checking with your doctor.

If you are allergic to a sulfa drug, you may likewise be allergic to Rauzide antihypertensive and diuretic.

Regroton antihypertensive and diuretic

Manufacturer: USV (P.R.) Development Corp.
Generic Name: chlorthalidone, reserpine
Equivalent Products: None
Dosage Form: Tablets: chlorthalidone, 50 mg; reserpine, 0.125 mg (pink)
Use: Treatment of high blood pressure
Minor Side Effects: Constipation, cramps, diarrhea, headache, itching, loss of appetite, nasal congestion, nausea, numbing or tingling of fingers or toes, palpitations, vomiting
Major Side Effects: Chest pain, depression, dizziness, drowsiness, elevated blood sugar, glaucoma, impotence, muscle spasms, nightmares, restlessness, sore throat
Contraindications: Allergy to sulfa drugs, severe kidney disease, pregnancy
Warnings and Precautions: Depression, diabetes, gallstones, gout, peptic ulcer, ulcerative colitis, bronchial asthma, liver and kidney diseases
Interacts With: amphetamine, colestipol hydrochloride, decongestants, digitalis, levodopa, lithium carbonate, monoamine oxidase inhibitors, oral antidiabetics, steroids
Comments: A doctor probably should not prescribe Regroton antihypertensive and diuretic or other "fixed dose" products as the first choice in the treatment of high blood pressure. The patient should receive each of the individual ingredients singly, and if response is adequate to the fixed doses contained in Regroton antihypertensive and diuretic, this product can then be substituted. The advantage of a combination product such as Regroton antihypertensive and diuretic is based on increased convenience to the patient.

Take Regroton antihypertensive and diuretic with food or milk.

Regroton antihypertensive and diuretic causes frequent urination. Expect this effect; it should not alarm you.

The effects of Regroton antihypertensive and diuretic therapy may not be apparent for at least two weeks.

Mild side effects (e.g., nasal congestion) are most noticeable during the first two weeks of therapy and become less bothersome after this period.

Regroton antihypertensive and diuretic can cause potassium loss. To avoid potassium loss, take Regroton antihypertensive and diuretic with a glass of fresh or frozen orange juice. You may also eat a banana each day. The use of Diasal or Co-Salt salt substitutes helps prevent potassium loss.

Regroton antihypertensive and diuretic may cause drowsiness; to prevent oversedation, avoid the use of other sedative drugs. If you feel continually tired or depressed, consult your doctor.

While taking this product (as with many drugs that lower blood pressure), you should limit your consumption of alcoholic beverages in order to prevent dizziness or light-headedness.

If dizziness or light-headedness occurs when you stand up, place your legs on the floor and "pump" the muscles for a few moments before rising.

Persons taking this product and digitalis should watch carefully for symptoms of increased toxicity (e.g., nausea, blurred vision, palpitations).

While taking Regroton antihypertensive and diuretic, do not take any nonprescription item for cough, cold, or sinus problems without first checking with your doctor.

If you are allergic to sulfa drugs, you may likewise be allergic to Regroton antihypertensive and diuretic.

Reserpine causes cancer in rats. It has not yet been shown to cause cancer in people.

reserpine antihypertensive

Reserpine is a generic drug.

Equivalent Products: reserpine antihypertensive (various manufacturers); Raurine antihypertensive (O'Neal, Jones & Feldman); Rau-Sed antihypertensive (E.R. Squibb & Sons); Reserpoid antihypertensive (The Upjohn Company); Serpasil antihypertensive (CIBA Pharmaceuticals Company)

Dosage Form: Tablets: 0.1 mg, 0.25 mg, 0.5 mg (usually white)

Use: Treatment of high blood pressure

Minor Side Effects: Diarrhea, itching, loss of appetite, nasal congestion, nausea, palpitations, rash, vomiting

Major Side Effects: Chest pain, depression, drowsiness, glaucoma, nightmares

Contraindications: Pregnancy

Warnings and Precautions: Depression, gallstones, peptic ulcer, ulcerative colitis, liver and kidney diseases

Interacts With: amphetamine, decongestants, levodopa, monoamine oxidase inhibitors

Comments: Reserpine antihypertensive is a powerful drug that may persist in the body for several months after the medication is discontinued, and patients must be watched for signs of drug-induced depression which might lead to suicide.

Take reserpine antihypertensive with food or milk.

The effects of reserpine antihypertensive therapy may not be apparent for at least two weeks.

Mild side effects (e.g., nasal congestion) are most noticeable during the first two weeks of therapy and become less bothersome after this period.

Reserpine antihypertensive may cause drowsiness or depression; to prevent oversedation, avoid the use of other sedative drugs or alcohol. If you feel continually tired or depressed, consult your doctor.

If dizziness or light-headedness occurs when you stand up, place your legs on the floor and "pump" the muscles for a few moments before rising.

While taking reserpine antihypertensive, do not take any nonprescription item for cough, cold, or sinus problems without first checking with your doctor.

Brands of reserpine antihypertensive vary widely in cost. Ask your pharmacist to fill your prescription with the least expensive brand.

Reserpine causes cancer in rats. It has not yet been shown to cause cancer in people.

Reserpoid antihypertensive (The Upjohn Company), see reserpine antihypertensive.

Ritalin adrenergic

Manufacturer: CIBA Pharmaceuticals Company
Generic Name: methylphenidate hydrochloride
Equivalent Products: None
Dosage Form: Tablets: 5 mg (yellow), 10 mg (green), 20 mg (peach)
Use: Relief of mild depression, treatment of hyperkinesis in children, treatment of narcolepsy
Minor Side Effects: Headache, insomnia, nausea, nervousness, palpitations, rash, vomiting
Major Side Effects: Chest pain, high blood pressure; in children, abdominal pain, impairment of growth, weight loss
Contraindications: Agitation, certain types of glaucoma, severe anxiety or tension, history of drug abuse
Warnings and Precautions: High blood pressure, pregnancy, epilepsy
Interacts With: acetazolamide, guanethidine, monoamine oxidase inhibitors, phenothiazines, sodium bicarbonate, antidepressants.
Comments: Do not take Ritalin adrenergic later than 3:00 P.M. to avoid sleeplessness.

While taking Ritalin adrenergic, do not take any nonprescription item for cough, cold, or sinus problems without first checking with your doctor.

Ritalin adrenergic may mask symptoms of fatigue and pose serious danger; never take Ritalin adrenergic as a stimulant to keep you awake.

Ritalin adrenergic has the potential for abuse and must be used with caution. Tolerance may develop quickly; *do not* increase the dose of this drug without first consulting your doctor.

If your child's teacher tells you your child is hyperkinetic, take the child to a physician for diagnosis.

A hyperkinetic child may need to take a dose of Ritalin adrenergic at noontime. Make arrangements with the school nurse to supervise administration of the drug.

Robamox antibiotic (A.H. Robins Company), see amoxicillin antibiotic.

Robaxin muscle relaxant

Manufacturer: A.H. Robins Company
Generic Name: methocarbamol
Equivalent Products: Delaxin muscle relaxant (Ferndale Laboratories, Inc.)
Dosage Form: Tablets: 500 mg, 750 mg (white)
Use: Relief of pain in muscles or joints
Minor Side Effects: Blurred vision, dizziness, drowsiness, headache, lightheadedness, nasal congestion, nausea, rash
Major Side Effects: Fever
Contraindications: Pregnancy
Warnings and Precautions: Liver or kidney diseases
Interacts With: central nervous system depressants
Comments: Robaxin muscle relaxant is not a substitute for rest, physical

therapy, or other measures recommended by your doctor to treat your condition.

Robaxin muscle relaxant may cause drowsiness; to prevent oversedation, avoid the use of other sedative drugs or alcohol.

A.H. Robins Company also produces a product called Robaxisal muscle relaxant and analgesic which is a combination of Robaxin muscle relaxant and aspirin.

Delaxin muscle relaxant is equivalent to Robaxin muscle relaxant, and buying it may save you money. Discuss this with your pharmacist.

Robaxisal muscle relaxant and analgesic (A.H. Robins Company), see Robaxin muscle relaxant.

Robitet antibiotic (A.H. Robins Company), see tetracycline hydrochloride antibiotic.

Ro-Chloro-Serp antihypertensive and diuretic (Robinson Laboratory, Inc.), see Hydropres antihypertensive and diuretic.

Ro-Chloro-Serp-500 antihypertensive (Robinson Laboratory, Inc.), see Diupres antihypertensive.

Ro-Chlorozide diuretic (Robinson Laboratory, Inc.), see Diuril diuretic.

Rocinolone steroid hormone (Robinson Laboratory, Inc.), see Aristocort steroid hormone.

Ro-Diet adrenergic (Robinson Laboratory, Inc.), see Tenuate adrenergic.

Rolabromophen antihistamine (Robinson Laboratory, Inc.), see Dimetane antihistamine.

Rolazine antihypertensive (Robinson Laboratory, Inc.), see Apresoline antihypertensive.

Ropred steroid hormone (Robinson Laboratory, Inc.), see prednisone steroid hormone.

Rosoxol antibacterial (Robinson Laboratory, Inc.), see Gantrisin antibacterial.

Ro-Thyroxine thyroid hormone (Robinson Laboratory, Inc.), see thyroid hormone.

Rozolamide diuretic (Robinson Laboratory, Inc.), see Diamox diuretic.

Salutensin antihypertensive and diuretic

Manufacturer: Bristol Laboratories
Generic Name: hydroflumethiazide, reserpine
Equivalent Products: None

Dosage Form: Tablets: hydroflumethiazide, 50 mg; reserpine, 0.125 mg (green)

Use: Treatment of high blood pressure

Minor Side Effects: Abdominal pain, constipation, diarrhea, dizziness, headache, itching, loss of appetite, nasal congestion, nausea, palpitations, rash, tingling in fingers and toes

Major Side Effects: Depression, drowsiness, glaucoma, muscle spasms, nightmares, sedation, weakness, blurred vision

Contraindications: Allergy to sulfa drugs, severe kidney disease, pregnancy

Warnings and Precautions: Bronchial asthma, depression, gallstones, peptic ulcer, ulcerative colitis, liver and kidney diseases

Interacts With: amphetamine, colestipol hydrochloride, decongestants, digitalis, levodopa, lithium carbonate, monoamine oxidase inhibitors, oral antidiabetics, steroids

Comments: A doctor probably should not prescribe Salutensin antihypertensive and diuretic or other "fixed dose" products as the first choice in the treatment of high blood pressure. The patient should receive each of the individual ingredients singly, and if response is adequate to the fixed doses contained in Salutensin antihypertensive and diuretic, this product can then be substituted. The advantage of a combination product such as Salutensin antihypertensive and diuretic is based on increased convenience to the patient.

Take Salutensin antihypertensive and diuretic with food or milk.

Salutensin antihypertensive and diuretic causes frequent urination. Expect this effect; it should not alarm you.

The effects of Salutensin antihypertensive and diuretic therapy may not be apparent for at least two weeks.

Mild side effects (e.g., nasal congestion) are most noticeable during the first two weeks of therapy and become less bothersome after this period.

Salutensin antihypertensive and diuretic can cause potassium loss. To avoid potassium loss, take Salutensin antihypertensive and diuretic with a glass of fresh or frozen orange juice. You may also eat a banana each day. The use of Diasal or Co-Salt salt substitutes helps prevent potassium loss.

Salutensin antihypertensive and diuretic may cause drowsiness or depression; to prevent oversedation, avoid the use of other sedative drugs. If you feel continually tired or depressed, consult your doctor.

While taking this product (as with many drugs that lower blood pressure), you should limit your consumption of alcoholic beverages in order to prevent dizziness or light-headedness.

If dizziness or light-headedness occurs when you stand up, place the legs on the floor and "pump" the muscles for a few moments before rising.

Persons taking this product and digitalis should watch carefully for symptoms of increased toxicity (e.g., nausea, blurred vision, palpitations).

While taking Salutensin antihypertensive and diuretic, do not take any nonprescription item for cough, cold, or sinus problems without first checking with your doctor.

Products equivalent to Salutensin antihypertensive and diuretic are available and vary widely in cost. Ask your doctor to prescribe a generic preparation; then ask your pharmacist to fill it with the least expensive brand.

Reserpine causes cancer in rats. It has not yet been shown to cause cancer in people.

If you are allergic to a sulfa drug, you may likewise be allergic to Salutensin antihypertensive and diuretic.

Seconal sodium sedative and hypnotic (Eli Lilly and Company), see Nembutal sedative and hypnotic.

Sedralex sedative and anticholinergic (Kay Pharmacal Co., Inc.), see Donnatal sedative and anticholinergic.

Selsun seborrheic shampoo

Manufacturer: Abbott Laboratories
Generic Name: selenium sulfide
Equivalent Products: Exsel seborrheic shampoo (Herbert Laboratories); Iosel 250 seborrheic shampoo (Owen Drug Company); Sul-Blue seborrheic shampoo (Columbia Medical Co.)
Dosage Form: Shampoo
Use: Treatment of dandruff or dermatitis of the scalp
Minor Side Effects: Discoloration of hair (rare), dryness or oiliness of hair and scalp, eye irritation
Major Side Effects: No major side effects
Contraindications: Inflamed scalp
Warnings and Precautions: No major warnings or precautions
Interacts With: No significant drug interactions
Comments: Although there have been no reports of serious toxicity if Selsun seborrheic shampoo is swallowed, call your doctor or your pharmacist immediately.
Selsun Blue seborrheic shampoo is a weaker product and can be purchased without a prescription.

Septra antibacterial (Burroughs Wellcome Co.), see Bactrim antibacterial.

Ser-Ap-Es antihypertensive and diuretic

Manufacturer: CIBA Pharmaceutical Company
Generic Name: hydralazine hydrochloride, hydrochlorothiazide, reserpine
Equivalent Products: Hydrotensin-Plus antihypertensive and diuretic (Mayrand Inc.); Unipres antihypertensive and diuretic (Reid-Provident Laboratories, Inc.)
Dosage Form: Tablets: hydralazine hydrochloride, 25 mg; hydrochlorothiazide, 15 mg; reserpine, 0.1 mg (salmon)
Use: Treatment of high blood pressure
Minor Side Effects: Abdominal pains, constipation, diarrhea, dizziness, headache, loss of appetite, nasal congestion, nausea, palpitations, tingling in fingers or toes, vomiting
Major Side Effects: Depression, joint tenderness, muscle spasms, rash, sedation, weakness, blurred vision, drowsiness
Contraindications: Allergy to sulfa drugs, coronary heart disease, peptic ulcer, suicidal tendencies, severe kidney disease, pregnancy

Warnings and Precautions: Bronchial asthma, suspected coronary heart disease, diabetes, gout, liver and kidney diseases, depression, peptic ulcer, ulcerative colitis

Interacts With: amphetamine, antidiabetics, colestipol hydrochloride, decongestants, digitalis, levodopa, lithium carbonate, monoamine oxidase inhibitors, steroids

Comments: A doctor probably should not prescribe Ser-Ap-Es antihypertensive and diuretic or other "fixed dose" products as the first choice in the treatment of high blood pressure. The patient should receive each of the individual ingredients singly, and if response is adequate to the fixed doses contained in Ser-Ap-Es antihypertensive and diuretic, this product can then be substituted. The advantage of a combination product such as Ser-Ap-Es antihypertensive and diuretic is based on increased convenience to the patient.

Take Ser-Ap-Es antihypertensive and diuretic with food or milk.

Ser-Ap-Es antihypertensive and diuretic causes frequent urination. Expect this effect; it should not alarm you.

The effects of Ser-Ap-Es antihypertensive and diuretic therapy may not be apparent for at least two weeks.

Mild side effects (e.g., nasal congestion) are most noticeable during the first two weeks of therapy and become less bothersome after this period.

Ser-Ap-Es antihypertensive and diuretic can cause potassium loss. To avoid potassium loss, take Ser-Ap-Es antihypertensive and diuretic with a glass of fresh or frozen orange juice. You may also eat a banana each day. The use of Diasal or Co-Salt salt substitutes helps prevent potassium loss.

Ser-Ap-Es antihypertensive and diuretic may cause drowsiness; to prevent oversedation, avoid the use of other sedative drugs. If you find that you are continually tired or depressed, consult your doctor.

While taking this product (as with many drugs that lower blood pressure), you should limit your consumption of alcoholic beverages in order to prevent dizziness or light-headedness.

If dizziness or light-headedness occurs when you stand up, place your legs on the floor and "pump" the muscles for a few moments before rising.

Persons taking this product and digitalis should watch carefully for symptoms of increased toxicity (e.g., nausea, blurred vision, palpitations.)

While taking Ser-Ap-Es antihypertensive and diuretic, do not take any nonprescription item for cough, cold, or sinus problems without first checking with your doctor.

Products equivalent to Ser-Ap-Es antihypertensive and diuretic are available and vary widely in cost. Ask your doctor to prescribe a generic preparation; then ask your pharmacist to fill it with the least expensive brand.

If you experience numbness or tingling in your fingers or toes when taking Ser-Ap-Es antihypertensive and diuretic, your doctor may recommend that you take vitamin B_6 (pyridoxine) to relieve the symptoms.

If you are allergic to sulfa drugs, you may likewise be allergic to Ser-Ap-Es antihypertensive and diuretic.

Serax sedative and hypnotic

Manufacturer: Wyeth Laboratories
Generic Name: oxazepam

Equivalent Products: None
Dosage Forms: Capsules: 10 mg (pink/white), 15 mg (red/white), 30 mg (maroon/white); tablets: 15 mg (yellow)
Use: Relief of anxiety, nervousness, tension, relief of muscle spasms, withdrawal from alcohol addiction
Minor Side Effects: Confusion, constipation, depression, difficult urination, dizziness, drowsiness, dry mouth, fatigue, headache, nausea, rash, slurred speech, uncoordinated movements
Major Side Effects: Blurred vision, decreased sexual drive, double vision, jaundice, low blood pressure, stimulation, tremors
Contraindications: Certain types of glaucoma
Warnings and Precautions: Pregnancy, suicidal tendencies, liver and kidney diseases, potential for abuse
Interacts With: central nervous system depressants
Comments: Serax sedative and hypnotic currently is used by many people to relieve nervousness. It is effective for this purpose, but it is important to try to remove the cause of the anxiety as well. Phenobarbital is also effective for this, and it is less expensive. Consult your doctor.

Serax sedative and hypnotic may cause dryness of the mouth. To reduce this feeling, chew gum or suck on a piece of hard candy.

Avoid the use of other sedative drugs or alcohol. Serax sedative and hypnotic taken alone is a safe drug; when it is combined with other sedative drugs or alcohol, serious adverse reactions may develop.

Serax sedative and hypnotic has the potential for abuse and must be used with caution. Tolerance may develop quickly; *do not* increase the dose of this drug without first consulting your doctor.

Serax sedative and hypnotic may cause drowsiness; try to avoid driving or operating machinery while taking it.

Sereen sedative and hypnotic (Foy Laboratories, Inc.), see Librium sedative and hypnotic.

Serpasil antihypertensive (CIBA Pharmaceutical Company), see reserpine antihypertensive.

Servisone steroid hormone (Lederle Laboratories), see prednisone steroid hormone.

Setamine sedative and anticholinergic (Tutag Pharmaceuticals, Inc.), see Donnatal sedative and anticholinergic.

Sherafed adrenergic and antihistamine tablets (Sheraton Laboratories, Inc.), see Actifed adrenergic and antihistamine.

Sherafed-C expectorant (Sheraton Laboratories, Inc.), see Actifed-C expectorant.

Sinequan antidepressant

Manufacturer: Pfizer Laboratories Division
Generic Name: doxepin hydrochloride

Equivalent Products: Adapin antidepressant (Pennwalt Prescription Products)
Dosage Forms: Oral concentrate liquid (content per 1 ml): 10 mg; Capsules: 10 mg (red/pink), 25 mg (blue/pink), 50 mg (light pink/pink), 75 mg (light brown), 100 mg (blue/light pink), 150 mg (blue)
Use: Control of bed-wetting, relief of depression
Minor Side Effects: Diarrhea, dizziness, fatigue, hair loss, headache, loss of appetite, nausea, numbness in fingers or toes, palpitations, rash, uncoordinated movements, vomiting, weakness, difficult urination, drowsiness, photosensitivity
Major Side Effects: Enlarged or painful breasts (in both sexes), imbalance, heart attack, high or low blood pressure, impotence, jaundice, mouth sores, ringing in the ears, sore throat, stroke, tremors, weight loss or gain (in children), fatigue, mild stomach upset, nervousness, sleep disorders
Contraindications: Recent heart attack
Warnings and Precautions: Certain types of glaucoma, certain types of heart disease, epilepsy, hyperthyroidism, pregnancy, difficult urination
Interacts With: alcohol, amphetamine, barbiturates, epinephrine, guanethidine, monoamine oxidase inhibitors, oral anticoagulants, phenylephrine, clonidine, central nervous system depressants
Comments: The effects of Sinequan antidepressant therapy may not be apparent for at least two weeks.

While taking Sinequan antidepressant, do not take any nonprescription item for cough, cold, or sinus problems without first checking with your doctor. Do not stop or start any other drug.

Sinequan antidepressant interacts with sedative drugs or alcohol. Avoid using them while taking Sinequan antidepressant.

Sinequan antidepressant may cause dryness of the mouth. To reduce this feeling, chew gum or suck on a piece of hard candy.

Sinequan antidepressant reduces sweating; avoid excessive work or exercise in hot weather.

Products equivalent to Sinequan antidepressant are available and vary widely in cost. Ask your doctor to prescribe a generic preparation; then ask your pharmacist to fill it with the least expensive brand.

Avoid long sun exposure while taking Sinequan antidepressant.

Immediately before taking Sinequan antidepressant oral concentrate liquid, it should be diluted in about a half-glassful of water. Do not mix your dosage until just before you take it.

SK-Lygen sedative and hypnotic (Smith Kline & French Laboratories), see Librium sedative and hypnotic.

SK-Niacin vitamin supplement (Smith Kline & French Laboratories), see nicotinic acid vitamin supplement.

SK-Phenobarbital sedative and hypnotic (Smith Kline & French Laboratories), see phenobarbital sedative and hypnotic.

SK-Pramine antidepressant (Smith Kline & French Laboratories), see Tofranil antidepressant.

SK-Prednisone steroid hormone (Smith Kline & French Laboratories), see prednisone steroid hormone.

SK-Soxazole antibacterial (Smith Kline & French Laboratories), see Gantrisin antibacterial.

SK-Triamcinolone steroid hormone (Smith Kline & French Laboratories), see Kenalog steroid hormone.

Slo-Phyllin expectorant and smooth muscle relaxant (Dooner Laboratories, Inc.), see Quibron expectorant and smooth muscle relaxant.

Slow-K potassium replacement (CIBA Pharmaceutical Company), see potassium chloride replacement.

Sodestrin estrogen hormone (Tutag Pharmaceuticals, Inc.), see Premarin estrogen hormone.

Solfoton sedative and hypnotic (Wm. P. Poythress & Co. Inc.), see phenobarbital sedative and hypnotic.

Soma Compound muscle relaxant and analgesic

Manufacturer: Wallace Laboratories
Generic Name: carisoprodol, phenacetin, caffeine
Equivalent Products: None
Dosage Form: Tablets: carisoprodol, 200 mg; phenacetin, 160 mg; caffeine, 32 mg (orange)
Use: Relief of pain in muscles or joints
Minor Side Effects: Diarrhea, dizziness, drowsiness, fatigue, light-headedness, nausea, rash, vomiting, ringing in the ears
Major Side Effects: Fainting, flushing, palpitations, rapid heartbeat, kidney disease
Contraindications: Porphyria, bleeding ulcers, pregnancy
Warnings and Precautions: Liver or kidney diseases, potential for abuse
Interacts With: central nervous system depressants
Comments: Soma Compound muscle relaxant and analgesic is not a substitute for rest, physical therapy, or other measures recommended by your doctor to treat your condition.
 Soma Compound muscle relaxant and analgesic may cause drowsiness; to prevent oversedation, avoid the use of other sedative drugs or alcohol.
 Soma Compound muscle relaxant and analgesic has the potential for abuse and must be used with caution. Tolerance may develop quickly; *do not* increase the drug without first consulting your doctor.

Somophyllin bronchodilator (Fisons Corporation), see aminophylline bronchodilator.

Sopor sedative and hypnotic (Arnar-Stone Laboratories, Inc.), see Quaalude sedative and hypnotic.

Sorbide antianginal (Mayrand, Inc.), see Isordil antianginal.

Sorbitrate antianginal (Stuart Pharmaceuticals), see Isordil antianginal.

Spalix sedative and anticholinergic (Reid-Provident Laboratories, Inc.), see Donnatal sedative and anticholinergic.

Spen-Histine Elixir adrenergic and antihistamine (Spencer-Mead Inc.), see Novahistine Elixir adrenergic and antihistamine.

Spentane antihistamine (Spencer-Mead, Inc.), see Dimetane antihistamine.

Stelazine phenothiazine

Manufacturer: Smith Kline & French Laboratories
Generic Name: trifluoperazine hydrochloride
Equivalent Products: None
Dosage Form: Tablets: 1 mg, 2 mg, 5 mg, 10 mg, (all blue)
Use: Management of certain psychotic disorders, relief of excessive anxiety or tension
Minor Side Effects: Blurred vision, change in urine color, constipation, diarrhea, drooling, drowsiness, dry mouth, jitteriness, menstrual irregularities, nasal congestion, nausea, rash, restlessness, uncoordinated movements, vomiting
Major Side Effects: Difficulty in swallowing; enlarged or painful breasts (in both sexes); fluid retention; impotence; involuntary movements of the face, mouth, tongue, or jaw; muscle stiffness; sore throat; tremors; jaundice; rise in blood pressure
Contraindications: Coma, drug-induced depression, shock, blood disease, Parkinson's disease, liver damage, jaundice, kidney disease, stroke, pregnancy
Warnings and Precautions: Asthma and other respiratory disorders, epilepsy, exposure to extreme heat
Interacts With: alcohol, antacids, anticholinergics, depressants
Comments: The effects of Stelazine phenothiazine therapy may not be apparent for at least two weeks.

Stelazine phenothiazine has sustained action; so never take it more frequently than your doctor prescribes. A serious overdose may result.

While taking Stelazine phenothiazine, do not take any nonprescription item for cough, cold, or sinus problems without first checking with your doctor.

Stelazine phenothiazine interacts with sedative drugs and alcohol. Avoid using them while taking Stelazine phenothiazine.

Stelazine phenothiazine may cause dryness of the mouth. To reduce this feeling, chew gum or suck on a piece of hard candy.

Stelazine phenothiazine reduces sweating; therefore, avoid excessive work or exercise in hot weather.

If dizziness or light-headedness occurs when you stand up, place the legs on the floor and "pump" the muscles for a few moments before rising.

As with any other drug that has antivomiting activity, symptoms of severe disease or toxicity due to overdose of other drugs may be masked by Stelazine phenothiazine.

Sub-Quin antiarrhythmic (Scrip-Physician Supply Co.), see Pronestyl anti-arrhythmic.

Sudafed adrenergic

Manufacturer: Burroughs Wellcome Co.
Generic Name: pseudoephedrine hydrochloride
Equivalent Products: Neofed adrenergic (The Vale Chemical Co., Inc.); Sudecon adrenergic (Corvit Pharmaceuticals)
Dosage Forms: Liquid (content per 5 ml): 30 mg; tablets: 30 mg (red), 60 mg (white); sustained-action capsules, 120 mg
Use: Relief of nasal or ear congestion
Minor Side Effects: Mild to moderate stimulation, nausea, vomiting
Major Side Effects: High blood pressure, chest pain
Contraindications: Severe heart disease, pregnancy
Warnings and Precautions: Diabetes, high blood pressure, hyperthyroidism
Interacts With: guanethidine, monoamine oxidase inhibitors
Comments: Sudafed adrenergic in 30 mg tablets and liquid may be purchased without a prescription.

While taking Sudafed adrenergic, do not take any nonprescription item for cough, cold, or sinus problems without first checking with your doctor.

Products equivalent to Sudafed adrenergic are available and vary widely in price. Ask your doctor to prescribe a generic preparation, and have your pharmacist fill your prescription with the least expensive brand.

Sudecon adrenergic (Corvit Pharmaceuticals), see Sudafed adrenergic.

Sul-Blue seborrheic shampoo (Columbia Medical Co.), see Selsun seborrheic shampoo.

Suldiazo antibacterial and analgesic (Kay Pharmacal Company, Inc.), see Azo Gantrisin antibacterial and analgesic.

Sulfalar antibacterial (Parke, Davis & Company), see Gantrisin antibacterial.

Sultrin vaginal anti-infective

Manufacturer: Ortho Pharmaceutical Corporation
Generic Name: sulfathiazole, sulfacetamide, sulfabenzamide, urea
Equivalent Products: None
Dosage Forms: Vaginal cream, vaginal tablets
Use: Treatment of vaginal infections
Minor Side Effects: Mild vaginal itching and irritation
Major Side Effects: No major side effects
Contraindications: Allergy to sulfa drugs, kidney disease
Warnings and Precautions: No major warnings or precautions
Interacts With: No known drug interactions
Comments: Triple Sulfa vaginal cream (E. Fougera and Co.) contains the same ingredients as Sultrin vaginal cream and tablets, but at different strengths.
Use until the prescribed amount of medication is gone.

Call your doctor if you develop burning or itching.

Refrain from sexual intercourse, or ask your sexual partner to use a condom until treatment is finished, to avoid reinfection.

See the chapter "The Right Way To Take Medications."

Sumox antibiotic (Reid-Provident Laboratories, Inc.), see amoxicillin antibiotic.

Sumycin antibiotic (E.R. Squibb & Sons), see tetracycline hydrochloride antibiotic.

Surfak stool softener

Manufacturer: Hoechst-Roussel Pharmaceuticals, Inc.
Generic Name: dioctyl calcium sulfosuccinate
Equivalent Products: None
Dosage Forms: Capsules: 50 mg (orange), 240 mg (red)
Use: Relief of constipation
Minor Side Effects: No minor side effects
Major Side Effects: No major side effects
Contraindications: Pregnancy
Warnings and Precautions: Liver or kidney diseases
Interacts With: No significant drug interactions
Comments: Take Surfak stool softener with at least a full glass of water. Drink at least nine to 10 glasses of water each day.

The effects of Surfak stool softener may not be apparent for several days. Surfak stool softener can be purchased without a prescription.

Although no exact generic equivalents are available, similar stool softeners are, and they may be less expensive. Talk to your doctor about using a substitute.

Synalar steroid hormone

Manufacturer: Syntex Laboratories, Inc.
Generic Name: fluocinolone acetonide
Equivalent Products: None
Dosage Forms: Cream; ointment; solution
Use: Relief of skin inflammation associated with such conditions as dermatitis, eczema, or poison ivy
Minor Side Effects: Burning sensation, dryness, irritation, itching, rash
Major Side Effects: Secondary infection
Contraindications: No absolute contraindications
Warnings and Precautions: Diseases that severely impair blood circulation, viral or bacterial skin infections
Interacts With: No significant drug interactions
Comments: If the affected area is extremely dry or is scaling, the skin may be moistened before applying the medication by soaking in water or by applying water with a clean cloth. The ointment form is probably better for dry skin. The solution is best for hairy areas.

Do not use Synalar steroid hormone with an occlusive wrap unless directed to do so by your doctor. See the chapter "The Right Way To Take Medications."

Synalgos-DC analgesic

Manufacturer: Ives Laboratories, Inc.
Generic Name: dihydrocodeine bitartrate, aspirin, phenacetin, caffeine, promethazine hydrochloride
Equivalent Products: None
Dosage Form: Capsules: dihydrocodeine bitartrate, 16 mg; aspirin, 194 mg; phenacetin, 162 mg; caffeine, 30 mg; promethazine hydrochloride, 6.25 mg (blue/gray)
Use: Relief of moderate to severe pain
Minor Side Effects: Constipation, dizziness, drowsiness, itching, lightheadedness, nausea, sedation, vomiting, dry mouth, nasal congestion, menstrual irregularities, jitteriness, blurred vision, flushing, palpitations, rash, sweating, odd movements, ringing in the ears
Major Side Effects: Sore throat, muscle stiffness, fluid retention, rise in blood pressure, kidney disease, jaundice, low blood sugar, tremors, rapid heartbeat, breathing difficulties, death
Contraindications: Bleeding ulcers, coma, drug-induced depression, shock, blood disease, Parkinson's disease, liver damage, jaundice, kidney disease, stroke, heart disease, pregnancy
Warnings and Precautions: Certain types of heart disease, peptic ulcer, potential for drug abuse, asthma and other respiratory problems, epilepsy, head injury, blood coagulation problems, exposure to extreme heat
Interacts With: alcohol, ammonium chloride, amphetamine, methotrexate, antacids, oral anticoagulants, oral antidiabetics, probenecid, steroids, sulfinpyrazone, anticholinergics, central nervous system depressants
Comments: Products containing narcotics (e.g., dihydrocodeine bitartrate) are usually not taken for more than seven to 10 days.

While taking Synalgos-DC analgesic, do not take any nonprescription item for cough, cold, or sinus problems without first checking with your doctor.

If you are also taking an anticoagulant ("blood thinner"), remind your doctor.

Synalgos-DC analgesic interacts with alcohol; avoid using alcohol while taking Synalgos-DC analgesic.

Synalgos-DC analgesic has the potential for abuse and must be used with caution. Tolerance may develop quickly; *do not* increase the dose of the drug without first consulting your doctor.

Although no product exactly equivalent to Synalgos-DC analgesic is available, similar products are, and buying them may save you money. Consult your doctor.

Take this product with food or milk.

If your ears feel strange, if you hear buzzing or ringing, or if your stomach hurts, your dosage may need adjustment. Consult your doctor.

Synthroid thyroid hormone

Manufacturer: Flint Laboratories

Generic Name: sodium levothyroxine
Equivalent Products: sodium levothyroxine (various manufacturers); Levoid thyroid hormone (Nutrition Control Products); Letter thyroid hormone (Armour Pharmaceutical Company); Ro-Thyroxine thyroid hormone (Robinson Laboratory, Inc.)
Dosage Forms: Tablets: 0.025 mg (orange), 0.05 mg (white), 0.1 mg (yellow), 0.15 mg (blue), 0.2 mg (pink), 0.3 mg (green)
Use: Thyroid replacement therapy
Minor Side Effects: None
Major Side Effects: Chest pain, diarrhea, headache, heat intolerance, insomnia, nervousness, palpitations, sweating, weight loss
Contraindications: No absolute contraindications
Warnings and Precautions: Heart disease, high blood pressure, diabetes
Interacts With: cholestyramine, digitalis, oral anticoagulants, oral antidiabetics, phenytoin
Comments: For most patients, thyroid hormone (see "thyroid hormone") tablets will do as well and cost only a fraction of the price of sodium levothyroxine products.

While taking Synthroid thyroid hormone, do not take any nonprescription item for cough, cold, or sinus problems without first checking with your doctor.

Persons taking this product and digitalis should watch carefully for symptoms of increased toxicity (e.g., nausea, blurred vision, palpitations).

Be sure to follow your doctor's directions exactly.

Most side effects from this drug can be controlled by adjusting dosage. Check with your doctor.

Tagamet antisecretory

Manufacturer: Smith Kline & French Laboratories
Generic Name: cimetidine
Equivalent Products: None
Dosage Forms: Tablets: 300 mg (pale green)
Use: Treatment of duodenal peptic ulcer and treatment of long-term excessive gastric acid secretion
Minor Side Effects: Diarrhea, muscle pain, dizziness, rash, confusion
Major Side Effects: Increased breast size (in both sexes), blood damage
Contraindications: Pregnancy
Warnings and Precautions: Do not take for longer than eight consecutive weeks to treat an ulcer. Use in children under age 16 with extreme care.
Interacts With: anticoagulants
Comments: Although Tagamet antisecretory is classed as a histamine receptor blocker, it has no action on histamine anywhere in the body except in the stomach and intestine. It should not be used for other purposes.

Tagamet tablets should not be crushed or chewed because cimetidine has a bitter taste and unpleasant odor.

Antacid therapy must be continued while taking Tagamet antisecretory.

Tagamet antisecretory therapy for four to six weeks can result in healing of ulcers. However, taking Tagamet antisecretory will make no difference in onset of future ulcer attacks. Tagamet tablets are extremely expensive ($22 to

$30 for a month's supply). Ask your doctor if some other medication will give similiar relief from your ulcer discomfort.

Talwin analgesic

Manufacturer: Winthrop Laboratories
Generic Name: pentazocine hydrochloride
Equivalent Products: None
Dosage Form: Tablets: 50 mg (peach)
Use: Relief of moderate to severe pain
Minor Side Effects: Constipation, diarrhea, dizziness, headache, insomnia, lightheadedness, loss of appetite, nausea, vomiting
Major Side Effects: Blurred vision, euphoria, nightmares
Contraindications: Pregnancy
Warnings and Precautions: Asthma and other respiratory problems, epilepsy, potential for drug abuse, head injury, liver and kidney diseases
Interacts With: alcohol, narcotics, phenothiazines, antidepressants
Comments: Talwin analgesic interacts with alcohol; avoid the use of alcohol while taking Talwin analgesic.

Talwin analgesic has the potential for abuse and must be used with caution. Tolerance may develop quickly; *do not* increase the dose of this drug without first consulting your doctor.

Tandearil anti-inflammatory (USV [P.R.] Development Corp.), see Butazolidin anti-inflammatory.

Tedral antiasthmatic

Manufacturer: Warner/Chilcott
Generic Name: theophylline, ephedrine hydrochloride, phenobarbital
Equivalent Products: Asma-lief antiasthmatic (Columbia Medical Co.)
Dosage Forms: Elixir (content per 5 ml): theophylline, 32.5 mg; ephedrine hydrochloride, 6 mg; phenobarbital, 2 mg. Sustained-action tablets: theophylline, 180 mg; ephedrine hydrochloride, 48 mg; phenobarbital, 25 mg (coral/mottled white); Tablets: theophylline, 130 mg; ephedrine hydrochloride, 24 mg; phenobarbital, 8 mg (white)
Use: Prevention and relief of bronchial asthma
Minor Side Effects: Difficult urination, insomnia, stimulation, nausea, vomiting, drowsiness
Major Side Effects: High blood pressure, chest pain, convulsions, difficult breathing, palpitations, cold and clammy skin
Contraindications: Severe heart disease, porphyria
Warnings and Precautions: Certain types of glaucoma, certain kinds of heart disease, enlarged prostate, hyperthyroidism, pregnancy, high blood pressure, diabetes, history of drug abuse
Interacts With: central nervous system depressants, griseofulvin, guanethidine, propranolol, lithium carbonate, monoamine oxidase inhibitors, oral anticoagulants, steroids, sulfonamides, tetracycline, antidepressants

216

Comments: Take Tedral antiasthmatic with food or milk.

Never take Tedral antiasthmatic more frequently than your doctor prescribes. A serious overdose may result.

Tedral antiasthmatic may cause drowsiness; to prevent oversedation, avoid the use of other sedative drugs or alcohol.

If you are also taking an anticoagulant ("blood thinner"), remind your doctor.

In many states, Tedral antiasthmatic tablets and liquid may be sold without a prescription.

This product may aggravate ulcers. Call your doctor if you develop stomach pain or vomiting.

While taking Tedral antiasthmatic, do not take other products for cough, cold, or sinus problems without first checking with your doctor.

Products equivalent to Tedral antiasthmatic are available and vary widely in cost. Ask your doctor to prescribe a generic preparation, and have your pharmacist fill your prescription with the least expensive brand.

Tega-Span vitamin supplement (Ortega Pharmaceutical Co.), see nicotinic acid vitamin supplement.

Teldrin Spansule antihistamine (Smith Kline & French Laboratories), see chlorpheniramine maleate antihistamine.

Tenax sedative and hypnotic (Reid-Provident Laboratories, Inc.), see Librium sedative and hypnotic.

Tenuate adrenergic

Manufacturer: Merrell-National Laboratories
Generic Name: diethylpropion hydrochloride
Equivalent Products: Ro-Diet adrenergic (Robinson Laboratory, Inc.); Tepanil Ten-Tab adrenergic (Riker Laboratories, Inc.); o.b.c.t. adrenergic (Pharmics, Inc.); diethylpropion hydrochloride (various manufacturers)
Dosage Forms: Tablets: 25 mg (blue); sustained-action tablets: 75 mg (white)
Use: Short-term treatment of obesity
Minor Side Effects: Diarrhea, dizziness, dry mouth, headache, insomnia, nausea, palpitations, restlessness, unpleasant taste in the mouth, vomiting
Major Side Effects: High blood pressure, overstimulation of nerves, chest pain
Contraindications: Certain types of heart disease, diabetes, high blood pressure, thyroid disease, glaucoma, pregnancy
Warnings and Precautions: Potential for drug abuse, liver and kidney diseases
Interacts With: acetazolamide, guanethidine, monoamine oxidase inhibitors, phenothiazines, sodium bicarbonate, antidepressants
Comments: Weight loss is greatest during the first three weeks of Tenuate adrenergic therapy. To be effective, Tenuate adrenergic therapy must be accompanied by a low-caloric diet.

The effects of Tenuate adrenergic on appetite control wear off; so do not take this drug for more than three weeks at a time. One way to get full benefit from Tenuate adrenergic is to take the drug for three weeks, stop for three weeks, then resume Tenuate adrenergic therapy. Consult your doctor about this regimen.

Do not take Tenuate adrenergic later than 3:00 P.M. to avoid sleeplessness.

While taking Tenuate adrenergic, do not take any nonprescription item for cough, cold, or sinus problems without first checking with your doctor.

Tenuate adrenergic may mask symptoms of extreme fatigue and decrease your ability to perform potentially dangerous or hazardous tasks, such as driving or operating machinery.

Never take Tenuate adrenergic sustained-action tablets more frequently than your doctor prescribes. A serious overdose may result.

Tenuate adrenergic has the potential for abuse and must be used with caution. Tolerance may develop quickly; *do not* increase the drug without first consulting your doctor.

Products equivalent to Tenuate adrenergic are available and vary widely in cost. Ask your doctor to prescribe a generic preparation; then ask your pharmacist to fill it with the least expensive brand.

Tepanil Ten-Tab adrenergic (Riker Laboratories), see Tenuate adrenergic.

Terramycin antibiotic

Manufacturer: Pfizer Laboratories Division
Generic Name: oxytetracycline hydrochloride
Equivalent Products: oxytetracycline hydrochloride (various manufacturers); Oxlopar antibiotic (Parke, Davis & Company); Oxybiotic antibiotic (Star Pharmaceuticals, Inc.); Oxy-Tetrachel antibiotic (Rachelle Laboratories, Inc.); Uri-Tet antibiotic (American Urologicals, Inc.)
Dosage Form: Capsules: 125 mg, 250 mg (both are yellow)
Use: Treatment of acne and a wide variety of infections
Minor Side Effects: Diarrhea, loss of appetite, nausea, vomiting, photosensitivity
Major Side Effects: Anemia, itching, sore throat, superinfection, rash, vaginal and rectal itching, irritation of the mouth, ''black tongue''
Contraindications: Pregnancy
Warnings and Precautions: Age (children under age nine), liver and kidney diseases
Interacts With: barbiturates, carbamazepine, dairy products, diuretics, iron-containing products, antacids, phenytoin
Comments: Take Terramycin antibiotic on an empty stomach (one hour before or two hours after a meal).

Do not take Terramycin antibiotic at the same time as milk or other dairy products or iron preparations. Separate taking the drugs by at least one hour.

Terramycin antibiotic should be taken for at least 10 full days, even if symptoms have disappeared.

While taking Terramycin antibiotic, avoid prolonged exposure to sunlight.

Products equivalent to Terramycin antibiotic are available and vary widely in cost. Ask your doctor to prescribe a generic preparation; then ask your pharmacist to fill it with the least expensive brand.

218

tetracycline hydrochloride antibiotic

Tetracycline hydrochloride is a generic drug.

Equivalent Products: Achromycin V antibiotic (Lederle Laboratories); Panmycin antibiotic (The Upjohn Company); Robitet antibiotic (A.H. Robins Company); Sumycin antibiotic (E.R. Squibb & Sons)

Dosage Forms: Achromycin V capsules: 100 mg, 250 mg, 500 mg (all are blue/yellow). Panmycin capsules: 250 mg (gray/orange); tablets: 250 mg, 500 mg (both are orange). Robitet capsules: 250 mg (brown/pink), 500 mg (red/white). Sumycin capsules: 250 mg (pink), 500 mg (pink/white); tablets: 250 mg (pink, oval), 500 mg (dark pink, oval)

Use: Treatment of acne and a wide variety of bacterial infections

Minor Side Effects: Diarrhea, loss of appetite, nausea, vomiting, photosensitivity

Major Side Effects: Anemia, sore throat, superinfection, rash, vaginal and rectal itching, irritation of the mouth, "black tongue"

Contraindications: Pregnancy

Warnings and Precautions: Age (children under age nine), liver and kidney diseases

Interacts With: barbiturates, carbamazepine, dairy products, diuretics, iron-containing products, antacids, phenytoin

Comments: Take tetracycline hydrochloride antibiotic on an empty stomach (one hour before or two hours after a meal).

Do not take tetracycline hydrochloride antibiotic at the same time as milk or other dairy products or iron preparations. Separate taking the drugs by at least one hour.

Tetracycline hydrochloride antibiotic should be taken for at least 10 full days, even if symptoms have disappeared.

While taking tetracycline hydrochloride antibiotic, avoid prolonged exposure to sunlight.

Brands of tetracycline hydrochloride antibiotic vary widely in cost. Ask your pharmacist to fill your prescription with the least expensive brand.

Theophozine tablets adrenergic, sedative, and smooth muscle relaxant (Spencer-Mead Inc.), see Marax adrenergic, sedative, and smooth muscle relaxant.

Theozine adrenergic, sedative, and smooth muscle relaxant (Henry Schein, Inc.), see Marax adrenergic, sedative, and smooth muscle relaxant.

Thorazine phenothiazine

Manufacturer: Smith Kline & French Laboratories

Generic Name: chlorpromazine hydrochloride

Generic Equivalents: chlorpromazine hydrochloride (various manufacturers); Chlor-PZ phenothiazine (USV [P.R.] Development Corporation); Promapar phenothiazine (Parke, Davis & Company)

Dosage Forms: Tablets: 10 mg, 25 mg, 50 mg, 100 mg, 200 mg (all brown); time-release capsules: 30 mg, 75 mg, 150 mg, 200 mg, 300 mg (all brown/clear with brown and white beads)

Use: Management of certain psychotic disorders; treatment of intractable hiccups, nausea, vomiting

Minor Side Effects: Blurred vision, constipation, diarrhea, drooling, drowsiness, dry mouth, jitteriness, menstrual irregularities, nasal congestion, nausea, rash, restlessness, uncoordinated movements, vomiting, change in urine color, reduced sweating

Major Side Effects: Difficulty in swallowing; enlarged or painful breasts (in both sexes); fluid retention; impotence; involuntary movements of the face, mouth, tongue, or jaw; muscle stiffness; sore throat; tremors; jaundice; rise in blood pressure

Contraindications: Coma, drug-induced depression, shock, blood disease, Parkinson's disease, liver damage, jaundice, kidney disease, stroke, pregnancy

Warnings and Precautions: Asthma and other respiratory disorders, epilepsy, exposure to extreme heat

Interacts With: alcohol, antacids, anticholinergics, central nervous system depressants

Comments: The effects of Thorazine phenothiazine therapy may not be apparent for at least two weeks.

Thorazine phenothiazine has persistent action; never take it more frequently than your doctor prescribes. A serious overdose may result.

While taking Thorazine phenothiazine, do not take any nonprescription item for cough, cold, or sinus problems without first checking with your doctor.

Thorazine phenothiazine interacts with alcohol; avoid using alcohol while taking Thorazine phenothiazine.

Thorazine phenothiazine may cause dryness of the mouth. To reduce this feeling, chew gum or suck on a piece of hard candy.

Thorazine phenothiazine reduces sweating; avoid excessive work or exercise in hot weather.

If dizziness or light-headedness occurs when you stand up, place your legs on the floor and ''pump'' the muscles for a few moments before rising.

As with any other drug that has antivomiting activity, symptoms of severe disease or toxicity due to overdose of other drugs may be masked by Thorazine phenothiazine.

Products equivalent to Thorazine phenothiazine are available and vary widely in cost. Ask your doctor to prescribe a generic preparation; then ask your pharmacist to fill it with the least expensive brand.

Thyrar thyroid hormone (Armour Pharmaceutical Company), see thyroid hormone.

Thyrocrine thyroid hormone (Lemmon Pharmacal Company), see thyroid hormone.

thyroid hormone

Thyroid preparations are generic drugs.

Equivalent Products: thyroid hormone (various manufacturers); Thyrocrine thyroid hormone (Lemmon Pharmacal Company); Thyrar thyroid hormone (Armour Pharmaceutical Company)

Dosage Forms: Tablets: 16 mg, 32 mg, 65 mg, 98 mg, 130 mg, 150 mg, 195 mg, 260 mg, 325 mg; chewable tablets: 195 mg; enteric-coated tablets: 32 mg, 65 mg, 130 mg; time-release capsules: 32 mg, 65 mg, 98 mg, 130 mg, 195 mg, 260 mg, 325 mg (various colors)
Use: Thyroid replacement therapy
Minor Side Effects: No minor side effects when taken as directed
Major Side Effects: Chest pain, diarrhea, headache, heat intolerance, insomnia, nervousness, palpitations, sweating, weight loss
Contraindications: No major contraindications
Warnings and Precautions: Heart disease, high blood pressure, diabetes
Interacts With: cholestyramine, digitalis, oral anticoagulants, oral antidiabetics, phenytoin
Comments: Many other products regulate thyroid activity. These products have little advantage over thyroid tablets and are much more expensive.

While taking a thyroid preparation, do not take any nonprescription item for cough, cold, or sinus problems without first checking with your doctor.

Persons taking this product and digitalis should watch carefully for symptoms of increased toxicity (e.g., nausea, blurred vision, palpitations).

Brands of thyroid preparations vary widely in cost. Ask your pharmacist to fill your prescription with the least expensive brand.

Be sure to follow your doctor's directions exactly.

Most side effects from this drug can be controlled by dosage adjustment. Check with your doctor.

Tigan antinauseant

Manufacturer: Beecham Laboratories
Generic Name: trimethobenzamide hydrochloride
Equivalent Products: None
Dosage Forms: Capsules: 100 mg (blue/white), 250 mg (blue); suppositories
Use: Treatment of nausea or vomiting
Minor Side Effects: Drowsiness
Major Side Effects: No major side effects
Contraindications: Pregnancy
Warnings and Precautions: Liver or kidney diseases
Interacts With: No significant drug interactions
Comments: Tigan antinauseant may cause drowsiness; to prevent oversedation, avoid the use of other sedative drugs or alcohol.

Tofranil antidepressant

Manufacturer: Geigy Pharmaceuticals
Generic Name: imipramine hydrochloride, or pamoate
Equivalent Products: imipramine (various manufacturers); Imavate antidepressant (A.H. Robins Company); Janimine antidepressant (Abbott Laboratories); Presamine antidepressant (USV [P.R.] Development Corp.); SK-Pramine antidepressant (Smith Kline & French Laboratories)
Dosage Forms: Tablets: 10 mg, 25 mg, 50 mg (all coral); capsules: 75 mg (coral), 100 mg (coral/yellow), 125 mg (coral/bright yellow), 150 mg (coral)

Use: Control of bed-wetting, relief of depression

Minor Side Effects: Diarrhea, difficult urination, dizziness, drowsiness, fatigue, hair loss, headache, loss of appetite, nausea, numbness in fingers or toes, palpitations, rash, uncoordinated movements, vomiting, weakness, reduced sweating, photosensitivity

Major Side Effects: Enlarged or painful breasts (in both sexes), imbalance, heart attack, high or low blood pressure, impotence, jaundice, mouth sores, ringing in the ears, sore throat, stroke, tremors, weight loss or gain (in children), nervousness, sleep disorders

Contraindications: Recent heart attack

Warnings and Precautions: Certain types of glaucoma, certain types of heart disease, epilepsy, hyperthyroidism, pregnancy, difficult urination

Interacts With: alcohol, amphetamine, barbiturates, epinephrine, guanethidine, monoamine oxidase inhibitors, oral anticoagulants, phenylephrine, clonidine, central nervous system depressants

Comments: The effects of Tofranil antidepressant therapy may not be apparent for at least two weeks.

While taking Tofranil antidepressant, do not take any nonprescription item for cough, cold, or sinus problems without first checking with your doctor.

Tofranil antidepressant interacts with many other drugs and alcohol. Be careful about taking any other drugs while taking Tofranil antidepressant. Consult your doctor.

Tofranil antidepressant may cause dryness of the mouth. To reduce this feeling, chew gum or suck on a piece of hard candy.

Tofranil antidepressant reduces sweating; avoid excessive work or exercise in hot weather.

Products equivalent to Tofranil antidepressant are available and vary widely in cost. Ask your doctor to prescribe a generic preparation; then ask your pharmacist to fill it with the least expensive brand.

Tolectin anti-inflammatory

Manufacturer: McNeil Laboratories
Generic Name: tolmetin sodium
Equivalent Products: None
Dosage Form: Tablets: 200 mg (white)
Use: Relief of pain and swelling due to arthritis
Minor Side Effects: Bloating, cramps, diarrhea, flatulence, headache, heartburn, nausea, ringing in the ears, vomiting, drowsiness
Major Side Effects: Blood in stools, depression, fluid retention, hearing loss, jaundice, palpitations, tremors, visual disturbances, weight gain
Contraindications: Allergy to aspirin
Warnings and Precautions: Anemia, pregnancy, ulcers, heart disease, liver and kidney diseases
Interacts With: anticoagulants, aspirin, oral antidiabetics, phenytoin, sulfonamides
Comments: In numerous tests, Tolectin anti-inflammatory has been shown to be as effective as aspirin in the treatment of arthritis, but aspirin is still the drug of choice for the disease. Because of the high cost of Tolectin

anti-inflammatory, consult your doctor about prescribing proper doses of aspirin instead.

If you are allergic to aspirin, you may not be able to use Tolectin anti-inflammatory.

Do not take aspirin while taking Tolectin anti-inflammatory without first consulting your doctor.

Tolectin anti-inflammatory may cause drowsiness; avoid tasks that require alertness such as driving and operating machinery.

You should note improvement of your condition soon after you start using Tolectin anti-inflammatory; however, full benefit may not be obtained for as long as a month. It is important not to stop taking Tolectin anti-inflammatory even though symptoms have diminished or disappeared.

Tolectin anti-inflammatory is not a substitute for rest, physical therapy, or other measures recommended by your doctor to treat your condition.

Tolinase oral antidiabetic

Manufacturer: The Upjohn Company
Generic Name: tolazamide
Equivalent Products: None
Dosage Form: Tablets: 100 mg, 250 mg, 500 mg (all white)
Use: Treatment of diabetes mellitus
Minor Side Effects: Dizziness, fatigue, headache, nausea, rash, vomiting, weakness, diarrhea, loss of appetite
Major Side Effects: Jaundice, low blood sugar, sore throat
Contraindications: Acidosis, age (see "Comments"), coma, ketosis, severe infection, severe trauma, impending surgery
Warnings and Precautions: Liver or kidney diseases
Interacts With: alcohol, anabolic steroids, anticoagulants, aspirin, chloramphenicol, guanethidine, monoamine oxidase inhibitors, phenylbutazone, propranolol, steroids, sulfonamides, tetracycline, thiazide diuretics, thyroid hormone
Comments: Studies have shown that a good diet and exercise program may be just as effective as oral antidiabetic drugs. However, these drugs allow diabetics a bit more leeway in their life style. Persons taking Tolinase oral antidiabetic should carefully watch their diet and exercise program.

Oral antidiabetic drugs are not effective in treating diabetes in children under age 12.

Take the dose of this drug at the same time each day.

Ask your doctor how to recognize the first signs of low blood sugar and how and when to test for glucose and ketones in the urine.

During the first six weeks of Tolinase therapy, visit your doctor at least once a week.

A patient taking Tolinase oral antidiabetic will have to be switched to insulin therapy if complications develop (e.g., keto-acidosis; severe trauma; severe infection; diarrhea; nausea or vomiting; or the need for major surgery).

Tranxene sedative and hypnotic

Manufacturer: Abbott Laboratories
Generic Name: clorazepate dipotassium
Equivalent Products: None

Dosage Forms: Capsules: 3.75 mg (grey/white), 7.5 mg (red/white), 15 mg (grey); sustained-action tablets: 11.25 mg (blue), 22.5 mg (brown)

Use: Relief of anxiety, nervousness, tension; relief of muscle spasms; withdrawal from alcohol addiction

Minor Side Effects: Confusion, constipation, depression, difficult urination, dizziness, drowsiness, dry mouth, fatigue, headache, nausea, rash, slurred speech, uncoordinated movements

Major Side Effects: Blurred vision, decreased sexual drive, double vision, jaundice, low blood pressure, stimulation, tremors

Contraindications: Certain types of glaucoma

Warnings and Precautions: Pregnancy, suicidal tendencies, liver and kidney diseases

Interacts With: alcohol and other central nervous system depressants

Comments: Tranxene sedative and hypnotic currently is used by many people to relieve nervousness. It is effective for this purpose, but it is important to try to remove the cause of the anxiety as well. Phenobarbital is also effective for this, and it is less expensive. Consult your doctor.

Tranxene sedative and hypnotic has the potential for abuse and must be used with caution. Tolerance may develop quickly; *do not* increase the drug without first consulting your doctor.

Never take Tranxene sedative and hypnotic sustained-action tablets more frequently than your doctor prescribes. A serious overdose may result.

Taken alone, Tranxene sedative and hypnotic is a safe drug; when it is combined with other sedative drugs or alcohol, serious adverse reactions may develop.

Tranxene sedative and hypnotic may cause drowsiness; be careful about driving or operating machinery when taking it.

Triavil phenothiazine and antidepressant

Manufacturer: Merck Sharp & Dohme

Generic Name: perphenazine, amitriptyline hydrochloride

Equivalent Products: Etrafon phenothiazine and antidepressant (Schering Corporation)

Dosage Forms: Triavil tablets 2-10: perphenazine, 2 mg; amitriptyline hydrochloride, 10 mg (blue). Triavil tablets 2-25: perphenazine, 2 mg; amitriptyline hydrochloride, 25 mg (orange). Triavil tablets 4-10: perphenazine, 4 mg; amitriptyline hydrochloride, 10 mg (salmon). Triavil tablets 4-25: perphenazine, 4 mg; amitriptyline hydrochloride, 25 mg (yellow)

Use: Relief of anxiety or depression

Minor Side Effects: Aching or numbness of arms and legs, change in urine color, blurred vision, constipation, diarrhea, difficult urination, dizziness, drowsiness, dry mouth, fatigue, headache, increased salivation, loss of appetite, loss of hair, jitteriness, menstrual irregularities, nasal congestion, nausea, palpitations, rash, restlessness, weakness, vomiting, reduced sweating

Major Side Effects: Enlarged or painful breasts (in both sexes), fluid retention; heart attack; high or low blood pressure; imbalance; impotence; insomnia; involuntary movements of the face, mouth, jaw, and tongue; jaundice; mouth sores; muscle stiffness; ringing in the ears; sore throat; stroke; weight gain or loss; tremors; nervousness

Contraindications: Drug-induced depression, coma, shock, blood disease, Parkinson's disease, liver damage, jaundice, kidney disease, stroke, heart disease

Warnings and Precautions: Certain types of glaucoma, certain types of heart disease, epilepsy, pregnancy, difficult urination, exposure to extreme heat, asthma and other respiratory disorders

Interacts With: alcohol, amphetamine, barbiturates, epinephrine, guanethidine, monoamine oxidase inhibitors, oral anticoagulants, phenylephrine, antacids, anticholinergics, central nervous system depressants, clonidine

Comments: The effects of Triavil phenothiazine and antidepressant therapy may not be apparent for at least two weeks.

While taking Triavil phenothiazine and antidepressant, avoid using alcohol, and do not start ot stop taking any other drug, including nonprescription items, without consulting your doctor.

Triavil phenothiazine and antidepressant may cause dryness of the mouth. To reduce this feeling, chew gum or suck on a piece of hard candy.

Triavil phenothiazine and antidepressant reduces sweating; avoid excessive work or exercise in hot weather.

If dizziness or light-headedness occurs when you stand up, place your legs on the floor and "pump" the muscles for a few moments before rising.

As with any other drug that has antivomiting activity, symptoms of severe disease or toxicity due to overdose of other drugs may be masked by Triavil phenothiazine and antidepressant.

One product equivalent to Triavil phenothiazine and antidepressant is available and it differs in cost from Triavil phenothiazine and antidepressant. Have your doctor prescribe a generic preparation, and ask your pharmacist to fill your prescription with the least expensive brand.

Tri-Vi-Flor vitamin and fluoride supplement (Mead Johnson Nutritional Division), see Poly-Vi-Flor vitamin and fluoride supplement.

Tussionex cough suppressant

Manufacturer: Pennwalt Pharmaceutical Division
Generic Name: hydrocodone and phenyltoloxamine in a resin complex
Equivalent Products: None
Dosage Forms: Capsules (green/white), tablets (scored, light brown), suspension (content per 5 ml): hydrocodone, 5 mg; phenyltoloxamine, 10 mg
Use: Cough suppressant
Minor Side Effects: Blurred vision, confusion, constipation, diarrhea, difficult urination, dizziness, drowsiness, headache, insomnia, nasal congestion, nausea, nervousness, palpitations, rash, restlessness, vomiting, dry mouth, reduced sweating
Major Side Effects: Low blood pressure, severe abdominal pain, sore throat
Contraindications: Certain types of glaucoma, certain types of peptic ulcers, enlarged prostate, obstructed bladder, obstructed intestine, pregnancy, severe heart disease
Warnings and Precautions: Diabetes, high blood pressure, thyroid disease, liver and kidney diseases, history of drug abuse
Interacts With: phenothiazines

Comments: Tussionex suspension must be shaken well before measuring each dose.

Tussionex products are intended to be taken at 12-hour intervals. Never take more than one dose every 12 hours unless specifically directed to do so by your doctor.

Tussionex cough suppressant may cause drowsiness; to prevent oversedation, avoid the use of sedative drugs or alcohol while taking it.

Although Tussionex cough suppressant is sometimes prescribed for the prevention and treatment of the common cold, a government panel of experts has concluded that the product may not be effective for this use.

While taking Tussionex cough suppressant, do not take any nonprescription item for cough, cold, or sinus problems without first checking with your doctor.

Tussionex cough suppressant may cause dryness of the mouth. To reduce this feeling, chew gum or suck on a piece of hard candy.

Tussionex cough suppressant reduces sweating; avoid excessive work or exercise in hot weather.

Products containing narcotics (e.g., hydrocodone) are usually not used for more than seven to 10 days.

Tussionex cough suppressant has the potential for abuse and must be used with caution. Tolerance may develop quickly; *do not* increase the dose of this drug without first consulting your doctor. An overdose usually sedates an adult but may cause excitation leading to convulsions and death in a child.

Tuss-Ornade cough and cold remedy

Manufacturer: Smith Kline & French Laboratories
Generic Name: caramiphen edisylate, chlorpheniramine maleate, isopropamide iodide, phenylpropanolamine hydrochloride
Equivalent Products: None
Dosage Forms: Liquid (content per 5 ml): caramiphen edisylate, 5 mg; chlorpheniramine maleate, 2 mg; isopropamide iodide, 0.75 mg; phenylpropanolamine hydrochloride, 15 mg. Capsules: caramiphen edisylate, 20 mg; chlorpheniramine maleate, 8 mg; isopropamide iodide, 2.5 mg; phenylpropanolamine hydrochloride, 50 mg (white/clear)
Use: Relief of symptoms of allergy, sinusitis, or the common cold
Minor Side Effects: Diarrhea, dizziness, drowsiness, dry mouth, headache, heartburn, difficult urination, loss of appetite, nausea, rash, restlessness, vomiting, weakness, blurred vision, confusion, constipation, insomnia, nasal congestion, palpitations, reduced sweating
Major Side Effects: Low blood pressure, severe abdominal pain, sore throat, high blood pressure, chest pain
Contraindications: Asthma, some glaucomas, certain ulcers, enlarged prostate, obstructed bladder, obstructed intestine, pregnancy, severe heart disease
Warnings and Precautions: Diabetes, high blood pressure, thyroid disease, liver and kidney diseases
Interacts With: guanethidine, monoamine oxidase inhibitors
Comments: Although Tuss-Ornade cough and cold remedy is frequently prescribed for the prevention and treatment of the common cold, a

government panel of experts has concluded that the product may not be effective for this use.

Tuss-Ornade cough and cold remedy has sustained action; never take it more frequently than your doctor prescribes. A serious overdose may result.

While taking Tuss-Ornade cough and cold remedy, do not take any nonprescription item for cough, cold, or sinus problems without first checking with your doctor.

Tuss-Ornade cough and cold remedy may cause drowsiness; to prevent oversedation, avoid the use of other sedative drugs or alcohol.

Tuss-Ornade cough and cold remedy may cause dryness of the mouth. To reduce this feeling, chew gum or suck on a piece of hard candy.

Tuss-Ornade cough and cold remedy reduces sweating; avoid excessive work or exercise in hot weather.

Be sure to tell your doctor that you are taking Tuss-Ornade cough and cold remedy if you are scheduled for a thyroid function test. The drug may affect the results of the test.

Tylenol with Codeine analgesic

Manufacturer: McNeil Laboratories
Generic Name: acetaminophen, codeine phosphate
Equivalent Products: acetaminophen with codeine (various manufacturers); Coastaldyne analgesic (Coastal); Empracet with codeine analgesic (Burroughs Wellcome Co.)
Dosage Forms: Liquid (content per 5 ml): acetaminophen, 120 mg; codeine, 12 mg. Tablets: #1, #2, #3, #4: acetaminophen, 300 mg; codeine (see "Comments") (all white)
Use: Relief of moderate to severe pain
Minor Side Effects: Drowsiness, nausea, constipation, dry mouth, flushing, light-headedness, palpitations, rash, sweating, vomiting, urine retention
Major Side Effects: Jaundice, low blood sugar, tremors, rapid heartbeat, breathing difficulties
Contraindications: Pregnancy
Warnings and Precautions: Asthma and other respiratory problems, epilepsy, potential for drug abuse, head injury, liver and kidney disease
Interacts With: alcohol
Comments: Products containing narcotics (e.g., codeine) are usually not used longer than seven to 10 days.

For this and other preparations containing codeine, the number which follows the drug name always refers to the amount of codeine present. Hence, #1 has ⅛ grain (gr) codeine; #2 has ¼ gr; #3 has ½ gr; and #4 contains 1 gr codeine. These numbers are standard for amounts of codeine.

Tylenol with Codeine analgesic interacts with alcohol; avoid the use of alcohol while taking this product.

Tylenol with Codeine analgesic has the potential for abuse and must be used with caution. Tolerance may develop quickly; *do not* increase the drug without first consulting your doctor.

Products equivalent to Tylenol with Codeine analgesic are available and vary in cost. Ask your doctor to prescribe a generic preparation, and have your pharmacist fill your prescription with the least expensive brand.

Phenaphen with Codeine analgesic (A.H. Robins Company) differs from Tylenol with Codeine analgesic only in the amount of acetaminophen it contains.

Unipres antihypertensive and diuretic (Reid-Provident Laboratories, Inc.), see Ser-Ap-Es antihypertensive and diuretic.

Uri-Tet (American Urologicals, Inc.), see Terramycin antibiotic.

Urodine analgesic (Robinson Laboratory, Inc.), see Pyridium analgesic.

Valdrene antihistamine (The Vale Chemical Co., Inc.), see Benadryl antihistamine.

Valisone steroid hormone

Manufacturer: Schering Corporation
Generic Name: betamethasone valerate
Equivalent Products: None
Dosage Forms: Cream; lotion; ointment; spray
Use: Relief of skin inflammation associated with such conditions as dermatitis, eczema, or poison ivy
Minor Side Effects: Burning sensation, dryness, irritation of the affected area, itching, rash
Major Side Effects: Secondary infection
Contraindications: No absolute contraindications
Warnings and Precautions: Diseases that severely impair blood circulation, viral or bacterial infections of the skin
Interacts With: No significant drug interactions
Comments: When the spray is used about the face, cover the eyes and do not inhale the spray. The spray produces a cooling response which may be uncomfortable for some people.

If the affected area is extremely dry or is scaling, the skin may be moistened before applying the medication by soaking in water or by applying water with a clean cloth. The ointment form is probably better for dry skin.

Do not use Valisone steroid hormone with an occlusive wrap unless your doctor directs you to do so. See the chapter "The Right Way To Take Medications."

Valium sedative and hypnotic

Manufacturer: Roche Products Inc.
Generic Name: diazepam
Equivalent Products: None
Dosage Form: Tablets: 2 mg (white), 5 mg (yellow), 10 mg (blue)
Use: Relief of anxiety, nervousness, tension; relief of muscle spasms; withdrawal from alcohol addiction
Minor Side Effects: Confusion, constipation, depression, difficult urination, dizziness, drowsiness, dry mouth, fatigue, headache, nausea, rash, slurred speech, uncoordinated movements
Major Side Effects: Blurred vision, decreased sexual drive, double vision,

jaundice, low blood pressure, stimulation, tremors
Contraindications: Certain types of glaucoma
Warnings and Precautions: Pregnancy, suicidal tendencies, liver and kidney diseases, potential for drug abuse
Interacts With: central nervous system depressants
Comments: Valium sedative and hypnotic currently is used by many people to relieve nervousness. It is effective for this purpose, but it is important to try to remove the cause of the anxiety as well. Phenobarbital is also effective for this purpose, and it is less expensive. Consult your doctor.

Valium sedative and hypnotic has the potential for abuse and must be used with caution. Tolerance may develop; *do not* increase the drug without first consulting your doctor.

Taken alone, Valium sedative and hypnotic is a safe drug; when it is combined with other sedative drugs or alcohol, serious adverse reactions may develop.

Valium sedative and hypnotic may cause drowsiness. Be careful about driving or operating machinery while taking it.

Vasodilan vasodilator

Manufacturer: Mead Johnson Pharmaceutical Division
Generic Name: isoxsuprine hydrochloride
Equivalent Products: isoxsuprine hydrochloride (various manufacturers), Vasoprine vasodilator (Spencer-Mead Inc.)
Dosage Form: Tablets; 10 mg, 20 mg (both white)
Use: To increase blood supply to the extremities; prevention of threatened miscarriage; relief of cerebrovascular insufficiency
Minor Side Effects: Dizziness, nausea, vomiting
Major Side Effects: Palpitations, severe rash
Contraindications: The first trimester of pregnancy
Warnings and Precautions: Low blood pressure, palpitations, liver and kidney diseases
Interacts With: No significant drug interactions
Comments: Vasodilan vasodilator increases the flow of blood to the brain and other areas of the body, but this action has not been shown to be of benefit. Discuss the relative merits of the drug with your doctor. If you agree to take it, ask your doctor to prescribe a less expensive generic brand.

Vasoprine vasodilator (Spencer-Mead Inc.), see Vasodilan vasodilator.

Vasotrate antianginal (Reid-Provident Laboratories, Inc.), see Isordil antianginal.

Vectrin antibiotic (Parke, Davis & Company), see Minocin antibiotic.

Veltane antihistamine (Lannett Co., Inc.), see Dimetane antihistamine.

Vibramycin antibiotic

Manufacturer: Pfizer Laboratories Division

Generic Name: doxycycline hyclate
Equivalent Products: Doxychel antibiotic (Rachelle Laboratories, Inc.), Doxy-II antibiotic (USV [P.R.] Development Corp.)
Dosage Forms: Liquid (content per 5 ml): 25 mg; syrup (content per 5 ml): 50 mg; capsules: 50 mg (blue/white), 100 mg (blue)
Use: Treatment of a wide variety of bacterial infections
Minor Side Effects: Diarrhea, loss of appetite, nausea, vomiting, photosensitivity
Major Side Effects: Anemia, itching, sore throat, superinfection, rash, vaginal and rectal itching, irritation of the mouth, "black tongue"
Contraindications: Pregnancy
Warnings and Precautions: Age (children under age nine), liver and kidney diseases
Interacts With: barbiturates, dairy products, diuretics, iron-containing products, antacids, phenytoin, carbamazepine
Comments: Take Vibramycin antibiotic on an empty stomach (one hour before or two hours after a meal).
   Vibramycin antibiotic should be taken for at least 10 full days, even if symptoms have disappeared.
   Do not take Vibramycin antibiotic at the same time as milk or other dairy products or iron preparations. Separate taking the drugs by at least one hour.
   While taking Vibramycin antibiotic, avoid prolonged exposure to sunlight.
   Vibramycin antibiotic is taken on a once or twice a day dosage schedule.
Never increase the dosage unless your doctor tells you to do so.

Vioform-Hydrocortisone steroid hormone and anti-infective

Manufacturer: CIBA Pharmaceutical Company
Generic Name: hydrocortisone, iodochlorohydroxyquin
Equivalent Products: Cortin steroid hormone and anti-infective (C & M Pharmacal, Inc.); Formitone-HC steroid hormone and anti-infective (Dermik Laboratories, Inc.); Heb-Cort steroid hormone and anti-infective (Barnes-Hind Pharmaceuticals, Inc.); Iodocort steroid hormone and anti-infective (Ulmer Pharmacal Company); Vioquin-HC steroid hormone and anti-infective (Scott-Alison Pharmaceuticals, Inc.); Viotag steroid hormone and anti-infective (Tutag Pharmaceuticals, Inc.)
Dosage Forms: Cream; ointment
Use: Relief of skin inflammation associated with such conditions as dermatitis, eczema
Minor Side Effects: Burning sensation, irritation of affected area, itching (all rare)
Major Side Effects: No major side effects
Contraindications: No absolute contraindications
Warnings and Precautions: Diseases that severely impair blood circulation, viral or bacterial infections of the skin
Interacts With: No major drug interactions
Comments: If a thyroid function test is scheduled stop using Vioform-Hydrocortisone steroid hormone and anti-infective one month before the test date. Inform your doctor you have taken or are using this product; it may affect the results of this test.

230

If the affected area is extremely dry or is scaling, the skin may be moistened before applying the medication by soaking in water or by applying water with a clean cloth. The ointment form is probably better for dry skin.

Do not use an occlusive wrap with Vioform-Hydrocortisone steroid hormone and anti-infective unless your doctor instructs you to do so. See the chapter "The Right Way To Take Medications."

Vioquin-HC steroid hormone and anti-infective (Scott-Alison Pharmaceuticals, Inc.), see Vioform-Hydrocortisone steroid and anti-infective.

Viotag steroid hormone and anti-infective (Tutag Pharmaceuticals, Inc.), see Vioform-Hydrocortisone steroid hormone and anti-infective.

Vistaril sedative (Pfizer Laboratories Division), see Atarax sedative.

Wampocap vitamin supplement (Wallace Laboratories), see nicotinic acid vitamin supplement.

Zorane oral contraceptive (Lederle Laboratories), see oral contraceptives.

Zyloprim uricosuric

Manufacturer: Burroughs Wellcome Co.
Generic Name: allopurinol
Equivalent Products: None
Dosage Form: Tablets: 100 mg (white), 300 mg (peach)
Use: Treatment of gout
Minor Side Effects: Diarrhea, nausea, vomiting
Major Side Effects: Fatigue, paleness, rash, sore throat, visual disturbances
Contraindications: Pregnancy
Warnings and Precautions: Liver or kidney diseases
Interacts With: azathioprine, cyclophosphamide, mercaptopurine, oral anticoagulants
Comments: It is common for persons beginning to take Zyloprim uricosuric to also take colchicine for the first three months. Colchicine helps minimize painful attacks of gout.

If one Zyloprim uricosuric tablet three times a day is prescribed, ask your doctor if a single dose (either three 100-mg tablets or one 300-mg tablet) can be taken as a convenience.

The effects of Zyloprim uricosuric therapy may not be apparent for at least two weeks.

If you are also taking an anticoagulant ("blood thinner"), remind your doctor.

If a skin rash develops, call your doctor at once. A rash is often caused by an allergic reaction, and if allowed to continue, the reaction may become severe.

Drink at least eight to 10 glasses of water each day to help minimize the formation of kidney stones.

Glossary

abuse—wrong or excessive use of a substance

addiction—habituation to the use of a drug or other substance; produced by repeated consumption and characterized by an overwhelming desire to continue use of the drug and a psychological and (usually) a physical dependence on the drug's effects

adverse reaction—an undesirable effect from drug use; usually unintended and often dangerous

allergy—an unusual physical response to a foreign substance; allergic symptoms (such as nasal congestion, itchy eyes, certain rashes, and sneezing) are caused by the release of histamine

analgesic—a pain-relieving substance

anesthetic—a substance that causes loss of feeling and sensation

anorectic—a substance that decreases the appetite; usually a sympathomimetic amine

antacid—a drug that neutralizes excess stomach acid

antiarrhythmic—a drug that regulates abnormal heart rhythms

antibacterial—a drug that destroys and prevents the growth of bacteria

antibiotic—a substance that slows or stops the growth of bacteria; often derived from a mold

anticholinergic drug—a drug that blocks the passage of certain nervous impulses

anticoagulant—a drug that slows the clotting of blood

anticonvulsant—a drug used to treat or prevent seizures or convulsions

antidepressant—a drug used to treat symptoms of depression

antidiabetic—a drug used to treat diabetes mellitus

antidiarrheal—a drug used to treat diarrhea

antidote—a substance that counteracts the effects of an ingested poison

antiemetic—a drug used to control vomiting

antihistamine—a drug used to relieve the symptoms of an allergy; works by blocking the effects of histamine

antihypertensive—a drug that counteracts or reduces high blood pressure

anti-infective—an agent used to treat an infection

anti-inflammatory—a drug that counteracts or suppresses inflammation

antisubstitution law—a law in a few states which prevents pharmacists from substituting an equivalent product for a drug prescribed by brand name

antitussive—a drug used to relieve coughing

barbiturates—a class of drugs used as sedatives or hypnotics; can be addictive

bioequivalence—when two medications have the same biologic effect

bronchodilator—a drug used to help breathing; works by expanding the air passages into the lungs and relaxing bronchial muscles

capsule—a small gelatin container filled with a drug

cathartic—a substance that causes evacuation of the bowel; for all purposes, the same as a laxative

caution—a negative aspect of a drug; manufacturers are legally required to tell physicians and pharmacists the negative features of a drug, such as whether the drug is dangerous for people with certain conditions

central nervous system depressant—a drug that acts on the brain to decrease energy and concentration

central nervous system stimulant—a drug that acts on the brain to increase energy and alertness

chemical equivalents—drugs that contain identical amounts of active ingredients

contraindications—conditions for which a drug should not be prescribed; conditions in which the benefits of a given drug would be outweighed by its negative effects

decongestant—a drug that relieves congestion in the upper respiratory system

diuretic—a drug that stimulates the production and passage of urine

dosage—the amount of drug to take and how often to take it

drug—a compound used to diagnose, cure, treat, or prevent a disease

drug interaction—when one drug affects (diminishes or intensifies) the action of a second drug

elixir—an alcoholic solution in which a medication is dissolved

emetic—a substance that causes vomiting

emulsion—a liquid preparation, usually creamy, in which two liquids are mixed

expectorant—a drug used to increase the secretion of mucus in the respiratory system

generic—not protected by trademark

histamine—a substance produced by the body in an allergic reaction; causes dilation of blood vessels, constriction of smooth muscles in the lungs, and the stimulation of gastric secretions

hormone—a chemical substance produced by glands in the body; regulates the action of certain organs

humidifier—an apparatus used to add moisture to the air

hypnotic—a drug that causes sleep

immunity—resistance to a specific infection

indications—uses for a drug that the government has allowed the manufacturer to state

ipecac—a substance used to induce vomiting when poisons have been ingested

laxative—a substance that causes evacuation of the bowel; for all purposes, the same as a cathartic

monoamine oxidase (MAO) inhibitor—a drug used to treat severe depression; acts by inhibiting the production of enzymes called monoamine oxidases

narcotic—a drug derived from the opium poppy used to relieve pain and coughing; addictive

over-the-counter (OTC) drug—nonprescription medication; drug which can be purchased without a prescription

palpitations—rapid heartbeats; a side effect in which the drug user feels throbbing in the chest

pathology—the study of disease

pediculocide—a preparation used to treat a person infested with lice

pharmacology—the study of how drugs work

precaution—a specific event to watch for when taking a drug

prescription—a written formula for the preparation and administration of a remedy

salicylates—a class of drugs prepared from salts of salicylic acid; the most commonly used pain relievers in the U.S.; aspirin is a salicylate

scabicide—a preparation used in the treatment of scabies

sedative—a drug given to calm the patient and reduce nervousness, thereby producing sleep

side effect—any effect from a drug other than that for which the drug is taken; usually expected and not life-threatening; not as serious as an adverse reaction

sign—any evidence of disease that is collected by a health professional such as a doctor, pharmacist, or nurse

smooth muscle relaxant—a drug which causes the relaxation of smooth muscle tissue (i.e., muscle tissue such as that in the stomach and bladder, that performs functions not under voluntary control)

steroid—any one of a group of compounds secreted primarily by the adrenal glands; a drug used to treat allergic reactions and skin irritations

sulfa drug—an antibacterial drug belonging to the chemical group of sulfonamides; some diuretics and some oral antidiabetic drugs are similar to sulfa drugs

suppository—a dosage form specially made for insertion into a body cavity

suspension—a liquid preparation containing particles of a nonsoluble drug; must be well shaken before use

sympathomimetic amine—a drug that raises blood pressure, acts as a decongestant, improves air passage into the lungs, and decreases the appetite

symptom—any subjective evidence of disease; pain is a symptom

syrup—a liquid drug preparation to which a large amount of sugar has been added

tablet—solid dosage form of a drug made by pressing the medication between metal dies

therapeutics—the combination of pharmacology and pathology; clinical medicine

toxicology—the study of harmful effects of a drug or chemical

vaccine—a medication containing weakened, killed germs; stimulates the body to develop an immunity to those germs

vaporizer—an apparatus used to add moisture to the air; changes liquids into a vapor

vasoconstrictor—a drug that constricts blood vessels, thereby increasing blood pressure and decreasing blood flow

vasodilator—a drug that expands blood vessels to increase blood flow

vitamin—a chemical present in foods that is vital to normal body functions

warning—a specific danger that has been shown to occur from using a drug

Index

aminophylline, 99
Amitril, see Elavil
amitriptyline hydrochloride
    in Elavil, 134
    in Triavil, 224
ammonium chloride
    in Ambenyl, 98
Amoxil, see amoxicillin
amoxicillin, 100
amphetamine, 61, 89, 90
Amphojel, 55
ampicillin, 48, 101
analgesics, 61
anesthetics, local, 63
anorectics, 61, 89, 90
Antabuse, 88, 89
antacids, 55
antiarrhythmics, 51
antibiotics, 16, 23, 25, 26, 54, 58,
    72, 81, 82
anticholinergics, 55, 56
anticoagulants, 52
anticonvulsants, 72
antidepressants, 30, 89, 90
antidiabetic drugs, 88
antidiarrheals, 56
antiepileptics, 61
antihistamines, 30, 64, 70, 72
antihypertensives, 51, 89
anti-infectives, 58, 59
anti-inflammatory drugs, 62
antimalarial drugs, 79
antinauseants, 54
anti-Parkinson's agents, 61
antipyrine
    in Auralgan Otic Solution, 106
antiseptics, 59
antitussives, 63
Antivert, 102
Anturane, 89
Anusol-HC, 41, 102
Apresoline, 51, 74, 76, 78, 80,
    103
Aquatensen, see Enduron
Aristocort, 57, 73, 76, 77, 78, 87,
    103
Aristocort A, 40
Artane, 61
arthritis, 62, 73
Asma-lief, see Tedral

aspirin, 16, 22, 29, 30, 49, 62, 88,
    89, 90
    in Darvon Compound-65, 122
    in Empirin Compound with
        Codeine, 136
    in Equagesic, 138
    in Fiorinal, 141
    in Fiorinal with Codeine, 141
    in Norgesic, 173
    in Percodan, 184
    in Synalgos-DC, 214
asthma, 51
Atarax, 60, 73, 80, 104
atherosclerosis, 52
Ativan, 72, 77, 78, 79, 104
Atromid-S, 53, 74, 77, 78, 79, 105
atropine, 47, 55, 73
atropine sulfate
    in Donnatal, 131
    in Lomotil, 158
Auralgan, 54, 106
aerosol foam, 177
AVC, 106
Azathioprine, 90
Azo Gantanol, 106
Azo Gantrisin, 107
Azolid, see Butazolidin
Azo-Soxazole, see Azo Gantrisin
Azo-Standard, see Pyridium
Azo-Stat, see Pyridium
Azosul, see Azo Gantrisin

B

Bactrim, 88, 108
barbiturates, 31, 60, 77, 79, 89
Benadryl, 64, 73, 74, 75, 77, 78,
    79, 80, 108
Bendectin, 37, 72, 73, 74, 77, 79,
    109
Benemid, 63, 77, 79, 88, 109
bendroflumethiazide
    in Rauzide, 200
Bentyl, 73, 75, 77, 110
benzocaine, 11, 53
    in Auralgan Otic Solution, 106
benzoyl peroxide, 60
benzyl benzoate
    in Anusol-HC, 102
beri-beri, 64

betamethasone valerate
in Valisone, 228
bioequivalence, 46
Biphetamine, 61
birth control methods, 177
birth defects, 64
bismuth resorcin compound
in Anusol-HC, 102
bismuth subgallate
in Anusol-HC, 102
blood, 80
blood pressure medications, 72
Brethine, 78, 111
Brevicon, see oral contraceptives
Bromatane, see Dimetane
Brometapp, see Dimetapp
bromodiphenhydramine
hydrochloride
in Ambenyl, 98
brompheniramine maleate
in Dimetane antihistamine, 126
in Dimetane expectorant, 127
in Dimetane expectorant-DC, 128
in Dimetapp Extentabs, 128
Bronkodyl, see Elixophyllin
Bu-Lax Plus, see Peri-Colace
butalbital
in Fiorinal, 141
in Fiorinal with Codeine, 142
Butazolidin, 17, 62, 73, 74, 76, 79,
80, 89, 111
Butisol Sodium, see Nembutal

C

caffeine
in Darvon Compound-65, 122
in Empirin Compound with
Codeine, 136
in Fiorinal, 141
in Fiorinal with Codeine, 142
in Norgesic, 173
in Percodan, 184
in Soma Compound, 210
in Synalgos-DC, 214
cancer, 68
cancer-treating drugs, 72
Candex, see Mycostatin
Capade, see Ornade

capsules, 36, 37
caramiphen edisylate
in Tuss-Ornade, 226
carbenicillin, 80
Cardabid, see Nitro-Bid Plateau
Caps
cardiovascular drugs, 51-52
carisoprodol
in Soma Compound, 210
casanthranol
in Peri-Colace, 185
Catapres, 51, 73, 75, 79, 112
central nervous system drugs, 60
cephalexin
in Keflex, 152
cephalosporins, 59
Cerebid, see Pavabid Plateau
Caps
Cerespan, see Pavabid Plateau
Caps
cerumenex, 54
Cerylin, see Quibron
chemotherapeutics, 59
child-resistant caps and containers,
28
chloral hydrate, 47, 48, 60
chloramphenicol, 47, 84
Chlordiazachel, see Librium
chlordiazepoxide hydrochloride
in Librax, 156
in Librium, 157
Chloromycetin, 84
chlorophenothane (DDT), 86
chlorothiazide
in Diupres, 129
chlorothiazide sodium
in Diuril, 131
chlorpheniramine maleate, 73, 74,
77, 79, 113
in Naldecon, 167
in Novahistine DH, 174
in Novahistine Elixir, 175
in Ornade, 178
in Tuss-Ornade, 226
chlorpromazine hydrochloride
in Thorazine, 219
chlorpropamide
in Diabinese, 123
Chlor-PZ, see Thorazine
chlorthalidone

239

causing constipation, 75
causing diarrhea, 74
causing dizziness, 77
causing fluid retention, 76
causing headache, 78
causing mild rash, 79
causing photosensitivity, 79
central nervous system, 60
dangerous during pregnancy, 67
ears, 53
eye, 54
interactions, 88
respiratory, 63
side effects, 70-82
topical, 60
drug categories, 51-64
drug interactions, 88
drug profiles, 91-231
how to use, 91-93
D-S-S Plus, see Peri-Colace
Dulcolax, 41
Duohist, see Drixoral
Dyazide, 52, 73, 74, 75, 78, 79,
80, 133
Dymelor, 57
Dyrenium, 52, 88

E

eardrops, 39
Edecrin, 52
edema, 76
E.E.S., see erythromycin
Elavil, 30, 38, 60, 76, 79, 80, 134
Eldefed, see Actifed
Eldetapp, see Dimetapp
Eldezine, see Antivert
Elixophyllin, 135
Empirin Compound with Codeine,
62, 136
Empracet with Codeine, see
Tylenol with Codeine
E-Mycin, 37
see also erythromycin
Endep, see Elavil
Enduron, 52, 74, 77, 78, 79, 137
Enovid, 177
see also oral contraceptives
enzymes, 81
ephedrine, 90

ephedrine hydrochloride
in Tedral, 216
ephedrine sulfate, 64
in Marax, 160
epilepsy, 51, 61
epinephrine, 64
epsom salts, 56
Equagesic, 63, 138
Equanil, 60
see also meprobamate
Equanil Wyseals, 37
ergot, 53
erythromycin, 59, 74, 138
Esidrix, 52
see also hydrochlorothiazide
Eskabarb Spansules, see
phenobarbital
Eskatrol, 61, 139
Eskatrol Extentabs, 76
Estroate, see Premarin
Estrocon, see Premarin
estrogens, 48, 57
Estropan, see Premarin
Etafon, see Triavil
ethoheptazine citrate
in Equagesic, 138
Etrafon, 38
Ex-Lax, 56
expectorant, 63, 64
Exsel, see Selsun
eyedrops and ointments, 39
eye infections, 54

F

Fastin, 61, 140
Federal Trade Commission, 45
Femest, see Premarin
Fem-H, see Premarin
Fenbutal, see Fiorinal
fenoprofen calcium
in Nalfon, 168
Fenylhist, see Benadryl
Fernisone, see prednisone
Fiorinal, 141
Fiorinal with Codeine, 62, 142
Flagyl, 73, 74, 75, 77, 78. 143
fluocinolone acetonide
in Synalar, 213

fluocinonide
in Lidex, 157
fluorouracil, 59
flurandrenolide
in Cordran, 118
flurazepam hydrochloride
in Dalmane, 120
folic acid
in Poly-Vi-Flor, 191
Food and Drug Administration, 11,
48, 65
Formitone-HC, see Vioform-
Hydrocortisone
Furadantin, 59
furosemide
in Lasix, 155

G

Galen, 6
Gamene, see Kwell
gamma benzene hexachloride
(lindane)
in Kwell, 154
Gantanol, 143
Gantrisin, 59, 144
gastrointestinal drugs, 54-56
gastrointestinal system, 73
generic drugs, 44
glucagon, 56
glycerin, 40
gramicidin
in Mycolog, 166
in Neosporin Ophthalmic
Solution, 170
griseofulvin, 84
guaifenesin
in Actifed-C expectorant, 94
in Dimetane expectorant, 127
in Dimetane expectorant-DC, 128
in Novahistine expectorant, 176
in Quibron, 198

H

Haldol, 38, 60, 72, 73, 74, 75, 79,
145
haloperidol
in Haldol, 145
hay fever, 57

health care professional
how to select, 14
heart and circulatory system, 75
heart attack, 53
heart disease, 63
Heb-Cort, see Vioform-
Hydrocortisone
heparin, 53
Hippocrates, 6
histamine blockers, 55
hormones, 56-58, 72
HRC-Proclan expectorant with
Codeine, see Phenergan
expectorant with Codeine
Hydergine, 53, 145
hydralazine hydrochloride, 8
in Apresoline, 103
in Ser-Ap-Es, 206
hydrochlorothiazide, 52, 146
in Aldactazide, 95
in Aldoril, 97
in Dyazide, 133
in Hydropres, 147
in Ser-Ap-Es, 206
hydrocodone
in Tussionex, 225
hydrocortisone, 40
in Cortisporin Ophthalmic
Suspension, 118
in Cortisporin Otic Solution,
119
in Vioform-Hydrocortisone, 230
hydrocortisone acetate
in Anusol-HC, 102
HydroDIURIL, 52, 79
see also hydrochlorothiazide
hydroflumethiazide
in Salutensin, 204
Hydropres, 51, 147
Hydrotensin, see Hydropres
Hydrotensin-Plus, see Ser-Ap-Es
hydroxyzine hydrochloride
in Atarax, 104
in Marax, 160
Hygroton, 52, 80, 148
hyoscine hydrobromide
in Donnatal, 131
hyoscyamine sulfate
in Donnatal, 131
hypoproteinemia, 85

243

I

ibuprofen
  in Motrin, 165
Ilosone, see erythromycin
Imavate, see Tofranil
imipramine hydrochloride (or
  imipramine pamoate)
  in Tofranil, 221
Inderal, 51, 53, 72, 74, 75, 77,
  89, 149
Indocin, 62, 72, 74, 79, 85, 149
indomethacin
  in Indocin, 149
influenza, 56
insect bites, 57
insulin, 9, 10, 56, 150
intrauterine device, 177
iodochlorohydroxyquin
  in Vioform - Hydrocortisone, 230
Iodocort, see Vioform-
  Hydrocortisone
Ionamin, 61
  see also Fastin
Iosel 250, see Selsun
Ipecac, 39, 40, 41
iron tablets, 30, 88
Ismelin, 89
Isolait, see Vasodilan
isopropamide iodide
  in Combid, 116
  in Ornade, 179
  in Tuss-Ornade, 226
Isopto-Carpine, 19, 151
Isordil, 151
Isordil Tembids, 37
isosorbide dinitrate
  in Isordil, 151
Isotrate Timecelles, see Isordil
isoxsuprine hydrochloride
  in Vasodilan, 229
Isuprel, 64
itching
  rectal, 74

J

Janimine, see Tofranil

J-Gan-V.C., see Phenergan VC
  expectorant plain

K

Kaochlor, 52
  see also potassium chloride
Kaon-Cl, see potassium chloride
Kaopectate, 56, 75, 88, 89
Kay Ciel, see potassium chloride
Keflex, 74, 77, 78, 79, 152
Kelsey, Frances, M.D., 64
Kenacort, 57
  see also Aristocort
Kenalog, 40, 57, 153
Kestrin, see Premarin
kidney, 81
kidney disease, 27
K-Lor, 52
  see also potassium chloride
Klorvess, see potassium chloride
K-Lyte, 74, 88, 154
  see also potassium chloride
Korostatin, see Mycostatin
K-Phen expectorant with Codeine,
  see Phenergan expectorant
  with Codeine
K-Y Jelly, 42
Kwell, 154

L

Lasix, 155
Lanophyllin, see Elixophyllin
Lanorinal, see Fiorinal
Lanoxin, 21, 52
  see also digoxin
Larotid, see amoxicillin
laryngitis, 42
Lasix, 52, 80
laxatives, 55
Letter, see thyroid hormone
levodopa, 85, 89
Levoid, see thyroid hormone
Librax, 55, 73, 75, 76, 79, 87, 156
Librium, 30, 60, 75, 76, 79, 157
Lidex, 40, 57, 157
Lidinium, see Librax
lidocaine, 51, 53, 63
Lincocin, 88, 89

liquids, 38
Lisacort, see prednisone
liver, 81
Loestrin, see oral contraceptives
Lomotil, 47, 56, 77, 78, 79, 158
Lonox, see Lomotil
loop diuretics, 52
Lo/Ovral, see oral contraceptives
Lorazepam
  in Ativan, 104
Lotrimin, 159
low blood pressure, 51
lozenges, 42
Luminal Ovoids, see phenobarbital
lye, 31

M

Maalox, 55
Macrodantin, 59, 160
Mallergan expectorant with
  Codeine, see Phenergan
  expectorant with Codeine
Mallergan VC expectorant with
  Codeine, see Phenergan VC
  expectorant with Codeine
malnutrition, 85
Mandelamine, 89
Marax, 160
Marezine, 54
marijuana, 66, 88
measles, 59
meclizine hydrochloride
  in Antivert, 102
medications
  how to take, 36-43
Medrol, 57, 73, 76, 77, 78, 161
medroxyprogesterone acetate
  in Provera, 197
Mellaril, 38, 60, 73, 74, 75, 76,
  80, 162
Menogen, see Premarin
Menotab, see Premarin
meperidine hydrochloride
  in Demerol, 123
meprobamate, 74, 75, 78, 163
  in Equagesic, 138
Meprogesic, see Equagesic
mercaptopurine, 90

Metamucil, 56
methaqualone
  in Quaalude, 198
methocarbamol
  in Robaxin, 203
methotrexate, 59, 86, 89
methyclothiazide
  in Enduron, 137
methyldopa
  in Aldomet, 97
  in Aldoril, 97
methylphenidate hydrochloride
  in Ritalin, 203
methylprednisolone
  in Medrol, 161
Meticorten, see prednisone
metronidazole
  in Flagyl, 143
Mi-Cebrin, 64
miconazole nitrate
  in Monistat, 165
Midahist DH, see Novahistine DH
Midahist, see Novahistine
milk of magnesia, 57
Miltown, 60
  see also meprobamate
mineralocorticoids, 57
mineral oil, 16, 42, 84
minerals, 64
Minipress, 51, 72, 73, 74, 75, 77,
  78, 79, 163
Minocin, 74, 79, 80, 164
minocycline hydrochloride
  in Minocin, 164
Mi-Pilo, see Isopto Carpine
Mistura P, see Isopto Carpine
Modicon, 177
  see also oral contraceptives
Monistat 7, 165
monoamine oxidase inhibitors, 85,
  89
morning sickness, 55
morphine, 7, 62
motion sickness, 55
Motrin, 62, 74, 76
mumps, 59
mustard powder, 32
myasthenia gravis, 54
Mycolog, 40, 57, 166
Mycostatin, 167

245

N

Naldecon, 37, 73, 167
Nalfon, 62, 168
Naprosyn, 62, 169
naproxen
    in Naprosyn, 169
narcotics, 30, 56, 72
National Formulary, 65
Nebralin, 37
    see also Nembutal
NegGram, 59
Nembutal, 60, 79, 169
Neocurtasal, 52
Neofed, see Sudafed
neomycin sulfate
    in Cortisporin Ophthalmic
        Suspension, 118
    in Cortisporin Otic Solution,
        119
    in Mycolog, 166
    in Neosporin Ophthalmic
        Solution, 170
Neosporin, 170
Neo-Synephrine, 64, 90
nervous system, 76
Niac, see nicotinic acid
Niacalex, see nicotinic acid
niacin
    in Poly-Vi-Flor, 191
NICL, see nicotinic acid
Nicobid, see nicotinic acid
Nicocap, see nicotinic acid
Nico-400 Plateau Caps, see
    nicotinic acid
Nico-Span, see nicotinic acid
nicotine, 86
nicotinic acid, 73, 171
night blindness, 72
Nilstat, see Mycostatin
Nitro-Bid, 72, 77, 78, 172
Nitrobon, see Nitro-Bid Plateau
    Caps
Nitrodyl, see Nitro-Bid Plateau
    Caps
nitrofurantoin (macrocrystals), 59
    in Macrodantin, 160
nitroglycerin, 27, 37
nitroglycerin
    in Nitro-Bid Plateau Caps, 172

in Nitrostat, 172
Nitrospan, see Nitro-Bid Plateau
    Caps
Nitrostat, 72, 77, 78, 172
Noctec, 48
Noludar, 60
Norgesic, 63, 173
Norinyl, 58
    see also oral contraceptives
Norlestrin, 58, 177
    see also oral contraceptives
Norpace, 72, 73, 74, 76, 77, 78,
    79, 174
nose drops and sprays, 40
Novahistine, 175
Novahistine DH, 174
Novahistine expectorant, 64, 176
nystatin
    in Mycolog, 166
    in Mycostatin, 167

O

o.b.c.t., see Tenuate
ointments, 40
Omnipen, see ampicillin
oral antidiabetics, 72, 74, 77, 78,
    79
oral contraceptives, 58, 73, 74, 76,
    77, 80, 177
Orasone, see prednisone
organophosphate insecticides, 54
Orinase, 57, 80, 86, 178
Ornade, 73, 74, 77, 78, 79, 179
Ornade 2 Liquid for Children, see
    Novahistine Elixir
orphenadrine citrate,
    in Norgesic, 173
Ortho-Novum, 58, 177
    see also oral contraceptives
Otobione, see Cortisporin
Ovcon, see oral contraceptives
over-the-counter drugs, 11
Ovest, see Premarin
Ovral, 58, 177
    see also oral contraceptives
Ovulen, 58, 177
    see also oral contraceptives
Oxalid, see Butazolidin

oxazepam
  in Serax, 207
Oxlopar, see Terramycin
Oxybiotic, see Terramycin
oxycodone hydrochloride,
  in Percodan, 184
oxycodone terephthalate,
  in Percodan, 184
Oxy-Tetrachel, see Terramycin
oxytetracycline, 47
oxytetracycline hydrochloride,
  in Terramycin, 218
oxytriphylline,
  in Choledyl, 114

P

Palopause, see Premarin
Panmycin, 44, 45
  see also tetracycline
Panwarfin, see Coumadin
papaverine hydrochloride, 8
  in Pavabid Plateau Caps, 181
paracetamol, 44
Paracort, see prednisone
Parafon Forte, 63, 181
paregoric, 56
Pargesic Compound-65, see
  Darvon Compound-65
Pargesic-65, see Darvon
Parest, see Quaalude
Parkinson's disease, 61, 85
Parnate, 89, 90
Pavabid, 53, 74, 75, 77, 78
Pavabid Plateau Caps, 50, 181
Pavased, see Pavabid Plateau
  Caps
PBR/12, see phenobarbital
pellagra, 64
penicillins, 8, 27, 74
penicillin G, 182
penicillin potassium phenoxymethyl,
  183
Pentazine, see Phenergan
Pentazine expectorant with
  Codeine, see Phenergan
  expectorant with Codeine
pentazocine, 62
pentazocine hydrochloride,
  in Talwin, 216

Pentids, see penicillin G
pentobarbital,
  in Nembutal, 169
Pen-Vee K, see penicillin
  potassium phenoxymethyl
peptic ulcer drugs, 72
Percodan, 62, 75, 184
Periactin, 184
Peri-Colace, 185
perphenazine,
  in Triavil, 224
Persantine, 186
pertussis, 59
Peruvian balsam,
  in Anusol-HC, 102
Pfiklor, see potassium chloride
phenacetin,
  in Darvon Compound-65, 122
  in Empirin Compound with
    Codeine, 136
  in Fiorinal, 141
  in Fiorinal with Codeine, 142
  in Norgesic, 173
  in Percodan, 184
  in Soma Compound, 210
  in Synalgos-DC, 214
Phenaphen with Codeine, 62
  see also Tylenol with Codeine
phenazopyridine hydrochloride,
  in Azo Gantanol, 106
  in Azo Gantrisin, 107
  in Pyridium, 197
Phenergan, 38, 64, 79, 80, 186,
  187
Phenergan VC expectorant, 64,
  188
Phenergan VC expectorant with
  Codeine, 189
phenobarbital, 61, 190
  in Donnatal, 131
  in Tedral, 216
Pheno-Squar, see phenobarbital
phenothiazine, 55
phentermine hydrochloride,
  in Fastin Capsules, 140
phenylbutazone,
  in Butazolidin, 111
phenylephrine hydrochloride
  in Dimetane expectorant, 127
  in Dimetane expectorant-DC, 128

247

Salutensin, 51, 204
Sanorex, 61
Seconal, 60
Seconal sodium,
  see Nembutal
sedatives, 60
Sedralex, see Donnatal
selenium sulfide,
  in Selsun, 206
Selsun, 206
Septra, see Bactrim
Ser-Ap-Es, 51, 206
Serax, 60, 78, 207
Sereen, see Librium
Serpasil, see Hydropres
Servisone, see prednisone
Setamine, see Donnatal
sex hormones, 57
Sherafed, see Actifed
Sherafed-C, see Actifed-C
side effects of drugs, 70-82
Sigtab tablets, 64
Sinequan, 38, 60, 72, 73, 75, 208
skin, 78
SK-Lygen, see Librium
SK-Niacin, see nicotinic acid
SK-Phenobarbital, see
  phenobarbital
SK-Pramine, see Tofranil
SK-Prednisone, see prednisone
SK-Soxazole, see Gantrisin
SK-Triamcinolone, see Kenalog
sleeping aids, 31, 72, 87
Slo-Phyllin, see Quibron
Slow-K, 37
  see also potassium chloride
smallpox, 8, 59
Sodestrin, see Premarin
sodium bicarbonate, 55
sodium citrate,
  in Phenergan expectorant plain,
    186
  in Phenergan expectorant with
    Codeine, 187
  in Phenergan VC expectorant
    plain, 188
  in Phenergan VC expectorant
    with Codeine, 189
sodium fluoride,
  in Poly-Vi-Flor, 191

sodium levothyroxine,
  in Synthroid, 215
Solfoton, see phenobarbital
Soma Compound, 63, 210
Somophyllin, see aminophylline
sopor, see Quaalude
Sorbide, see Isordil
Sorbitrate, see Isordil
Spalix, see Donnatal
Spen-Histine Elixir, see Novahistine
  Elixir
Spentane, see Dimetane
Spironolactone
  in Aldactazide, 95
  in Aldactone, 96
sprays, 40, 42
stelazine, 38, 60, 73, 74, 75, 76, 79,
  211
steroids, 54, 57
stroke, 53
strychnine, 31
Sub-Quin, see Pronestyl
Sudafed, 64, 90, 212
Sudecon, see Sudafed
Sul-Blue, see Selsun
Suldiazo, see Azo Gantrisin
Sulfabenzamide,
  in Sultrin, 212
Sulfacetamide,
  in Sultrin, 212
sulfa drugs, 74, 76, 78, 79, 80, 81, 82
Sulfalar, see Gantrisin
sulfamethoxazole,
  in Azo Gantanol, 106
  in Bactrim, 108
  in Gantanol, 143
sulfanilamide,
  in AVC, 106
sulfathiazole,
  in Sultrin, 212
sulfisoxazole,
  in Azo Gantrisin, 107
  in Gantrisin, 144
sulfonylureas, 57
sulindac,
  in Clinoril, 115
Sultrin, 212
Sumox, see amoxicillin
Sumycin, see tetracycline
  hydrochloride

superinfection, 81
suppositories,
    rectal, 41
    vaginal, 43
Surfak, 213
Synalar, 40, 57, 213
Synalgos-DC, 62, 214
Synthroid, 56, 214
syrup of ipecac, 32

T

tablets, 36
Tagamet, 37, 55, 74, 77, 79, 80, 215
Talwin, 62, 72, 74, 75, 77, 78, 216
Tandearil, 63, 73, 76, 80
    see also Butazolidin
Tapazole, 56
Tedral, 37, 216
Tega-Span, see nicotinic acid
Teldrin Spansule, see
    chlorpheniramine maleate
Tenax, see Librium
Tenuate, 61, 217
Tenuate Dospan, 37
Tepanil Ten-Tabs, 37
    see Tenuate
terbutaline sulfate,
    in Brethine, 111
Terramycin, 218
testosterone, 57
tetanus, 59
tetracycline, 44, 45, 59, 60, 68, 74,
    78, 79, 90, 219
Thalidomide, 66
Theophozine, see Marax
theophylline,
    in Elixophyllin, 135
    in Marax, 160
    in Quibron, 198
    in Tedral, 216
Theozine, see Marax
Theragran-M, 64
thiazide diuretics, 52
thioridazine hydrochloride,
    in Mellaril, 162
Thiotepa, 59
thorazine, 8, 9, 38, 60, 73, 74, 75, 76,
    79, 80, 219
Thyrar, see thyroid hormone
Thyrocrine, see thyroid hormone

thyroglobulin,
    in Proloid, 195
thyroid hormone, 56, 68, 220
Tigan, 221
tinnitus, 72
tobacco, 66, 88
Tofranil, 30, 38, 60, 74, 77, 78, 79, 80,
    221
tolazamide
    in Tolinase, 223
tolbutamide,
    in Orinase, 178
Tolectin, 63, 76, 222
Tolinase, 57, 76, 80, 223
tolmetin sodium,
    in Tolectin, 222
tranquilizers, 60
Tranxene, 60, 223
triamcinolone,
    in Aristocort, 103
triamcinolone acetonide,
    in Kenalog, 153
    in Mycolog, 166
triamterine,
    in Dyazide, 133
Triavil, 38, 72, 73, 76, 77, 78, 79, 80,
    224
trifluoperazine hydrochloride,
    in stelazine, 211
triglycerides, 53
Trilafon, 60
Trilafon Repetabs, 37
trimethobenzamide hydrochloride,
    in Tigan, 221
trimethoprim,
    in Bactrim, 108
triprolidine hydrochloride,
    in Actifed, 93
    in Actifed-C expectorant, 94
Tri-Vi-Flor, see Poly-Vi-Flor
tuberculosis, 58
Tussionex, 72, 74, 75, 77, 78, 79, 80,
    225
Tuss-Ornade, 226
Tylenol, 30, 62, 72
Tylenol with Codeine, 62, 227

U

ulcerative colitis, 56
ulcers, 55

251

Unipres, see Ser-Ap-Es
United States Pharmacopoeia, 65
Uracil Mustard Capsules, 59
urea,
   in Sultrin, 212
Uri-tet, see Terramycin
Urodine, see Pyridium

V

vaccines, 59, 90
vaginal medications, 42-43
Valdrene, see Benadryl
Valisone, 40, 57, 228
Valium, 30, 60, 72, 73, 75, 78, 79, 228
Vaseline, 42
Vasodilan, 77, 229
vasodilators, 53
Vasoprine, see Vasodilan
Vasotrate, see Isordil
Vectrin, see Minocin
Veltane, see Dimetane
Vibramycin, 229
Vioform-Hydrocortisone, 40, 57, 230
Vioquin-HC, see
      Vioform-Hydrocortisone
Viotag, see Vioform-Hydrocortisone
Vistaril, see Atarax
vitamins, 16, 30, 64, 81, 84
vitamin A, 84

in Poly-Vi-Flor, 191
vitamin B_1,
   in Poly-Vi-Flor, 191
vitamin B_2,
   in Poly-Vi-Flor, 191
vitamin B_6, 84
   in Poly-Vi-Flor, 191
vitamin B_{12},
   in Poly-Vi-Flor, 191
vitamin C (ascorbic acid)
   in Poly-Vi-Flor, 191
vitamin D, 84
   in Poly-Vi-Flor, 191
vitamin E, 84
   in Poly-Vi-Flor, 191
vitamin K, 84
vomiting, 74

W

Wampocap, see nicotinic acid
warfarin, 53

Z

Zinc oxide,
   in Anusol-HC, 102
Zorane, 177
   see also oral contraceptives
Zyloprim, 63, 74, 79, 80, 231